Garden Cities 21

Garden Cities 21
Creating a Livable
Urban Environment

John Ormsbee Simonds, FASLA

McGraw-Hill, Inc.

New York   San Francisco   Washington, D.C.   Auckland   Bogotá
Caracas   Lisbon   London   Madrid   Mexico City   Milan
Montreal   New Delhi   San Juan   Singapore
Sydney   Tokyo   Toronto

1 2 3 4 5 6 7 8 9 0   KP/KP   9 9 8 7 6 5 4 3

ISBN 0-07-057620-3

*The sponsoring editor for this book was Joel Stein, the editing
supervisor was Peggy Lamb, the production supervisor was Pamela
A. Pelton, and the designer was Susan Maksuta. It was set in
Garamond on a Macintosh system.*

Printed and bound by The Kingsport Press.

To Marjorie,
    without whom…

CONTENTS

FOREWORD
BY SENATOR BOB GRAHAM

"Make no little plans," said noted architect, Daniel H. Burnham. "They have no magic to stir men's blood."

A century later, in the spirit of Daniel Burnham, John O. Simonds brings to us a bold and innovative guide to the reshaping of our cities for tomorrow.

The problems of our contemporary cities are manifold. They are crumbling under unprecedented stress. Ever-widening, gridlocked trafficways, and "urban-sprawl"—the dispersion of citizens and enterprises into the suburbs and beyond—is draining the vitality of the cities. Massive exodus has left declining cities pocked with vacancies, obsolescence and decay—the breeding grounds of poverty and violence. There is need to redefine and reestablish within the metropolitan context dynamic and thriving centers of commercial and cultural activity. Each center—such as those of government, healthcare, trade, finance, and education—must be ringed with supporting facilities and residential neighborhoods.

We need coordinated systems of transportation, transit, and transmission that move freely through the open countryside and around, not through, established communities.

We need well-planned and more livable neighborhoods and unified communities with schools, convenience centers and recreation areas reached on foot or by bicycle along safe and attractive pathways.

We need to protect the integrity of our farmlands, forests, and wetlands—our beaches, shores, rivers and historic landmarks—and our scenic-ecologic superlatives.

The author of *Garden Cities 21* speaks to these issues in a clear and positive way from a lifetime of land and community planning experience. He makes a convincing case that the metropolitan regions of the future can, and must, provide the framework for both sound economic development and managed growth within a protected rural and wilderness matrix. He knows whereof he speaks, for such planning has been his hallmark. He understands that planning for the future requires not only a team mastery of the physical planning principles, but also an understanding of the politics, economics, and psychology of converting vision into reality.

What makes this book outstanding is the author's ability to draw upon the rich tradition and lessons of the past without allowing the past to compromise the future. Many of the concepts presented are drawn from exemplary urban designs already in place. By photographs, diagrams, and expressive text he shows how we can build upon and expand upon the best that now exists in an orderly transition to that which lies ahead.

I am proud to be a friend of John Simonds. Through his writings and work he has done much to advance the cause of sensitive landscape planning and to show that people, their communities, and cities can be brought into more productive, compatible, and rewarding relationships with the Earth.

ABOUT THE AUTHOR

John Ormsbee Simonds is one of the deans of American landscape design and urban planning. With a distinguished reputation as both an educator and practioner, Mr. Simonds has garnered top awards and honors in a career spanning some 50 years. His firm, EPD of Pittsburgh, has served as planner of record for three new towns and more than 80 major communities throughout the United States. He served for 15 years on the faculty of Carnegie-Mellon University and was a member of the President's task force on Resources and the Environment. Mr. Simonds is the author of McGraw-Hill's *Landscape Architecture,* Second Edition, and *Earthscape: A Manual of Environmental Planning and Design.* His education at Michigan State and Harvard universities has been augmented by 'round the world study in travel.

PREFACE

This book on the future of cities had its beginnings 100 years ago. At that time, British author, Sir Ebenezer Howard, perceived the industrial metropoli to be unlivable, and foundering. Sinks of pollution, poverty, and degradation, they befouled the air and waters of the countryside for many miles around.

In his treatise, *Garden Cities of Tomorrow*, Howard developed proposals for a more efficient, and far more agreeable, kind of human habitation. Essentially, he would center within each region an intensive governmental, trade, and cultural core, surrounded by specialized satellite communities, or "new towns"—all within a protected farm/forest setting. The concept had immediate appeal and received worldwide acclaim.

Although many of Howard's principles have since been adopted in the planning of prototype communities—his central tenet—that of interconnected satellites of various types within an open space frame, has yet to be implemented. Today, with new understanding of growth and resource management, innovative modes of transportation and transit, successful examples of Metro-governance, and highly effective techniques of comprehensive planning—the stage is set for the realization of garden cities beyond the possibilities envisioned by Sir Ebenezer.

Historian Lewis Mumford, and noted journalist, Wolf Von Eckardt have long been staunch "Garden City" advocates. Anthropologist Margaret Mead, biologist Rachel Carson, and such environmentalists as Marsh, Muir, McHarg, and Brower have helped establish a sound ecologic groundwork. Further insights have been contributed by such discerning urbanists as Jacobs, Tunnard, Pushkarev, Spreiregen, Spirn, Clay, Whyte, Bradley, and Gore, among a host of others. There has been much creative thinking, too, in related fields—as in economics, land planning law, communications, engineering, and systems dynamics.

In sum, the parts are there—ready to be assembled into a conceptual model for the more workable, more livable, more expressive cities of the 21st Century.

John O. Simonds

ACKNOWLEDGMENTS

A professional reference book has its genesis in ideas gleaned from myriad, often unremembered, sources. It takes form in the classroom, library, the office, the field—and on the hard, ringing forge of experience. There is heat and light involved, and not a little pounding. In a way it is a compendium of trial and error lessons learned, workable principles discovered, and observations to be shared. In this regard it is personal.

A published book, however, must be a collective effort—requiring as it does the knowledge and creative thinking of many contributors. Of those who have shared ideas, materials, and counsel in making this work possible, special thanks must be given:

...to my lovely and perceptive wife, Marjorie, who has spent months on end at the electronically wonderful typing machine, and long hours in conversation helping to refine the points discussed and bring them into focus.

...to publisher James G. Trulove and editors Michael Leccese and J. William Thompson of *Landscape Architecture* magazine which under their visionary guidance has become a powerful influence for the responsible development of the American countryside and cities. It is no happenstance that many of the quotations included in this volume are derived from their writings and forums.

...to John Wiley & Sons, for permitting inclusion of material written for the section on Urban Design in the AIA *Encyclopedia of Architecture, Design, Engineering and Construction.*

...and to Peggy Lamb and her co-editors and co-workers at McGraw-Hill who have skillfully converted a bundle of drawings and manuscript pages into a proper book.

*Civilisation consists in grasping
imaginatively all that is best in the
thought of a time...*

KENNETH CLARK, IN *CIVILISATION*,
HARPER & ROW PUBLISHING, INC.,
NEW YORK, 1969, P. 132.

OVERVIEW

Garden City 21 is not the dream of a visionary. Nor does it propose the creation of pastoral or gardenesque "urbanas." It is rather a book of practical and proven ideas on how to transform our ailing cities into thriving regional centers. More efficient. More vibrant. More livable.

The news media these days decry increasingly the full array of urban problems. They dwell on the worsening traffic snarls, water shortages, crime, drugs, poverty, filth, overcrowding, the homeless, and mounting public debt. The media seldom suggest solutions or even that solutions are possible. Little is said of the good things that are transpiring to vastly improve the living conditions of many metropolitan areas. These include urban renewal, pollution abatement, resource management, open space planning, new types of parks, and new transportation-transit systems. Together, these give promise of far more workable and self-sustaining garden-park cities.

In looking ahead, it is proposed that our cities of the future will be superior in many ways. They will comprise more functional and expressive urban places and paths of movement. There will be well-defined and interconnected activity nodes of high intensity. Obsolescence will be squeezed out; pollution overcome. There will be a protected regional matrix of field and forest within which the city will live and breathe. There will be, too, internally, a blue and green open space framework around which the new cities will take their evolving form.

Here is a book to help point the way.

1
The urban dwelling

It seems reasonable that a discourse on urban living should start with the dwelling unit. In the city these are, or should be, quite different from those of the suburbs or open countryside. Why? For one thing their "footprint" is smaller because of the exorbitant land costs within urban areas, where property is bought and sold by the square foot rather than the acre. Living spaces are perforce compact. To compensate, everything possible is usually done to make them seem more spacious.

In the teeming city, privacy and quiet are highly prized; security is a very real concern; ambient temperatures tend to be more extreme; and glimpses of the natural world—earth, sky, and foliage—have intensified meaning. Without views of the open landscape, orientation is usually inward. Objects, colors, and symbols seen in such limited spaces take on added significance. These factors all have bearing on the size, shape, and character of the urban habitation.

Living space

Humans, like all of God's creatures, need a place to call their own—a "terrestrial fix," as it were— where they can find shelter, store their belongings, and spend a good part of their time. The nature of their dwellings depends largely upon the nature of *place,* for location determines not only the special conditions and requirements, but also size, shape, and building materials at hand. Cities, too, vary widely in response to location, climate, problems, and opportunities. With the city dwelling, however, the very fact of urbanity presents a unique set of constraints.

The essence of city life is *separate togetherness.* Togetherness has its positive side. For one thing, the group instinct is deeply instilled in our psyches. Wherever people have roamed the earth they have tended to band together. Early on, this was probably a matter of protection, but soon they would discover the values of cooperative enterprise, convenience, and social carryings-on. Group living has also provided, and can provide, the advantages of sharing, ease of communication, and available help. There are disadvantages also—such as too much sharing, too much communication, and too much or too little help. Then too, there's the matter of lack of identity and of privacy—even of personal safety.

In the design, or selection, of urban habitations the positive values are to be optimized; the negative factors avoided or overcome to the limits of ingenuity.

Space expansion

How can small spaces be made to seem larger? This is a problem common to most urban dwellings. Many means are familiar to the architect, landscape architect, and interior designer by which cramped quarters can be made to seem commodious.

Borrowed space
Spatial expansion can be achieved by the visual appropriation of adjacent, and even distant spaces. This is to say that what is seen from a space—the sky, streetscape, courtyard, or corner of the entryway—is visually added to the space and extends its apparent dimensions. If, for example, living, dining, and even sleeping quarters are open to each other, in full or in part, all borrow shared space and seem larger.

Compression-expansion
It is generally true that people feel freer and more expansive when released from confinement or when moving from darkness to light. Within a small apartment a series of tight-free, small-large, dim-bright spatial sequences can be planned. These not only add the interest of contrast and variety, they make the larger, lighter volumes seem more spacious. Roof types and ceiling treatments, too, can add both dimension and distinction.

Fenestration
The treatment of window openings affords infinite opportunities for spatial expansion. If the opening is small and the view is pleasant, the curtains or blinds, if used, are placed to the side to increase the apparent size of the window. If the view be unpleasant, a translucent panel or filmy curtain can block it while admitting light.

A large window opening or window-wall can open a room or apartment to an exuberant vista of city skyline, or perhaps to a busy street scene—or a building wall of interesting color, texture, or shadow pattern. Even the profile of

The urban habitation
In the city dwelling of constricted dimensions apparent and actual living space can be expanded:

- **By the elimination of interior walls**
- **By variations in ceiling and roof lines**
- **By sensitive fenestration**
- **By the judicious use of light, color, texture, and furnishings.**

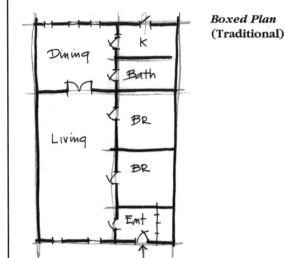

Boxed Plan
(Traditional)

Compartmented living areas. Interior walls limit visual space to the dimension of each room.

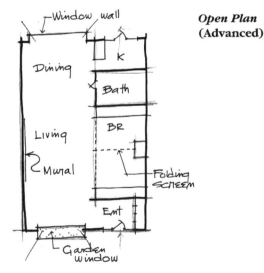

Open Plan
(Advanced)

Open floor plan with folding screens and counter height divider at kitchen.

"Borrowed space" can be attained by use of the open floor plan, the elimination of space-consuming doors, and by imaginative window treatment.

Sunlight and the Urban Dwelling
Aside from conventional fenestration sunlight can be admitted to a townhouse by a conservatory bay, solar dome, skylight, clerestory, or window wall.

From dark to light.
From compressed to free,
From rough to the refined.

With the same floor area, modulations of roofs and ceilings can give an increased sense of space and individuality.

nearby rooftops with their chimneys, water tanks, and fire escapes can have dramatic design appeal. Where illumination is wanted and the view is not, the clerestory, solar dome, or skylight have welcome application.

Simplicity

The curse of the townhouse is clutter.

The Japanese who live with compression have long ago learned the value of the simple elegant space. By use of sliding screens of natural wood and rice paper and floors of woven grass tatami mats, it is the occupants, rather than their possessions, who are featured. In these handsome shells of space—faces, dress, and even the simplest objects take on a striking intensity.

In the traditional Japanese home, all but a few belongings are carefully wrapped and stored away. In one area, however, there is placed an unpretentious shelf construction, or *tokonoma,* where, to brighten the room, honor a guest, or mark a special occasion, a chosen objet d'art is displayed, with or without a complementary flower arrangement. The delightful impact of these restrained displays, and their changing effect on the living space, have lessons for all chronic collector-exhibitors.

Texture

Large country places or suburban domiciles can sometimes carry the visual weight of heavy masonry walls, massive beams, coffered ceilings, deeply carved door frames and lintels, and bold patterns in paving, carpets, and draperies; but not the urban apartment. Here they would be overpowering.

In the city dwelling, simplicity of line and form is superior to the ornate. Refined wall textures, lightly framed furniture, and natural finishes are more fitting, as are hand-crafted ceramics and finely woven fabrics of linen, cotton, or wool. All furnishings, including dinnerware and utensils, can contribute to the sense of quiet good taste.

From the blocky boldness of the city streets to the inner sanctum of the urban home there is at best a studied sequential transition from heavy to light, from loud to quiet, from the rough to the highly refined.

Color

Colors, like textures, can run the gamut from the wild to the calm. If one enjoys an occasional blast of brilliance—of clashing hues and shocking contrast—as who does not, let these visual bracers be experienced at the circus, museum, or theater. There they can be seen and escaped. But to share the small city apartment with such insistent distractions would be tiring and eventually boring. Beyond this, bold colors are space-shrinkers. Subtle hues and tones, however, such as the off-whites, soft yellows, and warm grays not only defer to the other features or occupants of the room, they are relaxing, far more easy to live with, and expansive.

Light

To list but a few of the many qualities of light is to help one determine those which are more suited to application in the urban dwelling. For example, choices would hardly include the glaring, scintillating, oscillating, quavering, shooting, blinding, or dazzling. Nor the red, blue, sallow, mottled, hot, bright, or piercing. More likely one might select lighting that was soft, warm, and luminous, with perhaps a particular hue or intensity singled out for a special purpose.

A space can be bathed in light. A beam can be used to highlight the edges of a form, reveal modeling, or cast intriguing shadows. Light can be focused to feature a table setting or bring a work of graphic art to glowing intensity. It can harmonize. It can differentiate; it can unify. Within the simplest dwelling space light can expand not only the given dimensions but the range of visual experiences. The wrong choice can profane a space or series of spaces. The right choice can produce seeming miracles.

Graphics

Pictorial representations are especially suited to the urban home. Without usurping floor area they introduce welcome color and interest. They can establish or modify the basic character or a changing theme to suit the mood or season.

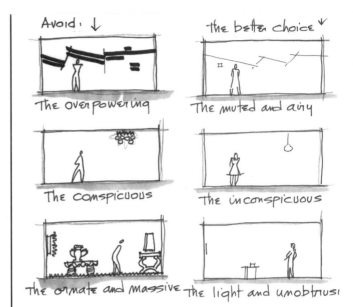

Space modifiers. Heavy form, rough textures, and bold patterns reduce the apparent size of living space. The muted, the inconspicuous, and the light are space expanders.

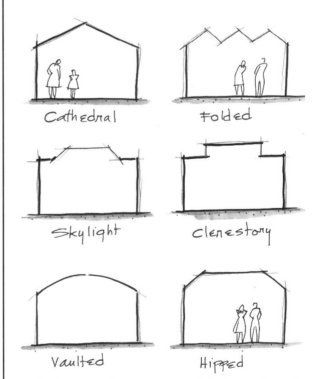

With the same floor area, modulations of roofs and ceilings can give an increased sense of space and individuality.

4

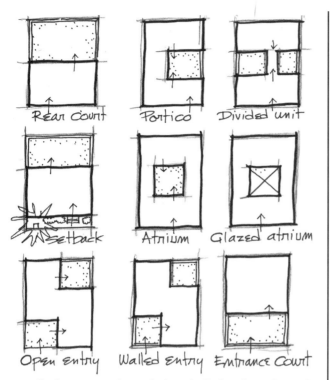

Walled courtyards and the skylighted or domed atrium add to city dwelling livability. All variations shown are superior to the conventional rear yard exposed to alley or neighbors.

They can set the color scheme for each subspace or the entire dwelling.

A single print or painting can brighten a wall. A composition of smaller prints—as those clipped from a magazine and mounted—may bring into the space the flashing hues of exotic birds, a rainbow flutter of butterflies, or a profusion of tropical bloom. For the sailor, a drawing or photograph may recall a favorite part of the world and set the imagination free to range far beyond the limiting walls of the city apartment. An illuminated mural of woodland, mountains, or sea can extend an end wall or living space to perceived infinity.

Symbols

A symbol is a graphic or three-dimensional representation of an object, place, or idea. Symbols embody and have the power to release intensified emotional responses. Such is the crucifix, the flag, the dove, the American eagle. Such, too, to a lesser degree, is the apple or apple tree, suggesting domesticity. A symbolic pine tree may invoke the feeling of wilderness—of mountains, trout, and the lumbering bear. Stones, flowers, or a seashell are among the host of symbols that convey the wonder of all nature.

In the small city dwelling, seemingly detached from nature, and where one is away from familiar surroundings and friends, pictorial or sculptural symbols can do much to bridge the distances and to set the spirit free.

Mystery

In the design of spaces, at any scale, one soon learns the value of partial concealment. If it's all out to be seen at a single glance, the glancing will soon be over. Discovery should come a bit at a time and is best if made sequential.

In plan layout, for example, attention is directed from one area or space to another in such a way that each succeeding experience of revelation is first introduced, then developed, and concluded—often as the best possible introduction of what will be coming next.

A sense of expectation and fulfillment can be induced in numbers of ways. All somewhat resemble a musical composition or the plot of a play. The simplest form of sequential revelation is a path of circulation, clearly defined or subtle, that leads from one viewing station to another. Or one may be introduced to an idea or theme which is then developed clue by clue until the story is complete. Sometimes seemingly unrelated clues are placed about to be comprehended gradually—with a culminating pleasure when relationships are realized. What has all this to do with expanding the limits of an urban domicile? Much, when fully comprehended.

Outdoors-in

We have considered several means of bringing nature into the urban living space as by views of trees and plantings from windows or the sky from an overhead solar dome. Scenes and subjects from nature may be portrayed graphically, as by drawings, paintings, or photographs. The use of natural materials and finishes also serves as a link, as does the introduction of symbols. There are other ways which are more direct:

Outdoor-living space

It doesn't take much exterior footage to yield a lot of outdoor living pleasure. A small setback of a building front may give room for a tree, a bench, a square of ivy and spring bulbs, or boxwood in a planter.

At ground level a walled and gated entrance court can provide security, privacy, and wide window views from the interior living quarters. There may be a place for a pool, a few squares of paving, furniture, and perhaps an herb garden. Or in the case of a deeper lot, there may be room for a larger courtyard or garden house.

A balcony, even if seldom used, gives extensional space to an upper-story apartment. For some apartment dwellers a spiral stairway leading aloft may give access to a full roof garden. Again, interior living space may be extended by a flying deck, exterior seat wall, or enclosed patio.

Indoor gardens

With or without a solar dome or skylight, interior gardens can be installed as delightful living attributes. A planter may be created against a window wall or under a lighted alcove near the center by the placement of an underlying waterproof tray. A recirculating spray pool or trickle of water over a stone adds sound and animation. Or a window bay may be designed as, or converted to, a mini-greenhouse-conservatory.

Foliage plants

Even if foliage did not freshen the air, it seems to. Tubbed or potted plants from around the world come in all shapes and sizes—some with interest in leaves and branches, others with fascinating flowers or attractive fruit. A single well-selected specimen can give welcome relief from the planes and angles of a room and serve as living sculpture. For those with a penchant for growing things, the nurture of container plants can bring a new dimension to city living.

Floral display

Flower arrangements need not be elaborate. A single blossom in a vase, or floating in a bowl of water, may be even

Interior space extension
Interior space can be expanded by an exterior balcony, flying deck, seat wall, or walled courtyard.

more effective than a profusion of blossoms. Perhaps, however, one of the highest of all art forms is the studied flower composition, combining as it does an understanding of nature, philosophy, and design. In its place a spray of autumn leaves will suffice, or a sheaf of heading grass, the pods of weeds, or, say, a branch of horse chestnuts in their opening husks. Lacking access to such as these, a basket of oranges, lemons, and limes from the grocery store, or a pineapple on display will provide a link to the orchard and field. It is hard to imagine a city home as complete without the grace of some recognition of the splendors of nature.

Creatures

Why do wispy-bearded elders of China sometimes carry about a cricket in a cage? Even they may not realize the strength of the bond between humans and the animal-insect kingdom.

In the rural communities of the United States there is no such need of caged crickets, for the pastures and barns are well-creatured. In sight, too, are the familiar swallows, crows, rabbits, raccoons, and perhaps an occasional deer. But in the city, too often, we humans feel isolated from other living things. We need not. Indoors, a dog, a cat, a parakeet on a perch, an aquarium—or, at the outside feeding tray, a visiting chipmunk, squirrel, or flurry of feathered friends—may sustain a link and give infinite satisfaction.

Attached dwellings

The city dwellings of Europe have for the most part shared common walls. So have the traditional city homes of urban United States—as in the typical townhouses of Baltimore, Philadelphia, Kansas City, and San Francisco. With the influx of families from rural areas there was a reluctance by them to huddle up so closely. Further, there was the expressed desire for more breathing space. This led toward a trend for requiring minimal sideyard spaces between individual homes. Ostensibly these narrow sideyard slots would "provide privacy, light, and air." In actuality they provided more often a cluttered outdoor storage space or dumping ground for refuse. As to privacy, many an American youth and adult was to learn or relearn the facts of life through the opposite neighboring windows.

In contemporary cities there is a marked return to the attached townhouse. Often it takes new forms and plan arrangements.

Why attached?

Why attached housing units? First and foremost because the cost of land within the more restricted limits of redeveloped

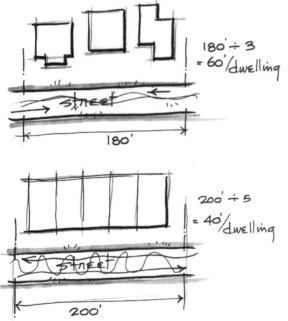

$180' \div 3$
$= 60'/\text{dwelling}$

$200' \div 5$
$= 40'/\text{dwelling}$

In a traditional townhouse plan, dwellings are aligned so as to face directly upon the noise and friction of the passing street.

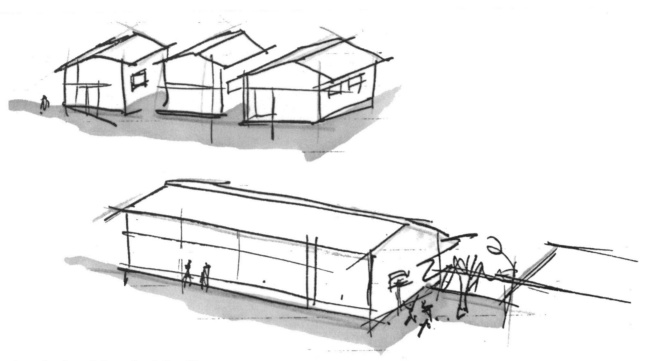

Attached and detached dwellings
Single-family homes on narrow city lots waste valuable space and afford less privacy than attached townhouses where useless sideyards can be combined to advantage.

cities encourages higher densities in designated residential neighborhoods. This density can only be accommodated by a preponderance of multifamily structures. Does this imply that detached housing will no longer be built in cities? Not so. Rather, within the more intensive inner city, land costs and real estate taxes will be so steep that only multifamily apartments will be economically feasible. In the restructured outer city, with a newly created open space framework, detached single family home neighborhoods will continue to have their place and appeal.

Other advantages

Aside from the fact of less land cost per unit when attached, there are substantial savings in construction and upkeep. By the sharing of common walls, one or two major exterior facings are eliminated in each dwelling, roofs are more or less continuous, and painting and other maintenance can be done for a number of units at one time. With something like half the exposure to weather, the cost of heating and cooling is also reduced.

Further, the narrow sideyard spaces can be combined and put to good use by dwelling owners or devoted to one or more additional dwellings within the same overall parcel dimension, thus reducing the cost of housing.

Disadvantages

Most of the disadvantages conceived to be inherent in townhouse living can be ameliorated, or eliminated, by innovative design. Sound transmission through walls is almost totally precluded by leaving an insulated air space (sealed at both ends) between abutting units. Recently, new types of technically advanced sandwich sheathing have further reduced the sound factor, and research continues.

As to privacy, the rediscovered zero lot line concept, popular with the ancient Romans and Greeks, permits totally walled enclosures for private indoor-outdoor living.

The most widely perceived disadvantage of attached homes living is that of too much togetherness. Propinquity in all forms of urban housing will remain a condition of city life. Propinquity can be and will be relieved by the combining and sharing of open space. By the consolidation of normally misused or underused areas into well-planned surroundings, new levels of land-use efficiency and livability can be attained.

Alternatives

Given a row of three to seven attached dwelling units, it would seem that choices in the external plan arrangement of the units would be limited. The typical early American "row house" or "townhouse" was a solid bar facing directly on the narrow street or sidewalk paving. Usually there were fenced-in backyards opening onto an alley. Rear yards, with access through the kitchen, pantry, and back door, were in the main used as service areas, sometimes for the growing of flowers and vegetables or the placement of a lawn swing or sandbox. This pattern was repeated, block after block after block.

In the simplest form of advancement the attached units were slid backward or forward to break the monotony of the street facade and provide more attractive entryways. With the advent of larger windows, weatherproof windowwalls and the idea of indoor-outdoor living, new plan arrangements evolved. This led to the forecourt garden or activity space and eventually to the dividing of the residence to enclose variformed courtyards. Presently, with the walled parcel concept, the integration of indoor-outdoor living space has been brought to new refinement.

Clustering

In the quest for a freer, more expansive lifestyle it was natural that in time residential structures and related living spaces should be more fully integrated. Many new plan arrangements have evolved; others are still emerging.

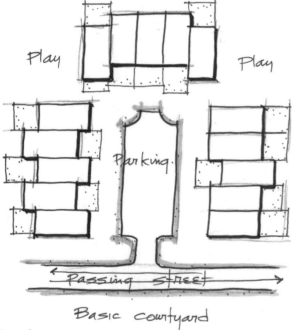

In a basic courtyard arrangement, buildings are grouped around an off-street court. The street is freed of parked vehicles, parking is convenient, and private dooryard courts may be attractively planted.

Of units

If the segmented bar townhouse seemed rigid—even when each dwelling segment had been made more open as a unit—the first step would be to slide the alternating units forward and back. This creates breaks in the building facade and allows for the play of light and shadow to differentiate each dwelling. It also provides a modicum of living or planting space at the front, reminiscent of British cottage housing. The next step would be to enlarge the building breaks into single or multiple entrance courts. Finally, in some cases, the rectilinear bar as a plan form would be abandoned altogether and the units, still attached, freely disposed in response to parcel shapes and topographical features.

Of buildings

Just as attached townhouse segments are increasingly grouped to better fit the topography and provide more agreeable living—so are entire building groupings now arranged much more freely in the city landscape. This highly desirable trend has been made possible by building regulations which relax the longstanding dictate that all buildings must face directly upon a public right-of-way. Instead, in most progressive municipalities they may now be fronted upon a pedestrian way or court or to a public park or other dedicated open space. By this one legislative stroke, city living can now be oriented away from the noise and fumes and hazard of the traffic-laden streets.

There are economic benefits, too. The heavy construction costs of the passing street, with its lighting, trunk sewers, and utility mains are normally assigned to the fronting buildings. This surcharge is often a very substantial part of the cost of housing. Facing homes instead upon an off-street court allows more dwellings to share the expense of a given length of the passing street .

As could be anticipated, entire buildings as well as individual dwelling units are turning their sides or backs to trafficways and parking compounds and embracing shared open space entrance courts, play lots, and parklets. Clearly, these new developments, and others yet to come, give promise of a whole new, better way of urban townhouse living.

Stacking

Just as urban homes and apartments can be attached horizontally, so are they by common practice stacked vertically, one on top of the other. Why? Again this is a factor of high land costs. Also, important, it is a means by which land coverage per unit can be decreased, thus accommodating

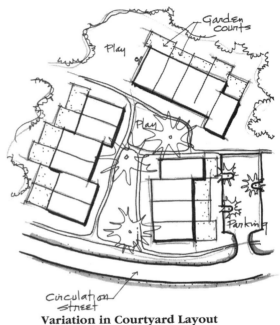

Variation in Courtyard Layout

Free disposition of townhouse dwellings. Such off-street residential courts presage a more livable city.

Evolution of the townhouse courtyard
The rigid bar row house facing directly upon the street is giving way to attached dwellings built around parking or garden courts with safe play spaces. The reduction in costly street frontage can effect an overall saving. The variations are infinite.

On-street living

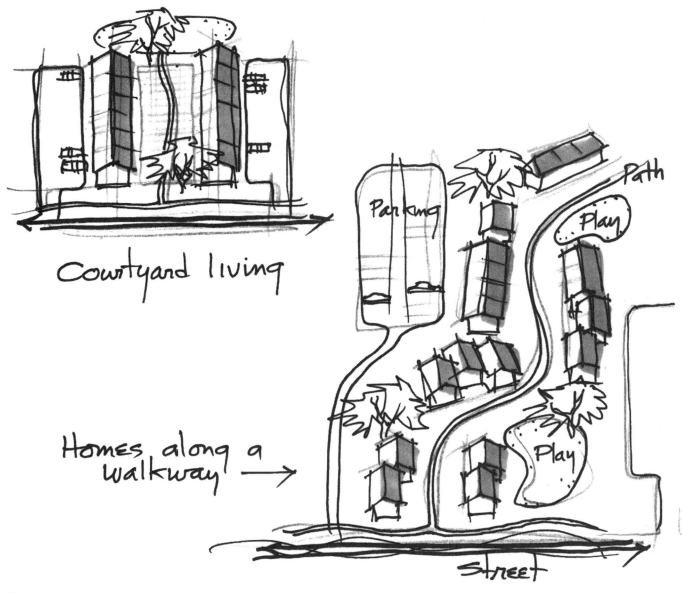

Courtyard living

Homes along a walkway →

Street versus nonstreet frontage
By tradition, homes have faced upon the street. With advanced PUD (Planned Unit Development) zoning, they may be aligned along a path—or follow the path to school, park, or shopping.

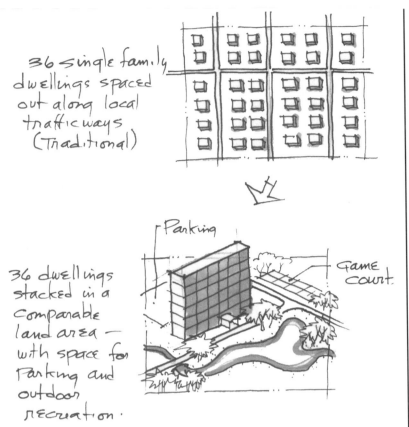

36 single family dwellings spaced out along local trafficways (Traditional)

36 dwellings stacked in a comparable land area — with space for parking and outdoor recreation.

Stacking yields shared open space
With the consolidation of dwellings into a multistory structure, the residents can live in a recreation park—often at considerable savings.

The single family home in our suburbs was designed for a family that consisted of dad, who went to work, mother, who stayed at home and ran the house, and 2.5 children. The family now is so small that both children and adults need to go out into the community and socialize with people from other families. That's a very good reason for other models of housing of higher densities, housing that provides some communal facilities.

Higher density doesn't mean you lose privacy. You can gain a lot of things, like a store or a coffee shop or a beautiful park or a place for the kids.

CLAIRE COOPER MARCUS

many more in-town dwellings. If, by developer choice or by governmental regulation the area gained is devoted to shared open space, the multistory residential areas can be made veritable urban parks.

Variations on a Theme

Within the past several decades the appearance and livability of multistory apartment buildings have undergone a remarkable transformation. From the stark monoliths spaced out at regular intervals along the urban trafficways, the plan arrangements for apartment buildings have been modified to produce a variety of handsome architectural groupings.

High-low combinations

Neither the high-rise, mid-rise, garden apartment, nor the townhouse is the best answer to multifamily housing. A combination of types in a building grouping gives more choices to potential users and adds interest and variety to the complex. The lower units can be faced to the more

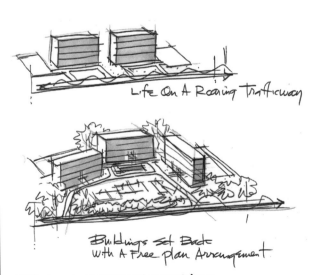

Life On A Roaring Trafficway

Buildings Set Back With A Free Plan Arrangement

Off-street apartment groupings
Apartment buildings can be set back from the street and grouped to provide welcome usable open space.

The use of high-rise and mid-rise housing suggests overlook viewing and the concentration of residential density to gain usable ground area and open space relief.

Garden apartments and townhouses are multi-family integrators, bringing people into closer contact with the trees, water features, and ground planes of a natural site.

Increasingly, single family urban homes are for the privileged few who are willing and able to pay the price of more privacy, more property, and its care.

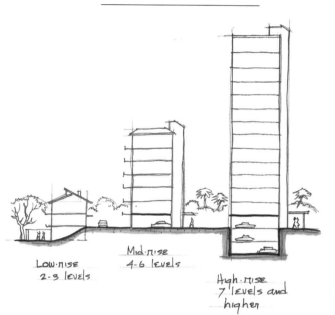

Multi-Story Building Type
Low and midrise dwelling are ground-related; high-rise to the skyline or distant view.

Families with children belong on the ground—not in high-rise apartments.

appealing of the immediate landscape features, and the higher apartments can face upon the longer-range views and prospects. Where higher apartments look down upon lower buildings, the roof treatment of the latter is obviously of importance. They can be designed as either recreation courts, horizontal murals, roof-top gardens, or combinations of the three.

What determines the optimum overall density of such apartment clusters? Not arbitrary maximums or restrictive zoning limits. Densities, rather, can only be site-specific and based upon a studied appraisal of projected impacts and performance. This presupposes that the uses proposed are in accordance with the long-range goals of the local jurisdiction. The right density requires the harmonious fit of the complex, or any building component thereof, into the immediate and extensional environs and assumes that all required trafficway improvements, utilities, and other services will be in place before the first occupancy is permitted. Finally, the optimum density must satisfy the reviewing

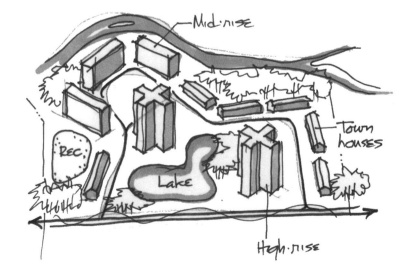

Mixed building types. As beside an urban waterway or nature preserve.

VARIATIONS IN HIGH-LOW APARTMENT COMBINATIONS

Monotonous streetfront canyons formed by buildings of uniform height and setback are giving way to freer and far more agreeable apartment plan arrangements.

agencies that the plan proposed represents the highest and best use of the land and that the long-term benefits to the community outweigh any significant negative stresses.

Space consolidation

Moving apartment buildings freely about (a practice encouraged by planned community development) enables planners to face apartment buildings upon off-road motor courts, entrance loops, or parklets. Where drainageways or watercourses are present, these may serve as lineal open space reserves lacing through the apartment grouping. All such related areas may be held and managed by an owners' association or dedicated as part of a public open space system. It can be seen that by the combining and shaping of the unbuilt-upon areas into a cohesive recreational and parklike surrounding, the apartments can be oriented to useful and refreshing open space.

There is no such thing as excessive density, provided all required facilities, amenities, and open space are at hand.

[As to nature] It seems people really do want to be reconnected—just having a stream or having a place where you can get to the water's edge, or feel the wind..."

RANDOLPH HESTER

Deeply ingrained in all of us
        is an instinctive feeling
        for the outdoors…
        for soil, stone, water,
        and the living things of the earth.
We need to be near them,
        to observe and to touch them.
We need to maintain
        a close relationship with nature,
        to dwell amid natural features
        and surroundings,
And to bring nature
        into our homes and lives.

2
The neighborhood

Besides an habitable dwelling, city living requires shared conveniences and amenities. Such are the grocery mart, the drug store, barber shop and beauty salon, the book stall, florist, restaurant, or tavern. Such, too, are the parklets, the meeting and greeting spaces—sometimes no more than a widened place in a walkway or a bench set out under a tree.

In the urban throng of nameless faces, the feeling of compatibility, of recognizing and being recognized, of belonging and sharing, has much to do with individual and group well-being. Accepted and applied, this truth can have telling expression in the plan arrangements of cohesive, convenient, and agreeable residential neighborhoods.

Togetherness

What, then, *is* a neighborhood? Actually, it's more a feeling than an area or layout. A neighborhood is simply a place where the people next door, or across the courtyard, or down the street, feel themselves to be "neighbors" rather than strangers. What, in planning terms, can be done to engender or strengthen this sense of compatibility?

Elimination of hassles

First, it might be proposed that all potential interhousehold annoyances be eliminated insofar as possible. These could include, for example, the need or temptation to cross another's property in order to go where one is routinely going. Or the placement of a game court in such a location that one neighbor is put upon by the needs, requests, or nuisance of the others. A good neighborhood plan induces pleasant relationships and experiences. If the layout is such as to generate undue frictions—or "rub"—it no doubt needs revision.

Induced compatibility

More positively, the sense of neighborhood can be fostered by the provision of well-placed activity nodes and paths of interconnection. Then, too, there's the all-important matter of how dwellings are related to each other. It was Catherine Bauer (Wurster), commissioned to undertake an analysis of the good and bad features of public housing, who focused upon the importance of group sizing. She pointed out that children peering from the shelter of a doorway and seeing strange children would instinctively close the door. Teenagers, too, felt (often with good reason) that gangs of unfamiliar neighbors of like ages posed a threat. Even adults, finding their urban domicile to be surrounded by people they didn't know, experienced feelings ranging from "uneasiness" to "fear."

It was the Bauer recommendation, based on her findings, that the most favorable assemblage of dwellings was from three to twelve in number, with sixteen as a very maximum. When household groupings within this range are brought together around a shared entrance court or other common focal point, the children get to know each other by their first names, men swap greetings and stories on meeting, and women exchange gossip and recipes. Friendships develop spontaneously when the conditions are right.

Sense of neighborhood

It is doubted that anyone has better defined the concept of *neighborhood* than William H. Whyte, Jr., in an early sociological study of Park Forest, Illinois. In it he showed by color-coded maps where the members of various social gatherings lived within the community. It demonstrated conclusively that most neighborly bonds are formed by families living beside or near each other along one or both sides of a residential street, around a common meeting ground, or along a mutually traveled path. Few friendships bridged rear property lines or trafficways intersecting the local street. Nor did friendships span many vacant lots or occur along major thoroughfares. Friendships tend to form where people meet and recognize each other.

Conformation

Is there an optimum neighborhood size and shape?

Until school busing came along, it was generally agreed that the most desirable plan diagram was an arrangement of housing clusters centered about an elementary school, with access by children along traffic-free walkways. In such neighborhoods, parents, children, young adults, and elders are drawn together on a daily basis—especially if the shop-

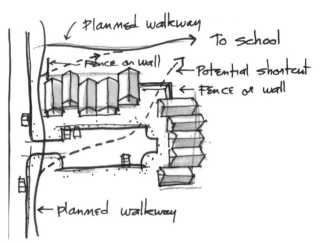

Avoidance of potential problems
Here, as an example, two potential shortcuts have been avoided.

Group encounter areas
Smaller neighborhood groupings promote closer interfamily ties.

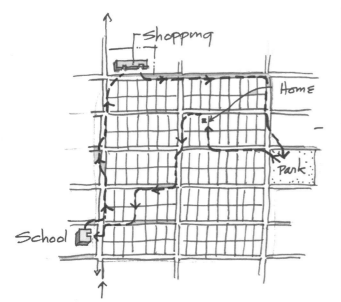

Life on the trafficway grid is fraught with noise, fumes, and frictions. To get from one block to another entails the danger of street crossings.

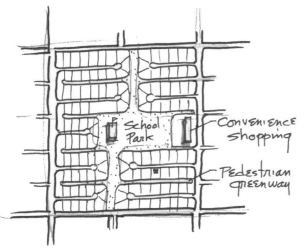

Here homes face inward to pedestrian pathways, bikeways, and park. There are countless variations to this theme.

Traditional versus traffic-free living
Advanced residential planning provides ready access by automobile and traffic-free paths of neighborhood interconnection.

ping and service centers are located within or bordering on the same central open space.

Variations

There are now many variations in neighborhood size and layout. Schools, recreation areas, convenience centers, and other amenities are commonly shared with adjacent neighborhoods. An accepted requisite, however, is that from the start the boundaries and buffers are to be predetermined and fixed, with either natural limits such as ridges, ravines, or waterways or trafficways or other constructions. Each neighborhood is to be planned as a unified residential entity and kept in balance.

The cardinal sin in neighborhood planning continues to be the division of an otherwise cohesive layout by on-grade vehicular throughways. This being so, one wonders at the traditional urban residential pattern of grid streets and highways with repetitive fronting blocks. We are finally learning the fallacy of such humdrum and insensitive planning. Neighborhood design is becoming at last the means of providing residents with the best possible living experiences. These include not only freedom from passing traffic but also the enjoyment of shared recreation areas and natural surroundings.

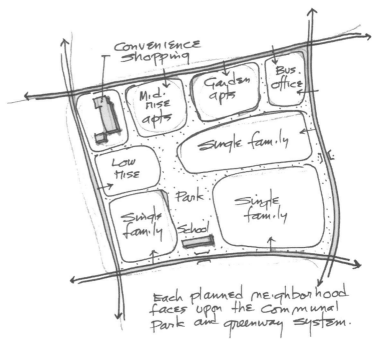

Shared amenities
Several diversified neighborhoods may share such common features as schools, playfields, shopping, and employment centers.
Vehicular approach drives and parking compounds are best kept to the perimeter.

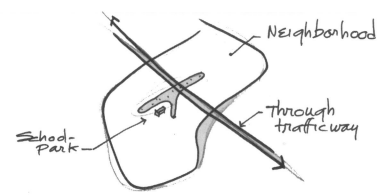

The cardinal sin
The disruption of an established neighborhood by a projected roadway is always to be avoided.

As to size, a subneighborhood need be no larger than a cluster of two to three homes, and a total neighborhood can be planned, in area and population, to the limits of convenient intra-area movement and harmonious group interaction. Shape is determined by topography, building composition, and the layout of interconnecting routes of travel. There is no longer a predetermined optimum size.

Automobile access

Vehicular access, circulation drives, and parking compounds are usually kept to the perimeter. When densities so warrant, as in multistory apartments, parking is often provided in decks below the living and pedestrian levels. Spacious or dense, the mark of well-conceived neighborhoods is that they face inward, or outward, to a safe, park-like pedestrian domain within which, and around which, neighborhood life takes place.

Places

Can one design friendships? Hardly. But certain it is that gathering and meeting places conducive to acquaintance-ship can be created. Such, for example, might be a swatch of paving under a tree, with benches and a table for chess or checkers. It could be a seat wall at the entrance of the school or an arbor and bicycle rack at the neighborhood store. It might be an area under a basketball hoop braced on the end wall of a building, or a space set aside for hop-scotch. Where tennis, handball, or boccie is played, a well-placed court could bring an otherwise dull housing area to exuberant life. Even the thought of such places conjures up a feeling of togetherness. They are the centers of neighborhood interaction—of camaraderie.

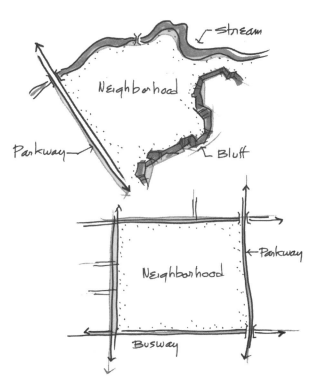

Neighborhood boundaries
The neighborhood edges are to be fixed and buffered—as by natural features or by trafficways.

Community planning means creating an environment that will enhance social contact and group pride.

Claire Cooper Marcus

Providing small gardens and comfortable places overlooking shared outdoor areas makes it easier for people to meet their neighbors.

Jane Holtz Kay

The dynamics of friendship

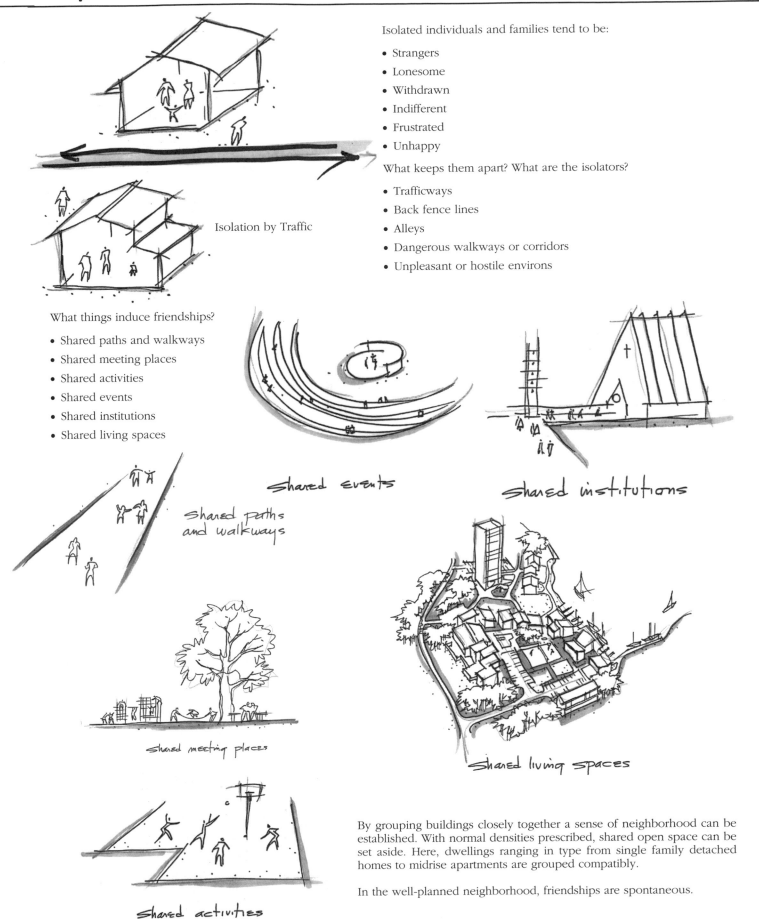

Isolated individuals and families tend to be:

- Strangers
- Lonesome
- Withdrawn
- Indifferent
- Frustrated
- Unhappy

What keeps them apart? What are the isolators?

- Trafficways
- Back fence lines
- Alleys
- Dangerous walkways or corridors
- Unpleasant or hostile environs

Isolation by Traffic

What things induce friendships?

- Shared paths and walkways
- Shared meeting places
- Shared activities
- Shared events
- Shared institutions
- Shared living spaces

shared events

shared institutions

Shared paths and walkways

shared meeting places

shared living spaces

By grouping buildings closely together a sense of neighborhood can be established. With normal densities prescribed, shared open space can be set aside. Here, dwellings ranging in type from single family detached homes to midrise apartments are grouped compatibly.

In the well-planned neighborhood, friendships are spontaneous.

shared activities

Empathy in planning

A neighborhood is more than a geometric layout of buildings, walkways, and parking lots. A neighborhood must entail more than just the efficient use of land. It must do more even than protect the residents from the noise and dangers of moving traffic. It must provide, in short, a well-conceived environs for living the good, full life. This includes considerations of safety, convenience, and pleasure. There should be something for everybody, and here is where empathy comes into play. Empathy is, in fact, a chief requisite of the designer of cities or any part thereof. To have empathy is to be able to put one's self in the place of the various potential residents—from children to the elderly, from swinging singles to large family householders, from the recluse to the socializer—and to provide for each, insofar as feasible, the opportunity to do those things which they most enjoy.

Obviously, all future neighbors can't have everything they want. The planner's selection involves the preparation of a checklist of possibilities and a decision as to priorities. The layout of dwellings and activity centers is studied in combination. Each such center is then designed—for its place, users, and budget—to come as close as possible to the perceived ideal.

Place into space

The design of place requires an understanding of space, for the nature of all places depends upon their volumetric qualities. To be meaningful, neighborhood use areas are to be translated into spaces. Each space—be it for a sandbox or a station of an exercise trail to a full-blown community—is to be designed to accommodate and express its use, with all the empathy, precision, and artistry at the designer's command. Spatial quality is determined by size, shape, type and degree of enclosure, materials, texture, color, light and sound levels and characteristics, and by symbols. One of the more telling signs of neighborhood livability is that each of its out-of-door spaces is well suited to its use.

Ways

Fully as important as places are the neighborhood paths of movement and interconnection. What should they be?

Efficient

Paths should be convenient connectors. Walkways, like bicycle paths and jogging trails, should take one where one wants to go, and that fairly directly. When they veer too far off course, a shortcut is in the making. The direction and

Empathy. Empathy. Empathy. The three keys to all successful planning.

The planner must be able to live, in his or her own imagination, the lives of those for whom the city is planned.

There's much more of an effort today to create a sense of place....

GEORGE PILLORGE

Place into space
To be best suited to their purpose, *areas* are converted into *volumes*.

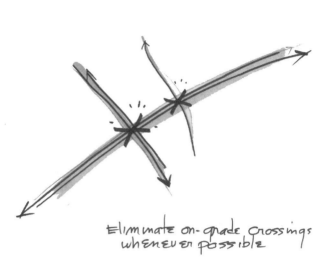

Elimmate on-grade Crossings whenever possible

Pathway-roadway crossings
Every intersection of a trail, jogging path, or bikeway with a road or street is a point of hazard.

alignment of a pathway must appear to make sense—providing obvious point-to-point connection along a course that follows a reasonable grade, avoids obstacles, and presents to advantage the area traversed and objectives attained.

Safe

At best there will be no crossing of major vehicular trafficways at grade. Further, the mischance of falls or hazardous contacts will be precluded. Shadowy lurking places along the ways are to be avoided and a safe level of lighting provided.

Comfortable

Comfort in the traveled way equates with ease of gradient, ample width for passing, nonslip surfacing, and protection from storms and extremes of temperature. Where possible, steps are replaced by ramps, and the short, steep pitch weighed against the longer, easier climb. Then, too, the needs of the handicapped are always to be accommodated.

Pleasant

Pleasure in walking, jogging, or bicycle riding implies enjoyment in the sensation of motion, satisfaction in convenient destination attainment, and delight in things seen, heard, or otherwise sensed along the way. Pleasure in motion is heightened by a horizontal alignment and vertical profile that induce a feeling of effortless gliding, looping, and swooping. Satisfaction implies that the relationships seem right and the objectives reached seem to be worth the haul. Delight is a matter of interest and a feeling of well-being. Travel along a path need never be boring. A proper path is exploratory; its use exhilarating.

Sequential

Linear movement along a path is sequential. It develops an evolving experience of transition from place to place and space to space—from sunlight to shade, from the open to the enclosed, from the general to the particular, from here to there. Such volumetric progression involves anticipation and achievement. Each segment along the pathway—as the path itself—should have its introduction and satisfying conclusion. Each integral space is designed not only to serve its own purpose but also to add interest and enjoyment to the experience of those who pass to it, through it, or by it along the way.

Every path has a story to tell. It is to be told simply, clearly, beautifully.

Character

What one likes or dislikes about a neighborhood can be largely ascribed to its character. Is the neighborhood like most of the others? Or, if it differs, does it differ in desirable ways? A good character bespeaks of individuality, of commendable traits, of qualities that lift it above the norm. What are some of the characteristics that can set a neighborhood apart?

Identity

First of all, does the neighborhood have a name? Why? Because a name imparts a certain flavor. Better, somehow, to live "in the Mews," or "on Signal Hill" than in "Block A of the Grant Street Project," or 726 44th Street, N.W. Streets, courts, and squares, even play lots and paths, will benefit from descriptive nomenclature. It might seem trite, but it's an effective touch to develop for any complex a system of naming based on a common theme. It may be nautical for a waterfront neighborhood, or perhaps elsewhere it might be of mountainous connotation, or historical, or such as Osprey, Heather, Hawthorn, or Hemlock taken from nature. If used, such names are to be appropriate to the locality, the feature named, and to the relative importance or magnitude. Such naming adds a certain sense of distinction; it also helps in giving and remembering directions.

Signage

This brings to mind the importance of signs, both for place identification and guidance. If brought on piecemeal and placed at random, signs can result in an unholy clutter. In general, the fewer the better. If designed as a coordinated "family" and strategically placed, however, signs can be an added attraction. Graphically, they are to be suited in size, shape, letter type, and color to the location and function.

Site furniture

Signage is often combined with site furniture—shelters, kiosks, lighting standards, game courts, and so forth. In neighborhood development there can be no better investment than site furnishings of the highest quality. For a small fraction of the total construction budget they can make the difference between shoddy surroundings and a handsome landscape environment. Furthermore, the initial cost of providing the best can effect substantial overall savings in long-term maintenance and replacement.

Those familiar with landscape construction have long ago learned the lesson of "site systems." Without a systematic approach to design, installation, and upkeep, a university campus, for example, would soon become a mismatched

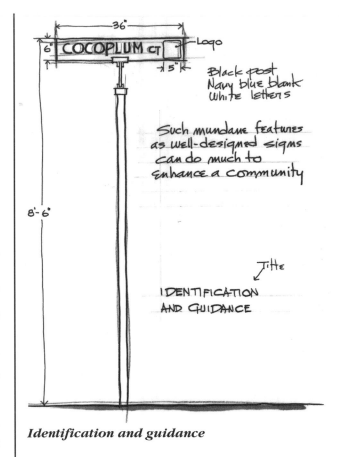

Identification and guidance

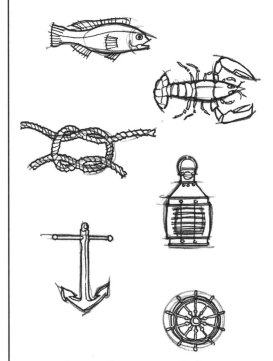

Logos bespeak a sense of place

collection of miscellaneous kinds of benches, light fixtures, waste receptacles, drinking fountains, signs, and even drainage inlets. Maintenance storage sheds would bulge with costly inventories of multitudinous replacement components, most of which would never be used. The solution lies in the standardization of parts, materials, and finishes reduced to a basic few. These, then can be "top of the line" and still effect significant savings.

Planting

In most cases the best "planting" is that which is growing naturally on the site. Clearly, this native vegetation is well suited to the growing conditions. Moreover, it is in place, thriving, and part of the natural scene. Experience has taught that it and the underlying ground forms should be preserved and protected insofar as feasible—with structures and site improvements fitted to and around them. Where the existing vegetation and contours are disturbed, new ground covers must be established, together with whatever planting may be needed—for plants are best installed only when and where they are needed and serve a purpose.

Planting has much to do with establishing the character of an area. For example, given three identical neighborhoods, each planted entirely with one of three different tree types—say one to Honey Locust, one to White Oak, and one to Monterey Cypress—their appearance would vary dramatically. Just so can the character of any site area be changed or modulated by the choice of plants used. Since a single tree by the entrance of a home may have more visual dominance than the building itself, plant materials must be used with great care and discrimination.

Some plants, like herbs and vegetables, are edible; some produce nuts and fruit; others are used for their timber, sap, or bark. Ornamental plants, native or introduced from all over the world, are prized for their varied contributions. Perhaps the greatest value of vegetation is its effect in ameliorating climate. By the introduction of planting in an area of masonry buildings and paving, the extremes of hot weather temperature can be reduced by as much as 30 degrees. In frigid winter the reduction in the wind chill factor can be almost as telling.

Too often in the development process, planting is treated casually—a bush or two here, a tree stuck in there, with more to come sometime later. Or, since installation is scheduled toward the last, when budgets sometime begin to pinch, it may be omitted altogether. But planting is far more than "horticultural parsley." It should never be incidental. It may be utterly simple, but it is absolutely basic to all fine landscape design—a powerful integrator of buildings, use areas, and site.

Increasingly, municipalities are passing laws offering both carrot and stick to protect their forests. In Cincinnati property owners can buy their street trees from the city to use as they please. But when the price tag reaches several thousand dollars, owners think twice about removal.

Studies show that houses on tree-lined streets command prices as much as 21 percent higher than homes in barren areas.

According to research (U. of California) three well-placed trees planted around a house can reduce air-conditioning needs by 10 to 50 percent.

MICHAEL LECCESE

Every home needs a place in which to set a plant. Every neighborhood needs a garden.

Ambience

A pleasant neighborhood ambience makes one feel good about the neighbors and life in general. It instills a sense of neighborhood spirit and pride. It is a product of good design and attractive surroundings. It bespeaks of healthful cleanliness—the absence of pollution. Of all negative features in a populated environs, pollution is the most insidious. Pollution spawns pollution. Weeds, litter, clutter, noise, glare, foul air, and contaminated water are all inconsistent with agreeable living. The prevention and elimination of pollution in any form is essential to commendable neighborhood character.

Neighborhood ties

Many neighborhoods are nondescript. In some it is difficult to tell where they begin and end. In other neighborhoods it is hard to decide what, if anything, holds it together. And again, there are those in which no one seems to know where to go for information or how to get things done.

Association

Few neighborhoods are organized politically to the point where they are chartered and have the authority to collect taxes or to exercise police power. Yet there is need to discuss local problems, study solutions, and to undertake improvements of mutual benefit on a shared basis. The proven mechanism is the neighborhood association, which comes in a variety of forms.

In the typical homeowners' association there is one vote for each household, with the majority ruling. Until a dwelling is sold or leased the landowner retains voting rights on each unit or platted parcel. A constitution is drafted, and officers are elected for staggered terms to ensure continuity. Matters dealt with are those of local interest not legally assigned to a superior jurisdiction, such as a borough, city, or county. Projects are paid for by annual dues and special assessments, as voted. Typical projects include the maintenance of common areas, the installation of new facilities or planting, petitions, news letters, and the staging of special events.

A place for convening

With or without an association, there is need for neighborhood meetings, as at the local school or church. There may be many smaller gatherings for special purposes or causes, but the vibrant neighborhood will have public meetings to which all residents are invited, reminiscent of the old town hall. Here, everyone has the opportunity to present his or her views in open discussion. If the meetings are held under the auspices of an association with elected officials, there is a better chance for order and constructive results.

Sociologists have long known that one of the most frustrating and debilitating aspects of urban living is that so many residents are never given the chance to express their opinions or to feel that their ideas or wishes have had an effect. In the neighborhood "town meeting" all will be given their chance.

Plan layout

Wherever one lives, it is reassuring to know where you are and how to get where you want to be going. This is a matter of simple plan organization. The best neighborhood diagram is probably some variation of a dominant spine or loop with off-set loops or spurs. Thus, with a short travel distance one is in the main stream and on the recognizable way. The nature of the spine or loop should not be accidental. It is the centerpiece, the theme piece, of the neighborhood. Along the spine's length should occur a series of meeting and activity nodes which in sum express and accommodate the best of neighborhood living.

The essence of neighborhood is togetherness in a healthful, well-organized environment that is unified and yet affords variety.

Planned economies

It might be supposed that any economies to be made in the plan layout of a neighborhood would somehow reduce livability. Happily, however, except where quality is sacrificed, significant savings can often be made while at the same time improving the neighborhood character.

Street frontage

Homes facing upon a public street must normally bear a prorata share of the costs of street and utility installation within the passing right-of-way. These costs include not only those of the heavier highway-type paving, drainage structures, and lighting but also outsize trunk sewers, gas mains, and water lines. Ranging more housing units along any given length of street diminishes the burdensome share of expense per dwelling. This can be accomplished by off-street court or cluster groupings or by loop streets and cul-de-sacs.

Off-street utilities

By long tradition, utilities—sewer, water, and gas mains, power and telephone lines, and more recently television cables—have been installed within the street and road rights-of-way and often under the paving. By all reason the

Street front economics
To face homes upon a major trafficway is to incur severe penalties in frontage costs, hazard, and pollution. Off-street living in clustered compounds has many advantages.

Street frontage is extremely expensive. Each dwelling carries the shared construction cost of heavy street paving, curbs, sidewalks, lighting, trunk sewers and outsize utility mains—often 20 percent of the cost of a home.

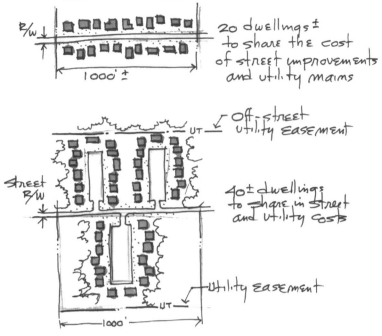

20 dwellings ± to share the cost of street improvements and utility mains

1000' ±

Off-street utility easement

40 ± dwellings to share in street and utility costs

Utility easement

Economies in cost sharing
The heavy construction cost of paving and outsize utility mains within the passing street must be shared by adjacent dwellings. This often unrealized surcharge is a major component of housing costs and rentals. The more homes that share a given length of street, the less cost per dwelling.

mains belong in off-street utility easements where connections or repairs do not necessitate the tearing up of the roadway and the frequent blocking of traffic. Off-street or rear lotline electric and telephone lines are also highly desirable, since there overhead wires are far less visible, do not interfere with the planting of street trees, and do not require their subsequent mutilation. With planning such easements can also accommodate interconnecting bicycle paths and lighted neighborhood walkways.

Stormwater runoff

Most tracts of land have well-established paths of surface runoff protected by the natural vegetative covers. Great savings can be effected by preserving these runoffs wherever possible. Where left intact they can often conduct storm water flow from residential groupings without need for a costly storm sewer system or expensive regrading and restabilization.

Existing ground forms

Plan with the contours. Let the existing land forms dictate the plan. Well-selected residential construction sites need little if any modification by excavation and grading. Where

To face homes upon a major trafficway is to incur severe penalties in frontage costs, hazard and pollution. Off-street living in clustered compounds has many advantages.

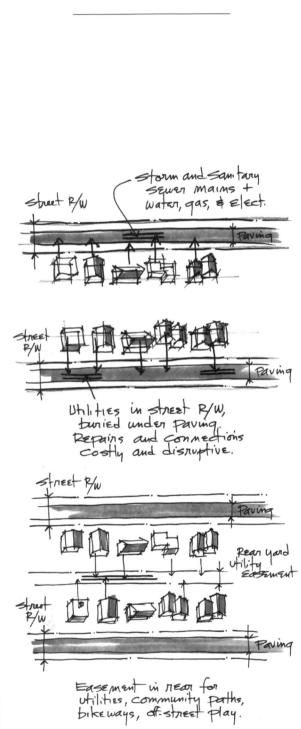

Storm and sanitary sewer mains + water, gas, & elect.

Street R/W

Paving

Street R/W

Paving

Utilities in street R/W, buried under paving. Repairs and connections costly and disruptive.

Street R/W

Paving

Rear yard utility easement

Street R/W

Paving

Easement in rear for utilities, community paths, bikeways, off-street play.

Traditional vs. advanced utility placement

buildings and paths of movement are fitted to the land, site construction costs are minimal, and landscape character is preserved.

Natural landscape features

Preserve the wetlands, meadows, and groves. Their presence and beauty were probably the reason for choosing the site in the first place. Plan around the waterways and water bodies, leaving ample bufferage to protect them. Ease into the edges of meadows and groves to blend with them while maintaining their essential quality. Such treatment not only precludes the cost of clearing, drainage, excavation, and the reestablishment of ground covers, it provides a ready-made landscape of a quality not to be replicated.

Open space

Create a neighborhood open space setting. Even in established urban neighborhoods slated for redevelopment, many topographical features can be preserved, or restored

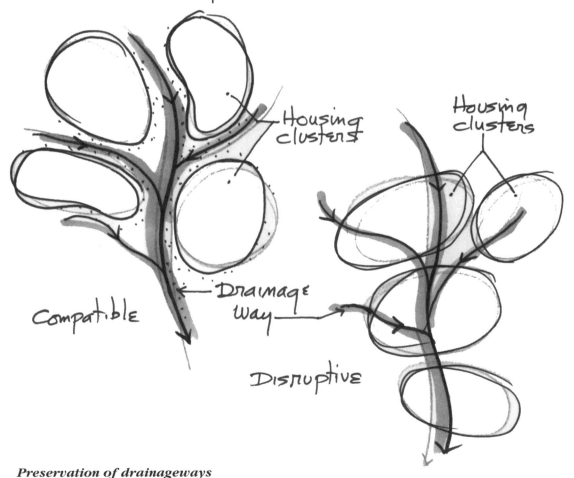

Preservation of drainageways
Where development blocks or disrupts the natural lines of storm water flow, increased costs and continuing problems are inevitable.

and included. In undisturbed development areas the possibilities are amplified. The features and areas to be preserved, when mapped, can be consolidated into an open space holding to provide neighborhood bufferage, natural drainageways, recreation opportunities, and paths of interconnection. By preplanning the total neighborhood, the costs of piecemeal design, multiple public hearings, and sporadic construction can be minimized.

Building by extension

In any land area to be developed in phases it is unwise and grossly inefficient to build section by scattered section. By doing so all the intervening connections of trafficways and utility lines must be installed to serve each section—often far in advance of needed capacity and at heavy installation, maintenance, and carrying costs. Far better to issue permits only for construction that extends existing lines and built-out areas. Existing dwellings are thereby spared the disruptions of intermittent construction, and overall costs are reduced.

The new neighborhood

The look and feel of the neighborhood is changing. The trend is toward the lighter, brighter, and freer in form. Less formal and less conventional. The linear row of single family homes or townhouses along the street is giving way to the freestanding pod or cluster. Dwellings of varying sizes and types are grouped around pedestrian spaces and interjoining paths, with cars stabled at the edges.

Architecturally, modular and prefab components of lighter, less permanent, and less costly materials are often assembled like Lego cubes into multifaceted structures of closed and open spaces around courts or a neighborhood center. In these minivillage compounds life is more gregarious. The elderly live side by side with the young; the wealthy with the less affluent. Residents often work where they live, with cubicles set aside for home offices, studios, craft shops, or the provision of community services. Such compounds are more complete and self-sustaining than the traditional, single-use neighborhoods. The more innovative are coming to resemble horizontal condominiums—with shared ownership and management of open space, gardens, and recreation areas. Many find these compounds more convenient, more affordable, and more pleasant.

In-fill, or the build-out of vacant properties in a neighborhood increases its vitality and the real estate values.

_____

Neighborhoods benefit from a mix of the young and the old. Isolated retirement villages—no matter how lavish or complete—are little more than "sweet hells." Unless those of a "golden age" can participate in community life, they pine away in boredom.

_____

The future may bring new concepts of neighborhood as in the cohousing of Denmark. There some households are sharing kitchens, dining space, child care facilities, and even commissaries.

_____

Cluster planning means simply that the same total number of dwellings allotted for a given site may be grouped more closely than under traditional subdivision regulations. A condition is that the land thus saved will be devoted to community open space or other amenities. The more compact arrangement provides savings in grading, paving, utilities, and other costs, and these may be shared with the prospective residents. It is good for all concerned.

_____

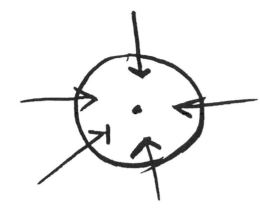

Togetherness
Neighbors need meeting and gathering places. Shown is but one example of block conversion possibilities.

Street dwellers.
Isolated by property lines.
Individual maintenance.

A sense of neighborhood
Shared spaces, ways and focal points all contribute to neighborly feelings.

Neighbors
Inward focus
Group participation

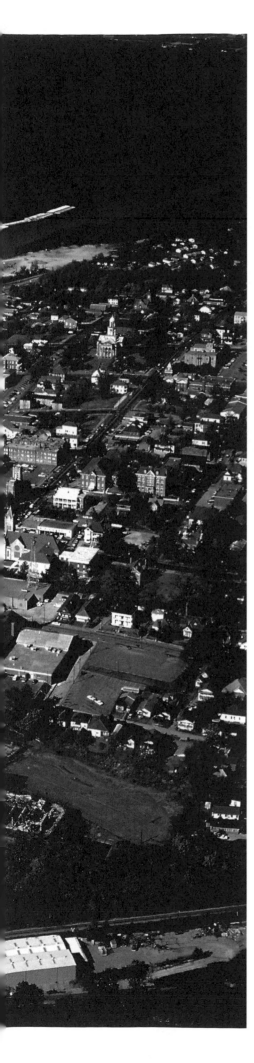

3
Communities

When one addresses the subject of urban communities, it is hard to know where to begin, for they vary so widely in character. Most cities have their substantial residential districts ranging from the posh estates and hilltop or waterfront apartment groupings to less swanky bedroom communities surrounding their shopping malls. Again in the older metropolitan sections are still to be found the homogeneous ethnic settlements of the Germans, Lithuanians, Poles, Dutch, Italians, and Greeks—or the more recent East Asians and Latinos. Where these settlements exist and thrive they are to be protected and their good features emulated. But in truth such agreeable enclaves are too often islands in a wasteland of humdrum mediocrity—or decrepit tenements and aching slums.

Within the massed and undifferentiated agglomerations there are wards or other political districts that function in some ways as nominal communities. They have their own schools and commercial areas, their own police and fire departments, and shared haunts and common landmarks, but here the sense of community ends. Although these teeming warrens have been extolled by some urbanists as being vibrant and exciting, they are for many inhabitants little short of living hells—fraught with poverty, disease, pollution, drugs, and mayhem in the streets.

Other residential districts fare better. In the main they are less impacted and somewhat cleaner and greener. There are, too, the formerly outlying subdivisions which have been encapsulated by the outward urban sprawl. Some have retained a trace of their individuality but lost much of their appeal by the fact of impinging traffic and the disappearance of the natural surroundings that were once their raison d'être. Many now slipping into obsolescence are crowded haunch to haunch with look-alike FHA minimum standard apartments or grid-locked blocks of once-proud single family homes, now converted to rooming houses. Signs in the windows offer zither lessons, dressmaking, palm readings....Most who must live in such surroundings yearn for something better.

Revitalization

Not long ago sagging communities had little hope of remedy. Once deterioration began to set in, the decay spread inexorably. It left in its wake the trashed remnants of better times and block after block of properties unreceptive to rehabilitation or new development. Should a venturesome entrepreneur with new housing or other uses in mind wish to take advantage of low property values and assemble a tract of sufficient size to stand on its own, there were always those holdout property owners who demanded exorbitant prices for key "out-parcels." As a result investors looked beyond the city limits to the countryside. This further weakened the city and further extended the sprawl.

Renewal

We Americans seem to act mainly in crises. In the past few decades the crisis of sick and sundered cities and of housing ills has demanded and received a whole legislative medicine chest of tourniquets, tonics, and cures. There are also provisions for major surgery. In sum, the new measures hold much of promise. There are now in most cities financial incentives for home owners to repair and improve. Government self-help and aided housing programs have become positive forces. Groups may apply for and receive low-interest loans for area upgrading. Tax-delinquent or vacated homes and other properties are offered to individuals or investment groups, on inviting terms, for rehabilitation.

In the early stages of obsolescence lesser measures are often enough. They may be fostered by neighborhood associations, by civic action groups, by service or garden clubs, or individual leaders. Sometimes city agencies become involved, as in sponsoring block-by-block cleanup drives, by the alteration of traffic routes, by street improvements, tree-planting programs, or the installation of parklets. City condemnation and resale of derelict buildings with "fix-up" incentives may also sometimes turn the tide—but it is mainly by individual efforts and example that urban renewal is initiated.

Clean up. Fix up

The cleanup of one yard or property often sets an example and starts the process rolling—from one neighbor or block to another. Neighborhood and community cleanup cam-

To live as a community is to live together in harmony and for the mutual good.

The community is a gathering of neighborhoods around a focal activity center.

The "quick-fix" single purpose endeavor to revitalize urban areas is giving way to a multi-faceted approach—as by aided neighborhood self-help projects, renewal incentives, and supportive public improvements.

To encourage the renewal of urban areas, it is helpful, and often necessary, to relax the stringent building standards. A two-section code—one for new construction, one for the renovation of existing structures—removes a major deterrent.

---

paigns—as sponsored by a club, church, or youth group—can lead first to the clearing away of trash, then to building and yard repairs, painting, window boxes, tree planting, and other improvements. A basketball hoop installed on a vacant lot or blank wall, a bench placed under an up-lighted tree, or a flower bed on a traffic island can create a sense of local pride and sharing. Municipal street repairs and bettered services tend to follow citizen efforts. The Philadelphia block garden program and "Pa Pitt's Partners," among many civic action projects, have started small and expanded to transform not only the appearance of whole communities but their attitudes as well.

Renewal does not always mean replacement, for new isn't always better. If something is broken it should be fixed. But often the bent, dented, faded, or stained has its own measure of charm. The weathered roof or discolored wall has a comfortable look of belonging, as does the swelling undulation of the once-level brick paving now heaved by roots or frost. Even the moss in the cracks lends a mellowing touch. The gnarled, misshapen tree with its lichens and burls has more character than would a younger, more symmetrical specimen that might be planted in its place. Nor is clearing and cleanup to be too thorough. Many volunteer vines and grasses have found a place where without care they thrive and add interest. Weed trees, too, such as ailanthus and mulberry or the osage orange, spring up of their own accord in neglected corners, which they soften with foliage and shade.

Many homes and neighborhoods are being regenerated—getting a new lease on life. Sometimes rehabilitation is sparked by external events but most often by a dynamic leader who enlists the help of others to form an improvement task force. Typically, as enthusiasm builds in group meetings, professional guidance is sought and the program gets into gear. The results may be slow in coming at first, but almost without exception, as momentum builds, the eventual gains are impressive, often spectacular.

Redevelopment

When decay has become endemic, more drastic measures are usually required. These combine the efforts of government and private enterprise. Local redevelopment authorities are granted enabling powers by the state, under which they can define areas in need of complete rehabilitation, acquire the properties by purchase (by condemnation if necessary), replan the street layout and land uses, reshape the topography where beneficial, and install new street paving and utility systems. Private developers are then invited to purchase parcels for approved types of construction within the new community framework. Where the

Perhaps what is needed is to forgo the suburbs and recapture the old towns in the old towns themselves, to downplay the car, tuck in more parks, put someone over the general store, use the street as a promenade, the sidewalk as a play area, and even—most traditional of all—create a total plan.

Jane Holtz Kay

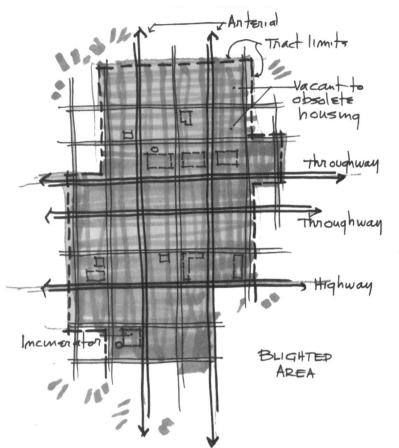

Labels on figure: Arterial / Tract limits / Vacant to obsolete housing / Throughway / Throughway / Highway / Incinerator / BLIGHTED AREA

Blighted area
This hypothetical in-city tract, plagued with dilapidated housing, vacant stores, abandoned factories, and rampant deterioration, has sagged beyond the help of renewal techniques. Every city has such diseased and infectious problem areas that rot away at the edges and drag the vicinity down. They are candidates for phased urban redevelopment. As such they can be acquired and consolidated by purchase with or without eminent domain. As alternative housing or business locations are made available to the remaining occupants the site can be progressively cleared except for historical buildings and other features to remain. A new community center can then be created by the redevelopment authority, working jointly with private enterprise.

redevelopment program is well conducted, everyone benefits. The tenants are interviewed, provided with social services if needed, and relocated (often temporarily) to more adequate housing. The transformed neighborhood provides a higher quality of living; entrepreneurs profit from their work; and the municipality recoups its investment through land sales, the savings in police and fire protection, and increased net yield in property taxes. The entire region gains in that such redevelopment is often the only means by which aging communities may be progressively reshaped and thus revitalized.

Neighborhood revitalization. First spontaneous neighborhood cleanup and improvement. Then aided self-help renewal programs if needed. Failing this, more drastic redevelopment can convert trashed neighborhoods into regenerative centers.

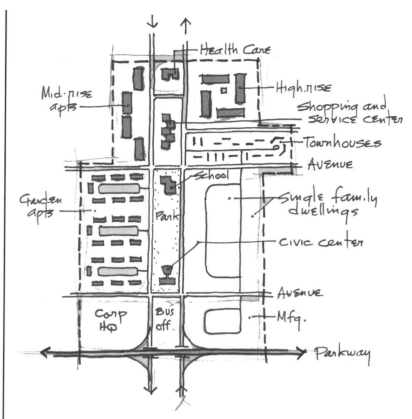

Revitalized community

Here the arterial throughways have been reconstructed as avenues with no residential frontage. All other trafficways have been vacated and replanned as local loop or cul-de-sac streets. The intensive mixed-use center is planned around shopping, business office, professional or health care plazas, a high school with recreation fields, and a community-civic-cultural compound. Such replanned community cores can convert problem sites into areawide assets.

Centering

A key strategy in community revitalization is that of regrouping scattered components into planned activity centers. The more successful have had a dominant purpose or theme, such as a commercial, business office, or medical complex. Typically they, together with supporting amenities or services, are grouped around a central pedestrian plaza, with direct access by rapid transit or busway and with various types of housing close at hand. An external roadway loop provides an automobile approach for let-off and parking while serving as a fixed boundary to keep the center compact and lively.

The figure page 36 depicts a typical urban condition of offices and other commercial buildings scattered throughout a predominantly residential neighborhood. Such a conventional disarray is laced with frictions. Homes are separated from shopping, schools, and playgrounds. Businesses tend to be marginal.

Today we're aiming for a much richer mixture of uses—not just office and retail, but a full array of residential, commercial, civic and institutional uses, linked and orchestrated by a renewed focus on … the pedestrian experience.

Alan Ward

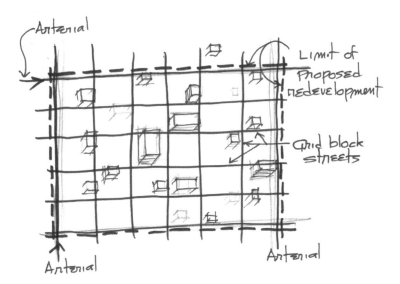

Scattered commercial uses
In this too-typical example, commercial enterprises have been located throughout a declining neighborhood as parcels became available.

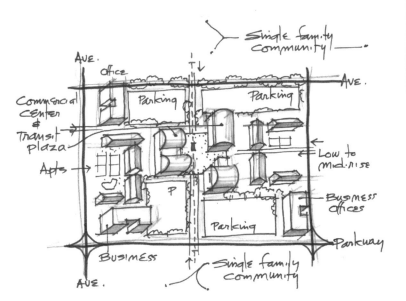

A planned business center (Consolidated Superblock)
Such a new or redeveloped aggregation, planned around a transit plaza, has the advantages of convenience, intensity, and unity with diversity.

With redevelopment, the commercial and business office functions can be centralized to their advantage and the grid street housing replaced with more livable neighborhoods and communities. In such a planned center the office buildings are directly related to the peripheral parkway, the service and convenience shops, and residential clusters.

Suburbs are becoming … small towns, because industries are moving from downtown out, restructuring trip-to-work patterns. These are the next generations of small towns, a gathering together of sprawl into nodes or other patterns.

ROGER TRANCIK

There is a real need to be conceptually aggressive, willing to go out on a limb and fight for a position ...

PETER ROTHSCHILD

You have to jolt the system in order to get somewhere.

RICHARD HAAS

You don't need to go on building Gothic courtyards or Georgian courtyards. The ones that are there preserve wonderful spaces of quiet and a sense of the past. You can weave on that past, not replicate it.

DIANA BALMORI

There's a kind of good manners to design which says that we respect differences, we honor the past, we appreciate craftsmanship and those who built before us.

HARRY PORTER

Evolution

No community or city can be better than the program and plan by which it is guided. This is far from being empty rhetoric—for most U.S. cities have arrived at their present condition through lack of clear direction. There is no excuse for such a lack—especially since in the next 20 to 30 years the equivalent of all existing urban construction will be built or rebuilt. It would shock most good and trusting citizens if they were to learn what sort of future city their leaders have, or have not, planned for them. Only with enlightened leadership and astute long-range planning can our cities undergo a constantly improving transition of orderly evolution.

Belonging

The more successful neighborhoods and community centers, new or revitalized, have a number of features in common. As a first essential step, high-volume through traffic has been diverted. Ample parking for destination vehicles is provided in compounds or garage levels immediately adjacent to residential clusters, offices and shops, or within easy walking distance. Improvements include the consolidation of blocks as pedestrian domains with variformed walks, passageways, and courts. Attractive furnishings, lighting, and graphics add their appeal, as do sculpture, displays, flags, banners, and even such incidental touches as windbells, mobiles, or hanging flower baskets.

Older buildings, restored to life, give a welcome sense of locale. Those that have been around through the years lend a touch of the venerable, a built-in picturesqueness that's hard to replicate. Perhaps a gabled roof, a gingerbread cornice or wrought iron fence and elaborate gate, or a patinaed copper lamp and post may recall another time and way of living. As in the Georgetown section of Washington, the Old Town district of St. Augustine, the original riverwalk of San Antonio, or the Bourbon Street environs of New Orleans. Few new places have such engaging charm.

For a lesson in melding the old with the new we may look to the grand old city of Montreal. There the best features of *"La vieille cité"* still exist—not cleared or spoiled, but rather, enhanced, by the new upper story office-apartment buildings. These have been carefully fitted to and among the familiar streets and haunts and woven into the fabric. Workers and residents stream in and out of the new structures during the daylight hours and long into the evening to enjoy the good life and liveliness of their surroundings. It is the compatible blend of the new and the old that is so agreeable.

Where feasible, historic landmarks, favorite meeting

places and even street names are preserved to retain familiar neighborhood ties. While common building materials, paving, colors, signage, or symbols may be adopted to give a unifying theme, it is well that each area maintain its unique identity.

Perhaps the most telling feature of all in the regeneration is the provision of *uninterrupted* sequences of pleasurable experiences as one moves along and through the pedestrian ways and places. Uninterrupted by vehicular traffic frictions and crossings. Uninterrupted by the intrusion of on-grade delivery trucks. Uninterrupted by the ostentatious facades of banks or office buildings that so often blank out long stretches of first-floor shop fronts and displays. Only within an islandlike pedestrian realm can community centers be fully enjoyed and their vitality fully experienced.

Grid street syndrome

In looking to neighborhood or community redevelopment an early consideration is whether to accept and work within the constraints and handicaps of an existing "grid" street layout or to make a change. Where established, the grid blocks are often best left intact and the streets improved with minor modifications. Again, two or more existing blocks can be combined to form a replanned "superblock," with many advantages. In most cases, however, when a sizable tract of the community is scheduled for demolition and rebuilding, a new plat and trafficway plan is called for. "Why?" some may ask. "What's wrong with the grid? Most people grew up in a house along a street and seemed to like it."

True, most who have lived along a street remember it with nostalgia, for the passing way and the walks at its side were where everything seemed to happen. Like meeting the neighborhood kids after supper, jumping rope, chalking out the hopscotch frame, feeling and hearing the clickity-click of skate wheels on cracks, dodging in and out on a scooter chase, or the excitement of the first weaving bike ride through traffic.

But too, one remembers what happened to little Emily and her sister in the perambulator. Or the time when Donnie was chasing the ball and it rolled out between two cars. Or the white-haired man who lived next door and tried to get to the store for a quart of milk, and now isn't there anymore.

Most things that happened along the street had no better place to happen—as on an off-street play court or the bicycle path to school. Although streetside living is still the way for most families, many have found that things can be much better. In terms of day-to-day living, safety, traffic

Every vehicular trafficway is a lethal line of force.

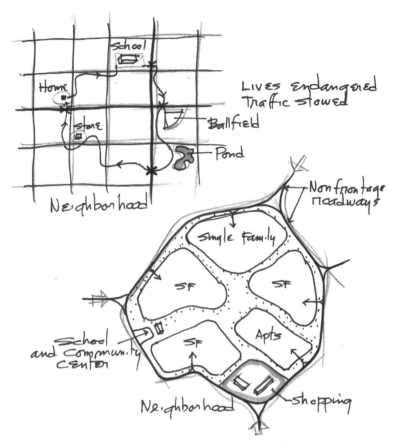

Street crossings or through-park walkways
Gridblock street crossings endanger life and limb. In superblocks and planned communities they can be eliminated.

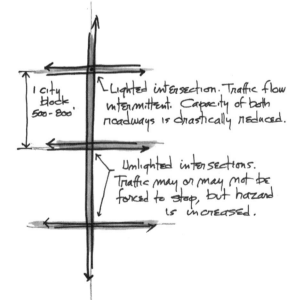

The urban traffic fiasco
It would be hard to conceive of a more hazardous or less efficient street pattern or traffic flow diagram than the conventional grid.

flow, or sheer economics, the gridblock layout of neighborhoods just doesn't make sense anymore—not since the days of the horse and buggy.

Suitability

When might the grid be more suitable? In many cases where it exists, and where related building patterns are established, the cost of short-term conversion to another street layout would be prohibitive. Here improvements and modification are in order to relieve the severity and to lessen the conflicts between moving vehicles and pedestrians. Where at all possible, vehicular traffic headed for other areas should be intercepted and bypassed. Reduction in street width, and widening of the walk paving would allow for street furnishings and planting—a boon to residential and commercial districts alike.

Again, the grid layout of streets may be well-suited to areas in which the land is relatively flat, with few landscape features to impede the geometric configuration. If used, the governing factor would be the size of the transected squares or rectangles to best accommodate the projected land uses, to reduce the number of intersections, and to avoid monotony.

The geometric grid would also seem to have more validity in districts of dominant architectural character, since buildings tend to the rectilinear. Where the blocks or superblocks are of sufficient size, those buildings which benefit from visibility can enjoy the prestige and exposure of avenue frontage, and residential buildings, pedestrian activities, spaces, and paths of interconnection may be focused inward to garden courts.

The curvilinear

A curvilinear roadway alignment is prescribed in those urban areas where the topography is rolling or irregular— for a rigid grid pattern imposed on even mildly rolling land not only inhibits the opportunity for landscape variety, it results in heavy costs in storm and wastewater system construction and earthwork. The more rugged the topography, the more rugged the costs.

In campus or community planning a freely curving street alignment and an undulating profile that rolls with the ground forms are much less disruptive and far more economical. Such curvilinear streets or roadways reveal the best views and provide the most buildable sites that the region has to offer. These streets are perfectly suited in spirit to the free and natural ambience that is so desirable. In a richly diverse landscape setting the grid street or roadway pattern would be anathema.

Grid block residential improvement

Dwellings on grid street blocks turn their fronts to the traffic-laden thoroughfares and their backs to each other, or to alleys. There is precious little, if any, outdoor living space, for up to half of such an urban neighborhood is usurped by paved roadway and parking areas, and buildings take most of the rest. As congestion increases, such neighborhoods tend to deteriorate. There are, however, a range of possibilities for improving livability and even reversing the trend.

Street closing

The temporary closing of a street can have long-term consequences. Sometimes it is brought about by enthusiasts who arrange a summertime block party or by the fact of ethnic homogeneity and the resolve to stage a street festival. City permission may be granted and barricades placed for the occasion. The spirit and good will engendered and the bene-

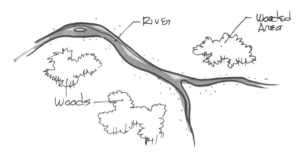

The natural site
A natural landscape setting is in harmonious equilibrium. To preserve and plan in response to its features is in all ways desirable.

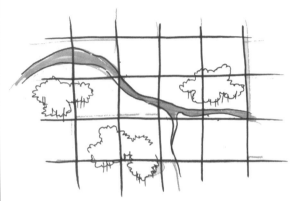

Grid street layout imposed
The imposition of a gridblock street pattern would destroy the natural quality of the site. Grading, drainage, and construction cost would be excessive.

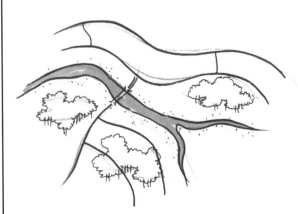

Curvilinear roadway alignment
Curvilinear streets flow with the land, preserving the topographical features and providing more livability at far less development cost.

If you can reclaim the street as a real space, in one act you have had more to say about the nature of community than anything else you could do.

BONNIE FISHER

A campus is an American invention. It strikes a balance between architecture and landscape. In a sense, the buildings are there in order to shape space.

DIANA BALMORI

In old Salisbury (England) the town plan layout featured "chequers," or large, named, rectilinear blocks, within which dwellings, shops, pathways and open spaces were freely arranged.

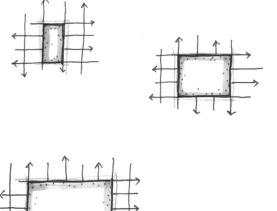

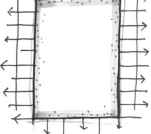

Creation of superblocks (By closing of streets)
With advance planning, or by street closings, superblocks are created.

fits of traffic-free living become so obvious that the initial request may lead to a petition for permanent street closing.

Rerouting

On a typical grid street network few drivers of vehicles have any desire to be where they are; they are simply taking a zig-zag shortcut to get somewhere else in a hurry. The closing off of selected street segments therefore has little negative effect except for the loss of a few minutes' driving time. It may in fact encourage through-area drivers to bypass the local residential streets in favor of the arterials where they belong in the first place. Each block thus closed off eliminates through traffic and provides the neighborhood with tree-shaded open space, safe recreation areas, and often local parking.

Blockage

Street interruption can be accomplished by the strategic placement of a building, park, or plaza on or across the roadway, with a bypass required. By eliminating the shortcut advantage, the former throughway is thus reduced to a local distributor street, and a whole new sense of "place" is engendered.

Superblocks

Still concerned with the troublesome and all-pervasive grid plan layout of existing streets, the urban designer must explore the various means of overcoming its drawbacks. One proven solution lies in the creation of superblocks. By this approach two or more single grid blocks are combined to form a larger, campuslike island. The best of existing buildings or other features may be preserved and augmented or a whole new grouping planned, complete with parking bays or compounds and open space

"Campus planning," as made possible by the conversion of urban grid blocks into more extensive superblocks—or by the larger redevelopment areas—will do much to "free up a city." Campus planning denotes a much more relaxed plan arrangement than the normal rigid street frontage. With the best of the landscape features preserved, the buildings can be clustered or grouped within and around pedestrian spaces. Approach drives and parking compounds are usually kept to the outer edges. Even the smallest such campus with the same or greater building densities can be made a garden park.

Widened corridors

Within the confines of the old grid matrix new freer traffic flow patterns and improved roadway-land use relationships

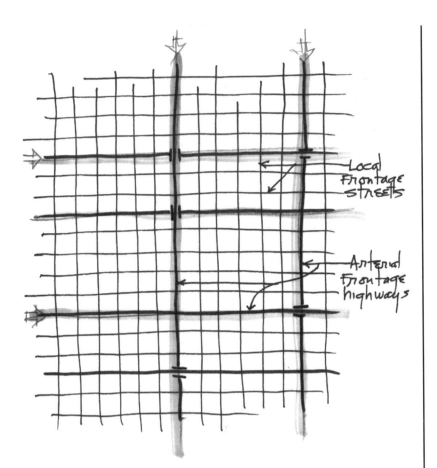

Local
Frontage
streets

Arterial
Frontage
highways

Grid street living
**The typical land use pattern in the older districts of most
U.S. cities. Life on such teeming trafficways has little to
commend it.**

are possible. With expanded, blockwide rights-of-way, the
rigid street alignments can be relaxed and many crossings
eliminated. (See figure on page 45.) But what of the rest of
the block area usurped? Is this not a waste of valuable
open space? It is not. First of all, the area of the blocks thus
used is more than replaced by the area of right-of-way
regained on the cross streets vacated. Moreover, the open
space flanking the paved roadways in these widened corridors can be devoted to water management swales and
ponds, mounded tree plantations, bikeways, walkways, jogging trails, game courts, and other recreation uses.

With advanced and ongoing planning, municipalities can
diagram evolutionary concepts of integrated trafficways,
communities, and the city itself and phase them into being.

Redesign of the trafficways

Trafficways are subject to change. Sometimes, on level terrain, with an existing grid pattern established, the conversion of two-way streets to alternating one-way routes will

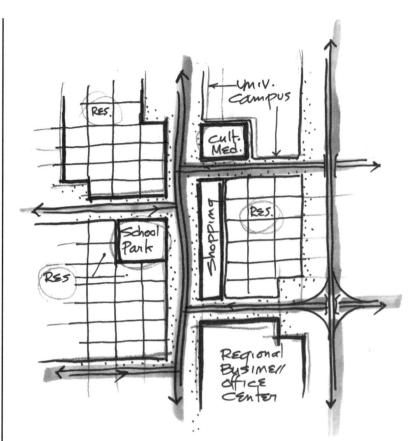

A restructured urban district (As by phased redevelopment)

Here, by the vacation of typical and obsolescent blocks the gridblock pattern has been converted to one of widened, non-frontage parkways serving unified neighborhood superblocks—each with its own internal circulation drives.

Highway widening is a village and small-town destroyer. Better the improved road swing out and around, with convenient access off-ramps.

Keeping traffic on the street in new suburban projects is not a goal for any functional traffic reason.

GEORGE PILLORGE

expedite traffic flow and reduce peripheral friction. Again, through traffic on local streets may be discouraged and shifted to nearby arterials by the reduction of speed limits, signalization, redesign, or by imposing blockage.

Alignment modification

Trafficways may be modified in design by the improvement of intersections, the introduction of curvature, or by complete realignment. With full neighborhood redevelopment or new community planning the possibilities are limitless. Relocated, the trafficways can be free form, following the valleys and skirting the waterways and other landscape features. They can be directed around, not through, cohesive residential, commercial, or cultural centers. They can be designed as limited access parkways for the safe movement of vehicles and the pleasure of passengers.

The planned community

Often, as part of urban restructuring, whole new communities are brought into being. When well located in relation to resources and needs and planned together with projected traffic patterns and transit routes, new communities can "free up" formerly overcrowded city districts. A new community can be part of the phased transition from the old "grid" city of the past to one more ideally suited to contemporary living.

New communities

Within recent years we have seen the advent of "planned communities" that hold much promise. They differ dramatically from the norm in that they are programmed and designed from the start as functional entities. The goal is to provide for a prescribed number of households in a receptive locale the best possible living environment. Some within or adjacent to the center city are wholly urban in character. Others of lesser densities are sited in outlying subdivisions. In every case the ultimate population is to be predetermined within broad limits—and brought on phase by phase, in keeping with demands, and land carrying capacity.

Such planned communities respond to the natural landscape features. They are designed to conserve water and energy. By a blend of lower and higher buildings, they provide a variety of building types, with relatively high land coverage, while preserving generous swaths of open space. Planned communities are built around their own schools, shopping centers, and industrial parks, with their own internal walks, bikeways, and recreation system. Their advantages over the conventional grid street living are so telling that large sections of our cities are being demolished and rebuilt in accordance with the new model.

Land-friendly communities

Although most newly planned communities have been built for the primary purpose of providing more desirable housing, they have had a propitious side effect by introducing a new sensitivity in large-scale land development. Some, like the "Greenbelt Communities" of the 1930s, represent conscious efforts by their sponsoring agencies and planners to fit unified and more complete settlements, compatibly, into the natural landscape. Following their early lead others have made their successive contributions. The benefits in livability, sustainability, and investment returns have been so telling that with knowledgeable landowners and agencies this approach is now becoming accepted planning procedure.

If we create physical environments that look very much like a gridded quadrant of downtown Philadelphia, do we really expect that 20 years from now they won't be functioning rather like downtown Philadelphia?

LEWIS D. HOPKINS

…to search for an order, to untangle the mix of ingredients and put them into like sets and then reassemble them in an interesting new way. …

WILLIAM JOHNSON

[As to community planning …] The thing you have to do is to figure out the kind of things you like to do and then make the kind of place where you can do them.

YVETTE MILLER, age 6

———————

Carrying capacity is the ability of a natural or constructed system—such as highway, utility, or public school—to sustain a given population without degradation.

———————

… public space will become the generator of form.…What makes me think that is the growing sensibility of people to the importance of public spaces for gathering, socialization, discussion, shopping.

PETER JACOBS

———————

We shape our communities and then they shape us.

———————

Free-form vs. grid communities

Most U.S. communities have been, by long tradition, divided into blocks. In the days before the automobiles this often made sense—provided the terrain was level or mildly undulating, and when there were no special landscape features to be avoided and preserved.

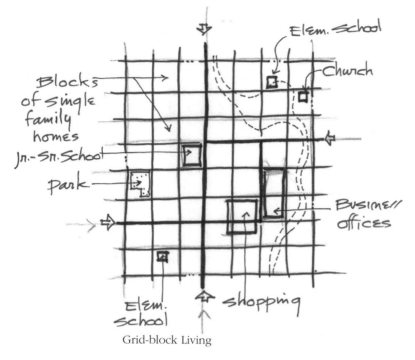

Grid-block Living

The automobile, however, has made gridblocks with their repeated "slow and go" intersections wholly inefficient for moving traffic. For children, the elderly, and other residents as well, the frequent crossing of checkerboard trafficways is distressing, dangerous, and often fatal.

That there is a better pattern for living and driving is being demonstrated in many recently planned communities. These comparative diagrams show but one hypothetical example.

Grid-block living
The typical urban grid-street community has little to commend it.

- Homes and schools face upon traffic-laden streets.

- Motorists and pedestrians are slowed and endangered at every intersection.

- Single family dwellings, being voracious land consumers, leave little room for open space, recreation, or natural features.

The Free-form community
New or redeveloped communities which include multi-family housing can, on a comparable land area, provide for many more people a much better way of life.

- Vehicular and pedestrian traffic can move more freely and safely.

- Clustered single family, townhouse, and apartment buildings can, without crowding, accommodate 2 to 10 times the number of families housed in single family neighborhoods.

- Schools, shopping, and all neighborhoods can be reached via park paths and lighted crossings.

The Free-form Community

The P-C-D approach

Given any candidate site for a new community, reconnoitering is in order. By aerial or other surveys, and mainly by exploring the property by air, land vehicle, and especially on foot, the planner will rough out the approximate limits of preservation, conservation, and potential development (P-C-D).

The preservation outlines are those including land, wetland, and water areas of high ecologic or landscape value. Of most concern are those outlines comprising an integral part of a working natural system such as dunes, tidal estuaries, bogs, streams, or water bodies. Outlined also will be areas of especially fertile soil, unique or prime vegetation, a specimen tree, a handsome grove, or other scenic superlatives. Also to be included are significant archeological finds and historic landmarks. All are to be preserved without disruptive intrusion.

Around them, as protective shields, are drawn the outline of conservation bands which, although not of preservation quality, are special in themselves. These transition buffers are to be devoted to such limited uses as trails, bicycle paths, parkways, or perhaps the community open space enframement. It is important that the uses imposed are compatible and require no extensive alteration of the landscape features.

Finally, the least sensitive, least productive areas—usually uplands—are outlined as suited to selective clearing, grading, and development.

This underlying pattern of preservation, conservation, and development areas is systematic in itself. Its process of P-C-D land classification is applicable not only in undisturbed natural terrain but also in highly urbanized districts slated for redevelopment. Where such preservation, conservation, and development areas do not exist, they may be created or recreated.

Environmental protection

We keep hearing more and more about the environment and the need to protect it—of the interdependency of all plant and animal creatures and organisms. At last it is beginning to sink in—the fact that we all share and contribute to the life-giving, life-sustaining biosphere. That we're all living, breathing inhabitants of nature's realm, that we're all in it together. We are coming to understand that as humans we have no inherent right to befoul the air, clear-cut the forests, dry up rivers, draw down the fresh water tables, or pollute the seas.

Our wanton and obdurate destruction is most evident in our cities, where little remains of the natural landscape. Not our choicest groves or wetlands. Not springs, or ponds, or

---

Until the planning commission has on the wall a generalized P-C-D map (the "want to be" of the land), it has no valid basis for planning.

Biotic communities consist of natural associations of plants, animals, and microorganisms that depend on each other for survival.

A thing is right for the land when it tends to preserve the integrity, stability, and beauty of the biotic community. It is wrong when it tends to do otherwise.

Aldo Leopold

Johnson Johnson & Roy

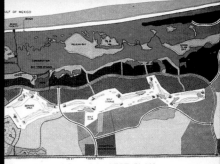

PROPOSED CONCEPT PLAN

PELICAN BAY

EPD: Environmental Planning and Design

Oehme, van Sweden & Assoc.

Robinson Fisher Associates

A TREE SPEAKS as MANY WORDS as IT has LEAVES

Peridian

COMMUNITY

Theodore Osmundson & Assoc.

Wallace Roberts & Todd (Paul Barton)

Peridian

Oehme, van Sweden/M. Paul Friedberg

Oehme, van Sweden & Assoc.

Oehme, van Sweden & Assoc.

WBA: William Behnke Assoc.

Garrett Eckbo

Oehme, van Sweden & Assoc.

EPD: Environmental Planning and Design

Von Hagge Design Associates

Thomas Church

Miami Lakes Community

Peridian

Robinson Fisher Associates

Royston Hanamoto Alley & Abey

Royston Hanamoto Alley & Abey

Clarke + Rapuano

Oehme, van Sweden & Assoc.

Sasaki Associates

COMMUNITY

EPD: Environmental Planning and Design

WBA: William Behnke Assoc.

Oehme, van Sweden & Assoc.

Royston Hanamoto Alley & Abey

J. Roland Lieber

Urban areas are the proving grounds for ecological experiments.

RICH PARIS

When the structure and form of the urban landscape are congruent with natural processes, cities will be more functional and sustainable.

ANNE WHISTON SPIRN

———————————

In the sphere of human behavior there have been three successive ethics. The first was that of the relationship between *individuals*. The second, still developing, is that of *individuals to society*. And at last people are rediscovering an inherent *land* ethic—of their ties to, and of their responsibility for the protection of, the human habitat.

———————————

Man's impact on the ecosystems occurs in small increments...careful monitoring is critical.

DEANE WANG

———————————

Environmental protection, to be meaningful, requires a system of monitoring. There is need in every region for a network of checkpoint stations to record data on the various types of use and development impacts. Such information can alert as to sources and levels before tolerances are exceeded.

———————————

even those hills which were graded out to smother the streams and drainageways. And now our cities are spreading out—inexorably, or so it would seem—to encompass more and more of the countryside. Is it then too late?

No, it is not too late.

Before any problem can be solved it must be recognized. Now, for the first time in history there is worldwide recognition of the urgent need to protect, and restore, a more wholesome living milieu for all living organisms. Let's call it a "new ecologic awareness."

George Perkins Marsh in his classic book, Man and Nature, first warned us, in 1864, of our destructive folly:

> —*of imprudence, and the necessity of caution in all operations which interfere with the spontaneous arrangements of the organic or inorganic world; of the possibility and importance of the restoration of disturbed harmonies, and the material improvement of wasted and exhausted regions.*

He went on to assert, and prove, that violations of natural law have catastrophic repercussions but that in the longer perspective, and given the chance, nature is healing and forgiving. We have learned some hopeful lessons and truths. That dustbowls *can* be stabilized. That watersheds *can* be reforested, springs regenerated, and streams returned to their former flows. That eroded farmlands *can* be restored to productivity—and that barren cities can be reshaped and rebuilt as thriving centers within an open space environs.

To protect and improve we must start with existing conditions. There is need to consider the problems and possibilities, to work out a program and plan for what a city might better be—and how best to achieve it. There is need also to monitor and to publicize the progressive results as notable urban achievements.

If "dying" Lake Erie can be resuscitated; if once hellish Pittsburgh can have its renaissance; if the sprawling Chicago region can be reformed around 100 square miles of new forest preserve—there is hope, and promise for every city.

No, it is not too late.

The conservation movement

Without "conservationists" we would have few, if any, state or national parks, wildlife preserves, wild rivers, lakes, or seashores in the public domain—or even the threatened remnants of our life-sustaining wetlands. Without the Muirs, Carharts, Pinchots, and Teddy Roosevelts our towns and cities would by now have "leached out" to infiltrate far more of the rural and wilderness countryside. Even the most remote of our mountain ranges and forested valleys, without protection, would have been subjected to over-grazing, clear-cutting, drilling for gas or oil, or uncontrolled mining.

Without the conservation tradition and momentum our cities by now would be largely barren expanses of brick and concrete—without the relief of hills, streams, or protected open space. Like the Biblical prophets, the early conservationists were fervent in their righteous resolve and persuasive exhortations. To them the American people owe a debt of gratitude.

How then could it be that today in many parts of the land and at many levels of society the local conservation groups are held in such low esteem? It is doubtless because in public meetings and hearings they are too often perceived as the vociferous no-growth, no-change, stop-all-progress contingent. Because too often, under the honored banner of conservation they campaign to achieve their own personal ends, which are not in the public interest. Such perceptions are counter-productive to the true conservation cause.

Again, often well-meaning conservation groups have unwittingly inflicted irreparable damage to the very lands they were seeking to protect. By their "block and delay" tactics they have forced the owners of large holdings to sell off their land in fragmented development parcels without an overall plan. The results have been higher densities, accelerated building, and ecologic disasters. Far better to encourage and cooperate in the long-range planning of such areas and reap the benefits.

The comprehensive planning of extensive land areas subjects them to strict environmental controls, regulations, and impact analysis. It requires the setting aside and preservation of such natural systems as dunes, prime woodlands, waterways, water bodies, and wetlands as prized community assets. It is the only means, short of outright acquisition, by which such naturally endowed tracts can be permanently sustained.

True conservationists have learned that for continuing success in their urgently needed endeavors a most promising opportunity lies in more active participation in the regional planning process. Here their expertise will be welcomed and applied. Here they can support, and help ensure, the preservation of the region's best natural and historic features while helping to formulate performance standards for the more compatible usage of the embracing lands.

Community components

Land use planning is simply the allocation for each broad community function or component an area of suitable size and shape in an appropriate place. Most areas will, of

Development versus conservation—a powerful issue in this country today.

Danielle Withrow

———————————

Enlightened conservation envisions the *wise use* and *enjoyment* of our natural resources while protecting and preserving them for future generations.

———————————

Sustainability implies that a given modification or development within the living landscape is so designed as to cause no significant long-term stress to the natural systems. In its expanded connotation sustainability touches upon such broader issues as pollution control, recycling, reclamation, regional planning, and resource management.

———————————

The conservation movement succeeds when it is positive and dynamic. It fails when, in a dynamic society, it is perceived to be static and wed to the status quo.

———————————

course, fall within the zone set aside for development. Shapes in this early phase are generalized and grouped in best relationship to each other and the topography. It is a trial-and-error process brought to ever greater refinement, until at last there is the best possible fit.

Circulation

Concurrently with the allocation of land use areas, their means of interconnection are to be established. There will be routes of vehicular movement, sometimes on grade, partially subsurface, or covered; sometimes elevated, sometimes aerial. Frequently their rights-of-way will be so aligned as to coincide with and accommodate storm drainage flow and sewer and utility mains. Other routes, lesser in scale but important, will be described for pedestrian walks, bikeways, and minivehicles. Where lakes or waterways are present boat routing is often incorporated in the circulation plan. The critical factor is that each route is to be coordinated with all others and with the land use area plan.

In the new and redeveloping cities of the United States, high-speed, rapid rail transit will play an important role. Most high-density urban areas soon will be served by a transit station with safe and convenient access from the surrounding communities. For many residents this will preclude the need of the family automobile. Their travel to and from the transit plaza will be on foot, by bicycle, or minitram. In such transit-focalized centers, limited home occupations such as resident offices, studios, child care, sewing, and crafts are to be encouraged as a means of further reducing the need for motorized travel. It is found that this practice also adds interest and sparkle to community life.

Residential uses

Clumping all residential development far off center in a community requires an inordinate amount of occupant travel. Probably it also puts too many people in one place. Rather, housing locations are to be composed in studied relationship to each other, to the topographical features, to circulation routes, to centers of employment, to the planned amenities, and within or near, but never astride, the paths of major vehicular trafficways.

Schools

Just as, ideally, the elementary school is central to neighborhood life and activity, so in the community are the secondary schools and perhaps a community college or university, together with their libraries, conference rooms, auditoriums, and athletic fields. With a concentration of

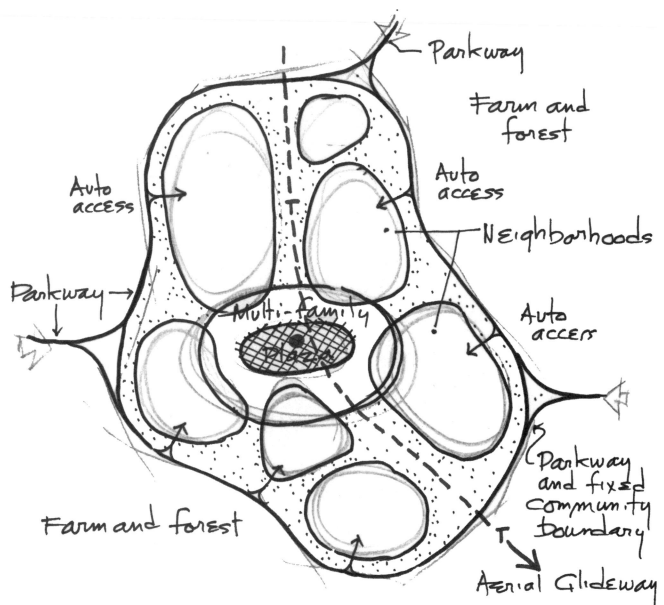

Parkway

Farm and forest

Auto access

Auto access

Neighborhoods

Parkway →

Multi-family
plaza

Auto access

Farm and forest

Parkway and fixed community boundary

Aerial Glideway

A transit-oriented community

Where sizable urban or suburban tracts become available for newly planned communities they may well be formed around a central transit plaza. In this example, neighborhoods of various types are grouped around an aerial glideway station.

As the major point of arrival-departure the plaza typically serves as the intensive community center. Ringed by apartment towers, with garden apartments just beyond, the station, plaza, shops, restaurants, and offices are within a few minutes walking distance for thousands of residents, who have no need of cars to get to other transit stops or the center city hub.

Residents of single family dwelling and townhouse neighborhoods, with automobile access from peripheral parkways, can approach the community center on foot, by bicycle, or by minitram through pleasant open space park and recreation areas.

pedestrian movement headed schoolward, it is reasonable that the paths thereto should be combined with parks or widened as community greenways.

Shopping

Complementing the schools as community destinations are the various convenience and commercial centers. They are therefore to be strategically located to provide access by those on foot or on bicycles as well as those who come by automobile along local streets. But also, since commercial centers are supplied by vans or larger transport vehicles, they need ready connections to and from the regional highway network.

Employment

The better planned communities and all more recent "new towns" have a sizable employment base. Aside from the nor-

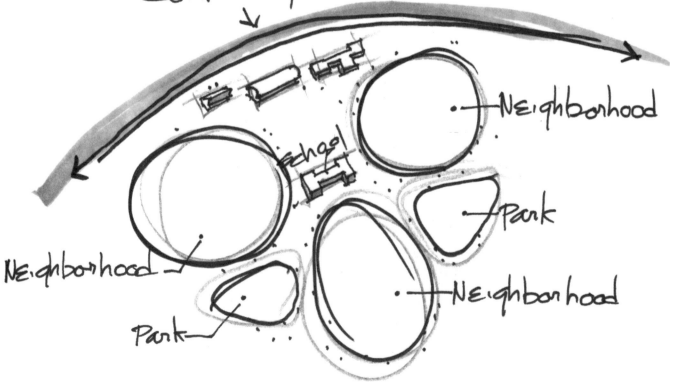

Shared community facilities
Neighborhoods can share parks, schools, and shopping-convenience centers.

mal labor force of clerks and service workers, there are those employed in the schools, recreation programs, professional and other business offices, and often in light industrial parks. Seldom are a majority of residents employed within the community bounds—for opportunities extend far beyond the borders. But for many the day's workplace is within a short walking distance of home. There are other advantages to built-in employment centers, for such workplaces add diversity and vitality to nearby living areas. Strictly "bedroom" communities are as drowsy as the name implies.

Recreation

Recreation need not be something one must go somewhere to find. At best it is part of the daily living experience. Although specific types of recreation—such as sports and court games—may need their own specialized areas, recreation may also be no more than a walk or jog down a pleasant path or a visit while minding the kids at a playground. A proper community abounds with enjoyable things to see and do—a "fun place in which to live."

Fundamentals

Most who decry the existing patterns of jumbled blight that mar our communities have blamed the results on uncontrolled growth. With good reason. Uncontrolled such growth has been, often to the detriment or ruin of adjacent landowners. In the absence of regulation, disruptions abound—the tavern next to the public school, the body shop next to the nursing home, the superette wedged between well-kept homes, the junkyard on the river. Each disruption introduces its measure of stress, discomfort, and various forms of pollution. Some such disruptions have been inadvertent. More commonly, however, they result from willful acts of obstinate independence. They reflect the U.S. penchant for nonconformance, for unquestioned rights in the use of land. They show little regard for neighbors. Too often they also show utter disdain for natural land forms, features, or forces. In short, these disruptions breach the accepted norms of human behavior and violate natural law. Such inappropriate land usage tells the rude story of raw opportunism—of gain for the individual or few to the detriment of the many.

Organic growth

Haphazard and disruptive development is a far cry from organic growth in the natural world, where all elements are marvelously suited to their location. In nature all elements fit and belong. They are interacting and mutually supportive. They are compatible to such an extent that groups of

A well-conceived development should increase, rather than diminish, the value of the surrounding land.

Modernism...treated the landscape as an abstract plane on which you disposed objects called buildings.

PETER JACOBS

Communities fail when human needs are allowed to give way to the pressures of profit making.

It is in the nature of living organisms to adapt themselves to nature's forms and forces.

Professional discourse resounds. On the one hand, open-space advocates endorse cluster housing and landscape architects pursue the contour of the land. Natural outcroppings of rock, cherished trees, and intact features dictate design. Organic is the operative word. On the other, a whole new school of architects favors reviving the right angle world....

PHILIP LANGDON

plants and animals within given terrestrial and aquatic limits are known as "communities." Moreover, in their form they demonstrate absolute economy in the use of energy and materials. As witness the irreducible structure of the blade of grass so ideally shaped to resist and flex with the blowing wind. Or the storm-braced grandeur of the towering oak whose trunk and limbing bring into dynamic balance every ounce of its mass. In nature all plan arrangements and structural forms are derived in sensitive response to surroundings and with utmost efficiency.

How can one build a clumsy structure after watching a spider spin its web? How can we so disrupt and corrupt the land after sensing the fitness of the grove or the meadow's harmony? How can we build discordant habitations and communities, as we do, when all about us to be learned are the lessons of the coral reef, the hill of ants, or the beaver dam? How can we fail to comprehend, and apply to our planning, the timeless principles of true organic growth?

Organic growth connotes a systematic organization of the parts. Philosophically, as applied to planning and design, it implies actions responding directly to need, time, and place—contributing to the well-being of the individual and the group. Organic growth is societal. Since communities and cities are first of all societal and since they aspire to systematic organization, it would follow that organic growth in their evolving formation is much to be desired.

If one wonders what lessons from the natural world might be applied to advantage in the design of our communities, the answer should be self-evident—the principles of organic form creation. The touted science of humanity is in truth no more than the perception, codification, and application of the universal principles of nature's way, or law. To violate is to engender problems and court disaster. To conform and apply is to experience harmony.

Precedent

History would suggest that as human habitations the most harmonious and livable communities of the world are not those of contemporary times but those of long-ago cultures.

The communities of early China, for example, were conceived in studied consonance not only with geologic forms, but as well with the courses of subterranean energy flow, the sweep of the sun, and the vast and intricate rhythms of the entire planetary system. Whole mountain ranges and river valleys were brought to a harmonious interweaving of natural vegetation, cultivated crops, villages, and urbanization.

In the civilizations of Egypt, Assyria, the Aegean Islands, Asia Minor, and Scandinavia, too, among many, every dwelling, town layout, and city plan was responsive to natural land forms, features, and forces. They were constructed extensions of nature, in all ways meticulously adapted to their locale and their building sites.

In more recent times and closer to home, the native Americans lived hand in hand with nature "as relative to all that lives." Their lives were guided day by day by the signs and seasons—the movement of game, the ripening of berries, the migrations of birds, the time of maple sap flowing. Native Americans took what was needed of the earth's bounty and left the land unblemished. The natural landscape not only was respected, it was revered. Snowcapped mountains were worshipped, as were the sun, constellations, and the spirits of the dark forest, deep lakes, and the roaring waterfall. Few today know the world of nature as keenly. In time, however, even city dwellers may come to experience once again the glowing satisfaction of lives attuned to the vital forces and nature's immutable way.

Today, sensing the urgent need for more articulate structures, more harmonious landscapes, and more agreeable communities, we are formulating an approach by which awareness of environmental factors is once again inherent in the planning/design process. The approach—instinctive for the earliest builders—has been repeatedly forgotten and repeatedly rediscovered. In earliest times an organic approach was probably considered to be no more than "common sense." Such an appellation as "scientific method" would be millennia in coming. In its current guise, after many centuries in limbo, it has come to be known as "comprehensive planning." We are only now beginning to relearn the fundamentals.

Comprehensive planning

In simplest terms, "comprehensive planning" means planning it all together. It starts with a broad survey of the regional environs and hones into a more detailed study of the specific project locale. Such planning examines all pertinent aspects of the land—its topographical features, geologic structure, vegetation, biologic communities, water supply, and drainage patterns. It further concerns itself with transportation and transit networks, with utilities, solid waste recycling, with tax yields, and alternative forms of governance. This planning deals with conservation and historic preservation, with education, health care, and recreation. It seeks the best possible social, political, and economic fit. It embraces the humanities and the arts. In the truest sense of the word it is, in fact, comprehensive planning.

Who?

Who does it? Who prepares for a community, city, or region a comprehensive, long-range plan? In the case of

In this day of reckoning, a few of us believe we have observed a limit to the ability of the natural world to recover from our excesses. If evidence of deteriorating ozone, emerging greenhouse effect and depleting non-renewable resources is not enough, certainly the realization that we have created a weapon that can destroy all life in a few hours should bring us to our senses. We must now teach and expound on essentials, not excesses, and replenishing, not exploiting.

MICHAEL FOTHERINGHAM

At every turn in the progressive design of cities there is need for experimentation and innovation. There is need, too, for a constant infusion of new ideas from the world of art and artists at the leading edge.

True urban design is not subject to fads, or styles, or "isms." It evolves in response to our understanding of people and the manifestations of nature. It is the art and science of preserving or creating compatible and synergistic relationships between people, their activities, their structures, and the natural world about them.

Planning the new community

Community planning, like all types of land planning, is an evolving process. It usually starts with the simple land use diagram, or graphic program. This sets down in a schematic way the approximate sizes and proposed "ideal" relationships of the various community components.

1. Diagram. In preliminary planning, land use areas can be indicated by outlines of the general shapes and sizes required to accommodate the various community activities. These will vary with the type of project. In this example they might well include two or more neighborhoods; a Jr.-Sr. high school with its campus, play courts, and athletic fields; a community shopping-service center; the cultural center; and perhaps a business office grouping. Depending upon the nature of the proposed community, it might also include the outline areas for such other land uses as a convention center, hotels/motels, a life care facility, hospital, or light industrial park.

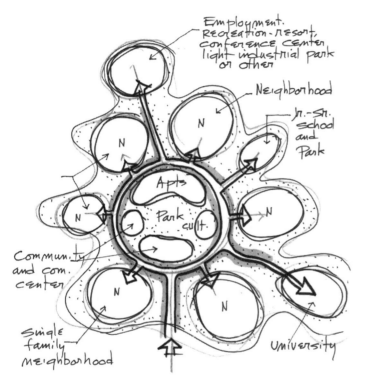

Diagram. Land Use Allocation.

At first the outlines are not to be positioned on a map of the proposed site but are rather drawn to approximate scale independently to give an idea of required sizes and best relationships. Together they give a first graphic indication of the community components and their proposed relationships.

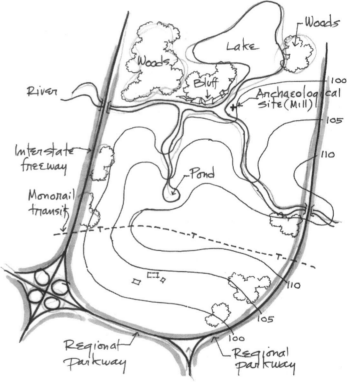

Topographical Survey Base Map (Simplified)

2. Survey. The topographic survey, a precise engineering document, outlines the property boundaries, easements, land and water conformation, and pertinent construction. If so specified, a complete topographic survey provides an accurate graphic portrayal of all salient surface and subsurface features—including structures, mines or tunnels, utility lines, vegetative covers, and other such data needed for detailed planning.

A superior community plan has an efficient component diagram, fits the terrain, and preserves the best landscape features for the used and enjoyment of the people.

3. *Analysis.* Taken into the field, the topographic survey is annotated to further indicate the constraints and possibilities. Upon this site analysis plan are outlined the "P-C-D" limits—or those areas of the site to be *preserved* intact without significant alteration, those to be *conserved,* with limited use, and those less ecologically productive or otherwise less valuable areas deemed most suited for *development.*

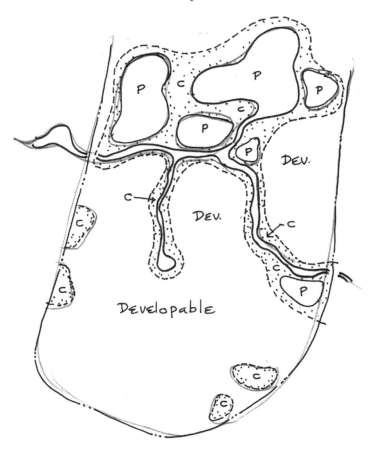

Analysis. Designation of the P-C-D Areas

4. *Concept.* The land use diagram is then tested against the annotated survey and adjusted or modified to achieve the best possible fit. The resulting plan, while still preliminary, records the basic community concept or "idea." It is known as the *conceptual community plan,* and is to be kept in simple outline form without fixed dimensions. Held for frequent reference, its expanded versions will be further adjusted and refined many times during the preparation of detailed construction drawings for the new community.

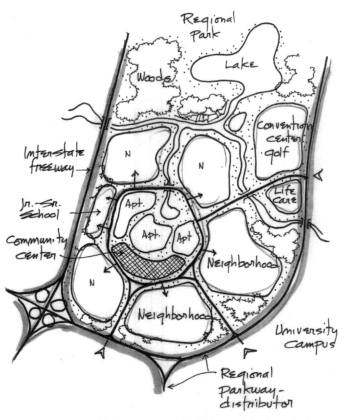

Concept. Conceptual Community Plan (A simplified version)

Only when the proposed *land uses* and connecting paths of movement have been adjusted to the topography is more detailed study in order. Only if the concept is sound can the project be successful.

Comprehensive land planning requires an inter-disciplinary team, including scientific advisors, to assure that proposals for change impose no excessive stress on existing ecosystems.

———————————

The relatively new interdisciplinary team approach—planners, landscape architects, architects and engineers, working together with scientific advisors—is the key to more effective urban planning.

———————————

Design critics regularly argue for a total plan to relieve the disorderly sprawl of the last generation.

Jane Holtz Kay

any political jurisdiction it is the work of a planning commission. Commission members are either appointed or elected, but in any case they should be, insofar as possible, politically independent and represent a broad-based spectrum of community leadership at its best. Citizen members discuss and determine goals and policy and review and guide the evolving plan. The actual planning is done by staff—hopefully under the direction of an inspired and inspiring generalist leader. An interdisciplinary team will be needed, often with the help of a supplementary panel of scientific advisors. No one person, not even a modern-day Leonardo, could have the breadth of knowledge required for total planning in its present dimensions.

Frequently, in smaller jurisdictions, a commission and planning director may engage and oversee the work of a team of planning consultants. This approach may have the advantage of bringing to any study a wider range of experience—of successes, failures, and lessons learned in other comprehensive planning endeavors.

Many landowners and private developers have, or engage, their own planning teams. In such cases it is evident that the private teams should work closely with the local planning commission and staff to their mutual gain.

Why?

Why plan our cities and communities? Why not let them come on, as in the recent past, in their own uninhibited, lackadaisical way? Simply because the results have been so disastrous and costly. Without planning, our communities will be built as before—on a parcel-by-parcel basis, without concern for what happens beyond the parcel limits, without provision for schools, shopping, workplaces, recreation areas or the means by which to get there. Lack of long-range planning results in "scatteration," bypassed lots, vacancies, strip commercial accretions, gridlocked neighborhoods, and clogged highways. Without planning, we could expect only more of the all-too-familiar same.

Only when all components are planned together, in balance and in harmony with the natural and built surroundings, can a salubrious living environment be expected.

How?

There is no mystery to the comprehensive planning process. It is orderly and logical, implemented step by step.

First, the goals. These will be broad, rather idealistic statements as to what is to be achieved. Then follows a listing of the more specific objectives—the actions by which the goals are to be realized.

There will be the preparation of a coordinated series of base maps having to do with such things as the existing _topography, soil types_ and the location and logs of test drillings. There will be maps of local and regional _land uses, zoning,_ and _trafficways;_ of _utility mains, employment centers,_ and _commercial areas._ Schools, libraries, and museums will be shown, as will be hospitals, churches, auditoriums, and other cultural amenities. Additional maps will show the _climatological, ecological,_ and _environmental_ factors, which vary with the locality.

Research will entail a survey of the pertinent data available from planning departments, other public agencies, libraries, and private sources. The genius of data gathering is to collect and record _all_ but _only_ the information required. Then comes the _site analysis,_ gained from a patient and thorough exploration of the site—on foot, by car or jeep, boat and/or helicopter.

Programming involves a painstaking listing and evaluation of all the necessary and desirable community components as to their nature, area requirements, and best relationships. The listing must be quite complete, for once components have been positioned on the conceptual plans it may be difficult to accommodate others that might have been omitted.

With program and annotated mapping on hand, the _land use and circulation studies_ begin, exploring all possibilities. These studies are then tacked to the walls for comparative analysis, review, and revision based on such considerations as performance, economic cost and yield, foreseeable political support, and public acceptance. The evolving studies will lead in time to the best possible _conceptual plan,_ together with its supporting exhibits and data.

What?

Just what is the _conceptual plan_ and how is it to be used? It is only what its title implies. It is a graphic representation of the team thinking as to the optimum long-range possibilities. It is not a "master plan," complete in detail and rigidly fixed. It is not to be officially "adopted" by the public agencies, for such adoption would rob it of its essential flexibility. Once so adopted and made part of the public record, not even the slightest change or improvement would normally be allowed without an advertised public hearing. Better that it be reviewed and "accepted" by officialdom as the long-range "conceptual guideline," against which all phased and more definitive construction proposals will be compared and tested. To receive the necessary development approvals and permits, more specific proposals must comply in spirit and demonstrate equal or superior performance. If in their presentation it is ascertained that these advanced and more detailed plans _are_ clearly superior, they are to be granted approval. The conceptual plan is then

The planning process is a systematic means of determining where you are, where you might better be—and how best to get there.

———

All sound planning starts with a goal and objectives—a clear statement of what is to be accomplished, and the intended means by which to make it happen.

———

The best planning sets the essential framework and leaves room for creative individual expression.

Until quite recently city planning has dealt mainly with the two-dimensional layout of trafficways and its subdivision into blocks and lots controlled by restrictive zoning.

Zoning as commonly conceived is artificial and damaging. It is based on a colored overlay land use map which has little relationship to topographic systems, carrying capacity, or projected needs.

Incentive zoning is taking new forms. Aside from the benefits derived from "cluster planning" and PUD or "Planned Unit Deveopment," developers can now receive bonuses of additional dwelling units or increased floor area for a variety of reasons. In housing, these include the provision of low and moderate income dwellings, convenience centers, bikeways, recreation facilities, and open space. In other types of development the bonuses derived may be trade-offs for the inclusion of such features as ground level shopping along pedestrian ways, building setbacks, plazas, a day-care center, transient parking, or the preservation of historic buildings.

---

amended to conform, and its supporting documents updated. Only by this procedure can the evolving long-range community plan respond to new times, new techniques, new problems, and new opportunities.

Every metropolitan community is due for study on a progressive and progressing basis, for comprehensive planning is never-ending and ever-improving. With a flexible conceptual plan as a guideline, remarkable transformations can take place by orderly evolution.

Zoning

Zoning, as conceived by its promulgators, is the establishment, by law, of districts in which differing regulations prohibit unsuitable or injurious land uses and encourage the appropriate uses of property. Unfortunately, in its application, zoning's restrictive aspects have been exacerbated and the incentives to creative planning and innovation largely ignored. Since zoning was first enacted the form of most U.S. cities has resulted less from a stimulating concept or positive guidelines than from arbitrary "zone" delineation by officialdom and the overlay of a multiplicity of deadening restrictions.

Such zoning powers in the hands of opportunistic public officials—or applied by "go by the manual" staff members—can negate all hope for sensitive response to needs, opportunities, or ecological factors and block the way to progress.

Yet zoning has implicit within it the promise of essential land use control. When administered by astute professionals as an incentive to sound planning—and to ensure compliance with well-framed goals and standards—it can be a powerful instrument for good. Planned Unit Development (PUD) ordinances, Urban Service Districts, and Phased "Contour" Zoning are examples.

The term zoning is being replaced by entitlement—the proven right to make use of one's land. The meaning of entitlement too is changing—from the strictly legalized rights of ownership to that of demonstrated contribution to the long-range public good.

The new town movement

Our U.S. town planning tradition is founded upon a solid base—St. Augustine, Savannah, Williamsburg, the New England villages, and such well-ordered rural communities as those of the Shakers, stretching from Maine to Kentucky. With the expansion of statehood, new communities and towns were to be established—literally by the thousands—across the nation from sea to shining sea. Most were unplanned or loosely organized at best. Some have been thoughtfully contrived, from broad concept to detail. Each, with study, has its lessons for those who would plan the new towns of the future.

Garden cities

In seeking improvement and direction as we plan ahead we would do well to look back—especially to the early idealists. Among them, it is proposed, there were few to equal the stature of Sir Ebenezer Howard. A British sociologist, of sorts, he sought in the late 1800s an alternative to the oppressive life of congested and sordid industrial cities. His ideas were propounded in a treatise, Garden Cities of Tomorrow. A small volume, it was to have immense influence on all town planning to follow.

Although the title is bandied about in contemporary planning circles, few comprehend the book's central meaning. Lewis Mumford is one who did. Mumford, who has traced the history of towns and cities throughout the course of civilization and who has contributed so much to our understanding, was deeply stirred by Howard's writings. What was it in these pages that could have affected him so profoundly? Simply put, it was the remarkably old, yet remarkably new, idea of integrating the city and countryside.

Neither Howard nor Mumford saw hope for cities as entities isolated from their surrounding regions—nor for rural regions threatened by urban intrusion and denied an efficient working relationship with their trade and cultural centers. Howard sought not an amorphous mix of the two but rather a planned integration of urban communities fitted with care into the surrounding metropolitan area. They would comprise a ring of planned activity nodes or communities grouped around the center city.

In his diagrams—for Howard worked only in diagrams—each satellite community would be focused upon a central park, with adjacent housing and convenient marketplaces. This residential grouping would be surrounded by a wide green open space band or park embracing the schools and playfields while separating the neighborhoods. Beyond, between the circumferential avenue and railway, were to be located the various manufacturing and fabricating plants, business offices, storage yards, and service facilities. Within the overall boundary would be reserved ample room for allotment gardens, orchards, vineyards, and recreation areas. Further, within its fixed limits each community would "float" in a verdant sea of protected farmland and forest.

Applications and extensions

Much of the thinking of Ebenezer Howard was to be tried and tested during his lifetime. He helped first in the planning of the experimental town of Letchworth near London

Garden Cities of Tomorrow has done more than any other single book to guide the modern town planning movement and to alter its objectives.

Lewis Mumford

The "new town" of Radburn, New Jersey, was planned according to the principles of Ebenezer Howard and his "Garden City" concept. Called "the town for the motor age" it featured superblocks, cul-de-sacs, clustered buildings, interconnected open spaces, and traffic-free pedestrian walkways.

———————

and later in the founding of nearby Welwyn. Their success, coupled with his writings and exhortations, was to firmly implant in a receptive public mind the "garden city" idea. In 1927, the first American "new town" of Radburn, New Jersey, was planned by Henry Wright and Clarence Stein. Built in the garden city idiom, it was heralded as the community of the motor age. Among its notable features were a central traffic-free greensward which "budded out" into townhouse enclaves upon which the dwellings fronted. Service courts with automobile access and parking were located at the rear, thus separating those on foot from automobiles. Superblocks and pedestrian underpasses provided further segregation.

Radburn was to be followed in the 1930s by several demonstration "greenbelt" communities, sponsored by the federal Suburban Resettlement Administration. Located in Maryland, Ohio, and Wisconsin, these communities seeded numerous other communities of Garden City lineage—Chatham Village in Pittsburgh, Baldwin Hills of Los Angeles, and a mushrooming of garden-park subdivisions across the country.

Then came World War II.

European war towns

With the devastation resulting from the blitzkrieg and bombing retaliations, most European countries faced, after the armistice, an urgent need for housing. The best of the plans for the new communities more or less combined the garden city version with various of the innovations from the U.S. experiments. In the zeal for "clean and green," however, it is generally conceded that the early war towns went too far. This was especially true in England where mixed uses were frowned upon and look-alike housing compounds of various types stand aloof from each other and even from shopping areas, play lots, and cafes. No pubs or skittles were allowed within the precincts. It was little wonder that many residents became bored with their spacious new surroundings and opted for return to the crowded but more eventful city. Other war towns had their drawbacks, too. Some, like so many U.S. subdivisions, were peopled by families of a single class. Others were too tight or too loose in their plan organization, some repetitious to the point of monotony. Some were stiff and architectonic. Some like Cumbernauld of Scotland or the Gropius new town of Germany were overpowering, even cold and brutal. A common fault was the lack of things for people to do, pleasant places to be, or nearby employment.

All in all, however, the new towns of Europe were to make many advances over their U.S. predecessors. As an example, the new towns of Scandinavia particularly seem more sensitive to the existing land forms and to the creation of livable out-of-doors spaces. In their design they tend more to custom rather than "catalogue" site furniture and lighting and to the use of fountains, sculpture, and floral displays. Their central shopping plazas are a bustling delight.

In their sponsorship, too, the new towns of Europe have much to teach us. Instead of the driving profit motive of individual or corporate investors, they are often planned, funded, constructed, and operated by a consortium representing the interests of financial institutions, social organizations, labor, and government. The advantages are manifold—among them much more cooperation and a community enriched by residents with a wide range of economic backgrounds, avocations, and skills. In many communities families of wealth live side by side with indigent families whose undisclosed welfare stipends include an increment for supplemental rent.

The highly successful new town satellites of Stockholm are models for access and efficiency not yet equalled elsewhere. Their lively pedestrian centers at the central transit station are surrounded by multistory apartments whose occupants have little need for motor cars. Residents with automobiles are housed in dwelling courts and compounds somewhat removed from, but within easy walking or biking distance of, the central plazas and accessible from approach drives that circle the periphery. Interspersed throughout the neighborhood compounds are play courts, athletic fields, and frequent focal points of interest along the tree-shaded pathways. In addition to schools, churches, and theaters there are community meeting rooms, libraries, and day-care centers. These are working and living communities in the fullest sense.

American contemporary

Back in the United States, while the war towns of Europe were being planned and constructed, we were not standing still. Far from it. New settlements were springing up everywhere at astonishing speed and in an astounding array. Most in concept had echoes of the greenbelt garden city refrain. The degree and patterns of their greening varied greatly, as did their reasons for being. Some were almost entirely residential, as in redeveloped superblocks and inner city enclaves. Others were planned as a mixture, and sometimes a blend, of housing with other uses. There were mining towns, mill towns, harbor towns, and port cities. There were railroad towns and airport towns; lake and river towns, coastal towns, and newly planned mountain communities. Sea Pines would come on as a residential resort

What we're really doing is departing from Euclidean zoning based on separation of uses. Now people are realizing that separation of uses creates a fairly sterile suburban environment.

ROBERT KETTLER

to be followed soon by Hilton Head, Amelia Island, Pelican Bay, and a host of others along the Atlantic and Pacific coasts and in most states between.

The larger new towns of Reston and Columbia are still emerging. Columbia in its planning was as comprehensive as any of its time—with detailed provisions for health care, continuing education, and a broad range of people activities. Socially it came off well; economically, too, for it yielded handsome returns to many entrepreneurs. Politically it has not been so successful. From the start it has run into governmental opposition—largely because those of federal, state, and local agencies have yet to learn the preponderant benefits of large-scale comprehensive planning.

Commonly, mediocre parcel-by-parcel proposals slide through the agencies and local officialdom without question as long as they conform to established subdivision regulations and building codes which are often outmoded and which have consistently produced such dreary stretches of urbana. They seldom contribute their share of such things as public open space, schooling, off-site trafficways, freshwater well fields, or treatment plants. Yet, as a usual thing, well planned and innovative communities which would provide the full range of benefits are stymied at every turn. How better than by such large-scale planning can water resources be managed, open space networks provided, or cohesive neighborhoods formed?

Lessons

The European town planning experience has taught the advantage of relative isolation—at least to the extent that each new town has an identity of its own, with a surrounding reach of open countryside. Most are centered upon a plaza or shopping mall approached from all parts of the community along traffic-free pedestrian paths. All have their own schools and community centers, most with provision for medical services and day-school child care. In those with a transit loop or station the plaza is usually fronted by buildings with first floor shops and upper story offices and apartments. They are backed by lower profile structures tapering away toward the outer edges and encircling highway.

On the negative side, there has been in postwar towns a tendency toward monumentality, architectural uniformity, and a degree of sterility caused by the segregation of the various kinds of land uses. There has also been in some cases a lack of flexibility due to the imposed requirement of fully detailed master plans at the start, to be followed to the letter.

Continuing evolution

An obvious advantage of a new town is that in its planning and design there is opportunity for innovation and a fresh

Plaza—a focus for the life of the community.

MARK CHIDISTER

new look. This is bringing rewarding insights as to energy conservation, systems analysis, and environmental protection. Planning a new town encourages the use of new materials and methods of fabrication and induces modular construction. Perhaps even more of a breakthrough is the emphasis on plan arrangements which bring people into compatible relationships with the living landscape. There is a striving, too, in contemporary new town planning, to achieve a more meaningful sense of community. The communities and new towns of the future will build upon and extend the recent advances.

Sponsorship

Residential developments built on the profit motive solely—as by private investors—tend toward the exclusive. They favor the wealthy and provide little if any low- to moderate-income housing, as for office workers and service employees. These developments evince little concern for farmland usurped or people displaced. They ignore the plight of the cities and indeed hasten their erosion and decay. Clearly, the public good would be better served if such new communities were to be sponsored by a more representative and social-minded group.

Response to topography

Among the many advantages of building with and to the land are economies in construction and operation. The best site features are thus preserved for the enjoyment and use of the people. Land values are increased by reason of a more parklike setting. Negative impacts are lessened, neighbors are happier, public attitudes are more favorable, and approvals are sooner in coming. These are no small matters.

People orientation

The best planned habitat is that which provides, for all people affected, the most agreeable and rewarding experiences. Such for the residents and users are those of safety, comfort, efficiency, and a sense of well-being. An optimum habitat also involves a sense of belonging, sharing, and contributing to the larger community, which embraces the whole of the region.

The complete community

Since no community could possibly provide for all the residents' needs, the question arises as to what then should be planned in the way of amenity. The best answer is probably, "All that might reasonably be expected—and then somewhat more." The elements will vary with the nature

With the increasing understanding of our ecologic interdependency, sensitive land planning has become a matter of moral rectitude. Fortuitously, developers are finding that it is also more profitable.

and size of the complex, but the basics should no doubt include convenient access to transportation, schools, shopping and services, meeting places, entertainment and recreation—all in attractive surroundings. For many potential residents employment opportunities may be the deciding factor. Completeness also involves such intangibles as the options of variety and choice.

The planning process

Comprehensive planning in all types of land development first ensures that the land uses proposed are consistent with the long-range goals of the jurisdiction. Planning explores the possibilities through a progression of studies and comparative analysis and reduces to the minimum all significant negative impacts on the site and its environs and maximizes all positive values. Comprehensive planning builds in and responds to the ideas and thinking of the potential users, their neighbors, and elected officials. Proposals are presented in public forum for phased review and final approval.

Inherent in the comprehensive planning process is the preservation of the natural systems and superior landscape features, the conservation of adequate open space buffers, and the concentration of compatible development on the least sensitive areas of the site.

Design guidelines

Whereas the diagrammatic layout or conceptual plan of larger communities is established in the early planning stages, the detailed design of the various component parcels is best brought on phase by evolving phase in accordance with broad but clearly stated performance standards. Only in this way can continuing development respond, over the years, to changing needs and conditions, and advancing technology.

The cherished "unity with variety," the hallmark of superior design, is possible only when the participating designers are able to work within such a free and stimulating framework.

Traffic-free living areas

In the planning of more livable "motor-age" communities in the manner of Radburn and many to follow, a significant feature has been the segregation of moving vehicular traffic from pedestrian paths and gathering places. Where well handled, this has worked to the advantage of the motorists and those on foot alike. We continue to seek improvement in the relationships.

Accordingly, with this in mind, the planned community is usually centered upon an open space network leading to a central plaza or group of interconnecting courts. These are devoted to pedestrians and their doings, with all except emergency vehicles excluded. Passenger let-off and pickup points may be provided at one or more sides of the plaza groupings. Thus are created traffic-free domains of pedestrian scale and appeal.

To accommodate automobile owners, the circulation drives and approaches are planned to ring the pedestrian centers. On this parkway loop traffic can move freely with few if any on-grade crossing or intersections. When such communities are linked center to center by bus lanes, monorail, or other forms of rapid transit—motorist, passengers, and pedestrians can all enjoy unprecedented freedom of movement.

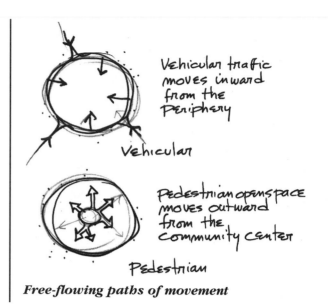

Vehicular traffic moves inward from the Periphery

Vehicular

Pedestrian openspace moves outward from the community center

Pedestrian

Free-flowing paths of movement

Can either the grid or the green
  provide a true sense of community?
Can we rid ourselves
   of the anti-social, car-bound environment
   of today's gridlocked suburbia,
   save the landscape
and make places where people mingle,
   play, and grow in new communities?

JANE HOLTZ KAY

4
City

It's a feeling that somehow won't go away. No matter what we hear to the contrary—of urban ills and problems—we still look to the city as the place to be—the there where the action is.

Why a city? Few if any who have studied the cities of history could conceive of a strong nation without them. That is a lesson of the past. Could it be, however, that in our dawning age of high technology, a polarized metropolis is no longer a valid premise? This is a possibility, and there is some rationale to support it. With data storage and retrieval systems so facile, and with communication so rapid, one wonders if the information and ideas could travel instead of so many bodies. To some extent this is feasible. Nuclear warfare has become a factor, too, as a deterrent to concentration. And there is always the question of just how much construction can be heaped on one spot—or how many activities brought into interplay without chaotic confusion. On balance, however, no evidence yet presented can refute the need for intensive activity centers where people can conduct their business "first hand" and where they may also experience much of the best that the region has to offer.

The city perceived

City life, at first hand, is experienced through all the senses. *Sight, sound,* and *smell* play their revealing roles. So does the sense of touch and feel, not only tactilely as by the hands and fingertips—muscles, lungs, and aching feet tell their story of the city, too.

The visible city conveys the most lasting impressions. It has been said that some 90 percent of what we perceive is registered through the eyes—those miraculous orbs which constantly scan the visual flux and bring into focus those aspects which for each individual have the most of meaning.

The audible city—of traffic noise; whirring, rumbling or roaring machinery; of street cries and crowd babble; of the occasional splash of a fountain, rustle of foliage, or the welcome song of a bird—provides a wealth of background information. Olfactory exploration, also, is more telling than one might think. Even with one's eyes closed and ears covered it would often be easy to identify a locality by its pervasive odors—as by the all-too-familiar stench of the packing plant, curbside refuse containers, exhaust fumes, sumps, or sewer outfalls. Or better, by the fresh breeze of park or waterway, the scent of a flower shop, the savory smells of the bakery, or of shish-kabobs broiling inside an open restaurant door.

Beyond the senses, the intellect takes its own probing measure of the urban scene, providing a running record of that which seems irrational or stupid, of that which is reasonable and fitting, of that which is awesome or inspiring. Then, too, the human emotions respond to, and color, that which is perceived. Attitudes of fear, anger, frustration, or despair can dull, or sharpen, perceptions—as can those of anticipation and pleasure.

Sight

First impressions are usually the most memorable. Therefore, since most citizens would like their city to be well perceived and remembered pleasantly, the approaches would be planned with this in mind. With but few exceptions they were not. Until the interstate freeways came into being the urban approaches were for the most part dreary excursions through fields of oil tanks, storage yards, commercial excrescences, and slums. With the freeways now looping within a mile or two of most city cores the opportunity exists for handsome connections to and around the urban center.

Introductions to a city can indeed be memorable, whether by ship or highway. Such examples come to mind as the port of New York, with its Statue of Liberty, the San Diego or Seattle harbors, the view to and from San Francisco's Golden Gate Bridge, or the Baltimore waterfront. From the highway, who could suppress an exclamation of wonderment and delight when following the Lake Michigan shore to enter Milwaukee, the upper Mississippi into Minneapolis–St. Paul, the Potomac into Washington, or when bursting through the bluff and tunnel upon Pittsburgh's Golden Triangle? Such visual experiences evoke a reaction similar to the auditory experience of hearing the opening bars of Beethoven's *Fifth,* or the *Hallelujah* chorus.

Future cities will witness more movement of images, signals, and ideas and less movement of people.

The advantage of the city is that of intensive contact amongst a diversified mix of groups and individuals.

The place to do the business of the center, it is being rediscovered, is the center.

WILLIAM H. WHYTE, JR.

The Carnegie Foundation for the Advancement of Teaching did a survey of 1,000 college-bound students, asking them what was the most important factor in choosing a college. Sixty percent said it was the visual environment.

RICHARD RIGTERINK

We perceive the landscape from the roadway more than in any other way. Even avid outdoorsmen spend more time driving through than walking in the landscape. It's hard to imagine something that has more impact on our environment and more impact on how we see the world around us.

WILLIAM D. RIELEY

The peripheral uses give life to a public space.

PAUL FRIEDBERG

Everybody would like to walk up and down a beautiful place, or go to a beautiful place....

ARTHUR COTTON MOORE

Beautiful, ordered, and humane surroundings are basic for everyone.

HARRY PORTER

Views

If scenic approaches are for some cities a while in coming, there is the more immediate possibility of capitalizing upon dramatic views. These may be related to new or existing buildings, congregating places, traveled ways, or overlooks. For the most part, exceptional views exist. It is a matter of bringing potential viewers into opportune relationships.

The passing scene

With planning, sustained and sequential viewing can be made a delightful part of the daily urban experience. It requires only the alignment of walkways, bicycle trails, parkways, and other routes of travel through or past scenic areas. New beltways and rapid transit routes also offer splendid viewing possibilities. Waterways especially await discovery in many cities. In San Antonio, Toledo, Cincinnati, Chicago, and Richmond—among many noteworthy examples—waterfront improvements have lifted the face of downtown.

The pedestrian experience

No doubt the greatest change to occur in our revitalized cities will be the reintroduction of pedestrian ways and places removed from the sight, sound, and presence of moving vehicular traffic. Freed of these intrusions the residents and visitors will rediscover the rich diversity of an urban scene designed to attract and please them. There will come into being diminutive courts, meandering byways, outdoor cafes, fountain patios, and flower-bedecked terraces within the urban centers. Tree-shaded walkways and plazas will be lined with shops exclusively at the pedestrian levels. Offices and residential apartments will occupy the upper floors. Water-edge paths and promenades will trace the waterfronts.

In the outlying neighborhoods and communities the internal greenways and the surrounding open space frame will provide a whole new prospect for pedestrian movement and recreation. Here people may rediscover the animal satisfaction of first-hand contact with nature.

Rooftop landscape

Almost without exception the rooftops of urban America lie starkly vacant. Exposed to the elements, they are frigid in northerly winters and in the summertime radiate stifling heat—adding immensely to the cost of air conditioning the buildings that support or surround them. In all seasons most are unsightly as viewed from adjacent upper story living and working spaces. When cluttered with the usual array of water tanks, machinery, and discarded miscellanies, they have the aspect of aerial slums or wastelands.

Wasted they are, for with in-town land so costly it seems incredible that so much valuable outdoor area is allowed to go unused.

Used for what? The possibilities are limitless. With a paved playing surface a wide variety of game courts can be marked off—shuffleboard, ring toss, paddle tennis, or boccie. Or how about a noontime or after-work game of volleyball in the sky? There can be exercise stations or, if room, a health course, glass-domed sauna, or year-round geodesic swimming pool and spa. Such recreation spaces can be made doubly attractive with landscape treatment and planting.

There can be rooftop gardens. With ample sun and a water source, hydroponic culture is a natural. Or with a light soil section or planters a roof area can produce a bountiful crop of herbs or vegetables for the table or even for sale in the markets below. Dwarf fruit trees in tubs, or espaliered, are not only decorative, they can also produce such welcome bounty as figs, pears, limes, and lemons. So, too, can the arbor yield its festoons of grapes or a tiered wall its cascades of strawberries.

Slatted decks, planting bins, and well-selected plants can convert an arid rooftop into a veritable bower of foliage and bloom. Succulents, bulbs, and annuals placed about in containers are an ideal solution for city gardeners, as are flowering vines on trellis or wall. The right trees, shrubs, and grasses can also thrive with but little care and add interest in all seasons. Plantings can be supplemented with irrigated ground covers, gravels, and other mulches. Here, too, is the place for water panels, spray basins, wall fountains, mosaics, and sculpture. Such transformed spaces not only brighten the day for all around but, with evening illumination, are favored places for relaxation, dining, sky watching, or viewing the city lights. Aside from the advantages of savings in building heating and cooling costs and the refreshing effects of plant transpiration, the visual upgrading of the neighborhood can add a measure of enjoyment to all city dwellers.

Climate moderation

To bring trees, ground covers, and open water into the city is not just for "pretties." They can significantly affect the ambient temperatures year 'round. The surface temperature of tree-shaded turf, an irrigated planting bed, or an expanse of open water, for example, can be some 30 degrees cooler in summer than that of sun-hot paving beside it. In winter, even bare-limbed trees can temper the chilling winds. Planting beds add their measure of moderation. It would follow that in the issuance of permits for any and all urban

Neglected

Utilized

City rooftops

Example:

80 dba. (decibels)
Airports, transport,
manufacturing

70 dba. Commercial,
business offices,
fabricating

60 dba. Residential

50 dba. Hospitals
schools, churches

development—be it a neighborhood, apartment complex, or high-rise tower, be it a shopping center or office park—a condition of plan approval might well be the provision of a specified number of sizable trees or a given area of planting. The sum of such climate modifiers would soon, and increasingly, make an appreciable difference.

Sun, shade, and shadow patterns affect the microclimate, also. Building height and bulk conformation, and the positioning of structures in relation to the seasonal sun-sweep are important considerations in the plan review. Not to be overlooked is their effect on the blockage of prevailing winter winds and the channelization of welcome summer breezes. Architecturally, the use of the canopied walkway, arcades, colonnades, the open atrium, protected courts, and roof gardens are also to be considered.

Without doubt, however, the greatest benefit to be gained in urban climate amelioration is that to be provided by the plantations and natural covers of the open space systems and forest preserves that surround and weave through the city.

Sound

Decibels are the unit measure of sound intensity. Sound can be good or bad. Unwanted sound is commonly known as "noise," with little to commend it. Desirable sound is akin to music. Even music, however, can be classified as noise by some listeners, especially when too loud or inappropriate as to time or place. As to noise of all types, the fewer decibels, the better.

Compatibility

Appropriate sound is that which produces no disturbance or discomfort and is agreeable to its listeners. Noise distracts, disturbs, and may become a hazard to well-being or even sanity. Within the urban context the best means of ensuring that sound levels are compatible is that of decibel zoning, which prohibits excessive noise within prescribed geographical limits. Hospitals, schools, churches, and conference centers are candidates for quiet. Residential areas, passive parks, botanic gardens, and office groupings can withstand a few more decibels, as can shopping and business compounds. Playgrounds and sports fields generate their own higher sound intensity and are best kept apart. Light manufacturing districts and transport centers with their noisy truckway traffic are also to be segregated—as are airports, the chief offenders.

Such decibel zoning cannot be arbitrarily applied and should be a major consideration in all long-range urban planning.

Noise control

Noise can be reduced by distance, by interception, by deflection, and by absorption. To move trafficways or point sources away from susceptible areas, or to isolate them, is desirable. Where this is not possible the construction of solid, perforated, or studded masonry barriers or earth mounding as a shield is surprisingly effective. Sound tends to rise, which gives reason to elevate such noise generators as playfields above the level of surrounding areas where quiet is appreciated.

Foliage absorbs sound, although not as much as might be expected. Psychologically, however, the visual screening of roadways by vegetation reduces apparent traffic noise as well as mitigating other negative features.

Acoustical perfume

Some disturbing noises such as those emanating from trafficways or mechanical equipment can be softened or masked by other counterbalancing sounds. Crowd chatter is a cover-up, as is suitable background music, a cascade, or waterfall.

Many distinctive and familiar sounds add much to the pleasure of city living. Such are those of rolling church bells, pealing chimes, the stirring beat of marching bands, or lilting strains of a concert in the square. We welcome, too, the vendor's calls, the strumming of a lone guitar, or the cadence of pickup musicians gathered in the evening at a corner. Increasingly city dwellers will come to enjoy such quiet sounds as the rustle of foliage in the breeze or the splashing of water in a wayside fountain.

Smell

If we think of the city as being malodorous, it is by reason of experience. Even in this era of tightened environmental controls we have as yet to eliminate the stench that pervades large sections of our cities. We need not bother to categorize the olfactory offenders. We know them only too well.

Pollution controls are having increasing effect and are to be supported to the utmost. Often, however, persistent offenders are best addressed on a case-by-case basis—by personal protests, boycotts, letters to the newspaper, petitions, and political pressure. Not long ago, many politicians approached for relief from such nuisances would have wondered what you were talking about. All are now aware of the problem and the need for positive action.

A problem of pollution control has been that those most able to institute change have seen little benefit to themselves. They must be made to see the advantage.

Touch

How does one feel a city? Through all the creature comforts and pains. The less of pain and more of comfort, the better the city "feels."

It has been the privilege of Americans to live in a free and well-ordered society. The freedom we take for granted. Lately, the "well-ordered" we have come to question.

Comfort is equated with agreeable sensations such as warmth and lack of exposure in winter—cool breezes and shade in the summertime. Distances to be traveled and ease of ascent or descent are functions of comfort also, as is the grip of the pavement under foot. Even the springiness or curvature of a bench, the slope of a ramp, or the height of a handrail can contribute to physical comfort. All are matters of planning and design.

The human animal never ceases the tactile exploration of the environment—mainly by hands and feet. The eyes, too, in an indirect way, are finely tuned tactile sensors, for they translate light and shadow into masses and textures, and colors into the "hots" and "cools." All individuals, young or old, from head to toe, are sensitive perceptors. And so we make our way from object to object and place to place repelled or attracted by our sensations and the way things feel.

Intellection

We are more than sensing creatures; we are thinkers, too. We are bothered when there are discrepancies between what things are and what we believe they might better be. Logic has taught us to seek a rational order. Experience has shown that when things are not operating in accordance with our ethical code, or with natural law, then disappointment, suffering, or total disaster may follow.

As animals, species homo sapiens, we reason that danger and unhealthful conditions are to be avoided, and so it is clear that in our living environment undue threats to our safety or well-being and all forms of pollution must be eliminated. We seek always those conditions closer to the ideal. By intellection and learning we find that as conditions improve, our concept of the "ideal" may change for the better—a fact that should lead to progressive improvement. For as we raise our levels of expectation, superior performance will usually follow.

Emotions

Emotions, also, are involved in impressions, for what is perceived is often affected by one's emotional state. Our emotional rheostats have an astounding range—from the base to the lofty, from brutal to tender, from the crude to the highly refined. Whole cities at times have been caught up in the baser emotions—as of blind rage and clamor for war. In damning testimony it can be pointed out that with few exceptions every civilization of history has been built upon the charred rubble of another. If intellection fails us here in crucial times, the charred remnants of *our* cities too may be all that we leave behind.

Whole cities have also been imbued with emotions that tend toward the sublime. How else can one explain the occasional passion of a people for great works of music and art, for magnificent garden-parks, or for such architectural superlatives as Salisbury Cathedral, San Marco, Rheims, or Chartres?

Civic pride

One of the higher emotions to be attributed to world citizens is that of civic pride. The Athenians had it with good reason and good measure. Their high-minded approach to all things in life—to their bodies, minds, temples, and city—is still considered a benchmark. The Romans gave further meaning to civilization—to law and to order. In turn, the people of Constantinople created a city perhaps yet unsurpassed in those qualities we have come to associate with urbanity. Such cities of the past give credence to the belief that the well-conceived and well-governed city is the highest form of human accomplishment.

Our triumph, if we are to have one, may not be the world's greatest cities but rather the advancement of knowledge by which greater cities are built.

Events

What is happening this week in the city? If the answer is, "Nothing," or "not much," then it's not much of a city. A thriving city is always eventful.

Events come in multitudinous forms—ranging all the way from celebrations to disasters. On the up side are the holiday parades and festivals when the bands are playing, the flags are flying, and all is in happy tumult. There are conventions, trade fairs, auto shows, and shows of homes, flowers, pets, and boats. There are sporting events in the stadium, matches and circuses in the arena, exhibitions in the galleries, and races on rivers and in the streets. Patrons flock to the city from far and wide to attend the symphony, the opera, plays, pageants, the ballet, and special religious services. There are lesser festivities, too, for each community or neighborhood will have its own athletic events, school plays, concerts, lectures, street fairs, club meetings, and bake sales. All help to give a sense of belonging and sharing—and that's what the good life is about.

In the tradition of the Mississippi showboat, a new fleet of show and music barges has become a familiar seasonal attraction along the urban riverways and waterfronts. By longer custom and at lesser scale we have the strolling players and performers. The loner strumming a guitar, the pop group with hat set out on the paving, the noontime string or wind ensemble seated by the plaza fountain—all add zest and life.

The great cities of their eras were the embodiment of an ideal—each the "ideal" city for its culture, place, and time.

———————————

Urbanism equates with variety. The more variety, the bigger the crowds. The bigger the crowds, and the longer they linger—the more successful the city.

———————————

The excitement of the city comes from its ceaseless activity.

RICHARD BROOKHISER

Climate, culture, religion, and history have all contributed to Mexico's strong tradition of plazas and public open spaces, where architecture and landscape meet to accommodate festivals, markets, and courtship.

MARIO SCHJETNAN

———————————

The city is a community of communities.

———————————

On the down side, there will be strikes, protests, rowdy political rallies, and out-of-control demonstrations.

What have these events to do with city planning? In the broad perspective, it could almost be said that town planning started here, for the old cities were built around the people-gathering places, the drill field, the market square, the cathedral plaza, the fountain-courts, and paths of interconnection. Every activity or event needs a suitable place—the more suitable the better. Therefore, in the programming of urban activity centers and the diagramming of their locations and characteristics, it is well to foresee and provide for all eventualities.

Participation

For a time citizen participation in civic matters regressed from the full and open discussions of the old town hall meetings to the closed door decisions of Tammany Hall. This, too, was to change. Partly because of the resulting abysmal urban conditions and partly to regain a voice, voters demanded and have acquired increasing opportunities to express their opinions. Most matters of local concern are now brought to the floor of the city council or other public forum for discussion and debate. At the regional level, issues affecting such matters as transportation, energy production, and environmental protection are routinely aired in public hearings. This trend not only restores to individuals the feeling that their opinions have weight, it also increases public awareness of current problems and alternative solutions.

At the design level, it has long been the tradition for professionals—architects, landscape architects, and engineers alike—to work "in camera" to the point of presenting their final proposals. This has the obvious advantage of a focused, expeditious approach. It is direct, unhampered, and self-satisfying to the designers. This process suffers, however, in matters affecting the public, from the lack of citizen input—and often results in a project that is unacceptable to those who may not understand the reasoning behind it, who might otherwise have their objections, or who might have a better idea.

Recently, and mainly in an effort to "bring the public along," or "develop a climate of acceptance," some design offices, on selected projects, have initiated a participatory approach. This involves free, round-the-table discussions with citizens of the community who first discuss the needs and program and then either describe or draw suggested solutions. Citizens are thus built into the process as contributors. Often, as the plans are developed, the participants are reconvened for phased reviews and comments up to and including the time of the final design presentations.

When the majority of people within an affected area understand, yet oppose, a projected happening, it probably shouldn't happen.

Too much architecture today is preoccupied with a self-referential discourse and a self-conscious dialogue with high culture. It aggrandizes the designer and client, but has lost touch with what architecture is all about; creating a vital, humane habitat that artfully expresses the conditions of its time and place and the dreams of its people.

ANNE WHISTON SPIRN

Designers have their talents enhanced by participating with the people who will inhabit their designs.

CHARLES MOORE

Although in some such instances the design solution may be somewhat diluted, and the process is bound to be more time-consuming, such involvement is often warranted. It can be seen that the odds of approval in such cases may be considerably enhanced.

Not infrequently the citizen input results in a plan that lies closer to the public need and to the public good.

Distinguishing features

What distinguishes one city from another? A New Orleans from San Diego? New York from Washington? Chicago from San Francisco? Seattle from Denver or Dallas? The name of each conjures up a vivid impression—not only to those who might visit, but to the people who live and work there as well. The image stems mostly from physical characteristics. Of these the topographical setting is predominant, with architectural character usually coming second. There are cultural attributes, too—foods, dress, music, dance, and the festivals. And then there's the imagery of special places remembered—a market square in the early morning, an exuberant sunlit plaza, or a waterside restaurant overlooking a sunset sky. And events—the St. Patrick's Day parade, the Mardi Gras, the World Series playoff, the mime by the fountain, the release of all those balloons at the fair....

In a homogenized nation of look-alike streets, of office buildings seemingly stamped by the same machine or motels that look each night like the one from the night before, differences are esteemed. Even in the shape of a street lamp, or the way seafood is displayed at one particular wharfside stall. How refreshing it is therefore to come upon a place, or whole city—like Santa Fe—that has a personality of its own. The more vivid, the more attractive. This being so, it is incumbent upon urban planners to preserve and build upon, to emphasize and dramatize, those features that make their city unique.

Dilemma

Cities, by one definition, are loci of concentrated human interaction. They have polar attraction and serve as the magnetic regional core. At least that's what most cities have been until recently. In our times, however, they are losing their gravitational pull. Why? Mainly because, with the advent of the automobile, they have literally exploded into the countryside, their activity centers dispersed—their magnetic pull dissipated.

If it were possible to scan the metropolitan regions with an activity-sensing device, most would appear as viscous blobs on a skein of strands spreading outward from an ill-defined mass, called the *center city*. The whole conglomer-

By taking participation beyond the stage of attending public meetings and serving on committees, community designers have given activism a new, creative dimension.

Sally B. Woodbridge

Involving people is part of the process—so, they, as a result, derive a sense of ownership of the recommendations.

Charles Law

The polar strength of the center city is measured by its intensity.

1. Limit of early city development

2. Expanding limit of development

3. Rampant Sprawl

Dispersion of urban centers
Without the benefit of established boundaries and zoning controls urban activity areas migrate outward along the trafficways.

URBAN ILLS

Before a sickness can be cured it must be recognized and diagnosed. Only then can effective treatment be prescribed. The common metropolitan maladies portrayed are symptomatic of debilitating conditions in urgent need of correction.

Unplanned redevelopment
Massive clearance has converted many once-lively city blocks into desolate wastelands. (*Grant Heilman Photography*)

Despoliation
Utility R/W gashes, an omni-present regional blight, are to be consolidated as planned transport-transmission corridors. (*Grant Heilman Photography*)

Fuming scatteration
This once superbly beautiful landscape is an all-too prevalent example of urbanization out of control. (*Grant Heilman Photography*)

Desecration
"Pollution on poles," or uncontrolled
wiring and signage, has for too long been
condoned. (*Grant Heilman Photography*)

Smog
Air pollution, contamination, and "acid rain"
are still facts of life in most metropolitan
areas. (*WestLight © Richard Fukuhara*)

Obsolescence
Vacant, obsolete structures usurp mile
after mile of formerly thriving
commercial districts. (*Grant Heilman
Photography*)

Sterility
Such deserts of asphalt and masonry
have lost their polar attraction. (*WestLight
© C. Moore*)

Pollution
Throughout metropolitan regions industrial
installations will be made to "clean up their
act." *(Grant Heilman Photography)*

Automobile invasion
Streaming trafficways and surface
parking rob the center city of its vital
interconnections. *(WestLight © Bill Ross)*

Decay
Diseased urban tissue infects everything
nearby. *(Grant Heilman Photography)*

Gridlock
By such divisive lines of force are cities
drawn and quartered. *(U.S. Coast and
Geodetic Survey)*

Vacuous monumentality
How not to plan a plaza.
How not to plan a boulevard.
How not to plan a city. *(Kenneth M. Wyner)*

Slums
Slum living and unemployment are
breeders of turmoil and crime. *(U.S.*
Bureau of Outdoor Recreation)

Monotony
Such dreary streetside clutter makes an
eloquent case for planned communities.
(Grant Heilman Photography)

Neglected waterways
Chicago's once-grim Wacker Drive (circa 1970)
has been transformed into a prestigious business-
apartment center. *(Grant Heilman Photography)*

If our present cities are failing, they can only be taken as evidence of the need for something better.

The natural advantages of downtown are enormous, but the simple fact is that downtown, as the core of the worn-out inner city, has become obsolete. In spite of all their creative vitality, Americans have failed to bring their downtowns up to date. The downtown is ugly, inconvenient, confusing and grim.

James ROUSE

Why do people flee the city?
Because of the breakdown of neighborhoods. Because of the dispersal of commerce and industry and places of employment. Because of higher taxes, poverty, blight, and the fear of crime. Because the fields beyond are fairer and greener. And because of the radial extension of the highway network that has hastened the getaway.

Besides, they see no reason to remain. Downtown is neither attractive nor enticing. Parking space when available is too far removed and too expensive. It takes too long a walk, with too many street crossings, to get where one wants to go.

When might people return to the city?

When it comes to have more advantages than where one is living now.

---

ation, superimposed on a web of trafficways, would seem formless, without discernible structure, without logic. This has not always been so. Something has gone drastically wrong to so disrupt the city form order.

Were the city a human being subject to physical examination, the findings would be depressing indeed. The vital organs have wasted away. The heart is perforated, the pulse weak, the veins and arteries clogged, the tissue diseased, the body deformed, the visage wan and haggard. The once-robust cities have aged beyond recognition. Debilitated, near the point of collapse, they slip further and further into decline. Tonics and poultices have failed. Even massive transfusions give scant relief. It is too much to expect of our ailing cities that they may somehow regain their lost vigor. We must look to a new generation.

How will the new cities differ? In what ways can they be better? We can hope that they will be handsome of form— lithe, clean-limbed, and healthful. We know that to prosper they must attain a position of dominance. To be dominant they must regain their regional centrality. These are worthy goals; how can they be achieved? As a first step, if our cities are faltering, it would help to discover the cause.

Exodus

Increasingly, for those of the city, opportunity has beckoned from the suburbs and beyond—sometimes from deep in the countryside. Home owners, alarmed at the general deterioration, sell while they can and move out. Department stores are vacating their city strongholds or establishing flourishing outposts that draw off their in-city trade. Office and manufacturing parks are springing up beyond the city limits. Cathedrals and churches are closing their doors to follow their migrating members. Colleges, sports arenas, performing arts centers are gravitating to less costly, more accessible, and more attractive locations. Even high-rise apartments are "going country."

The centrifugal flight of so many from the city centers is a sign that something has gone awry. What is causing the exodus? Stated bluntly, it is that most cities are slowly but surely "going to pot." Many long-time residents no longer perceive them to be the best place in which to live and work. Increasingly cities present a desolation of traffic-choked streets, parking deserts, and isolated towers of monumental proportions rising amidst blocks of dreary apartments in a backwash of slums. Service levels decline— as pollution, crime, and taxes mount. When those who have paid the most taxes leave, the increasing burden falls upon others who can less afford it. Many who gravitate to our cities to fill the vacuum can pay no taxes at all.

It is only to be expected. When the advantages of an

urban location no longer equal or exceed the negative factors, city dwellers will look for greener pastures. Finding them, they move out. This accelerating trend, known as "scatteration," or urban sprawl, poses a difficult problem.

Scatteration

A central premise of this treatise is that the current malaise of cities is due largely to the phenomenon of scatteration. *Scatteration,* or *urban sprawl,* is the creeping dispersion of the more successful enterprises and more desirable housing into the surrounding countryside. All sorts of support services follow along. Not only does this wreak havoc with the sagging centers, it infiltrates the outlying agricultural, forest, and wetlands with a network of incompatible roadways and ill-matched types of development.

How can this hemorrhaging of the city and the disruption of the surrounding region be precluded? Only by the imposition of fixed boundaries and development controls to check the outward pressures.

There are various types of boundaries. The political boundaries are those of the borough, township, city, county, or metro jurisdictions which may have their own codes and regulations by which they can manage growth. There are natural boundaries, including such physical barriers as the beaches and shores of extensive water bodies—or swamps, rivers, and delimiting mountain ridges. There are transmission corridors, canals, and railway lines and other linear lines of demarcation. The most common and most effective, however, are major highways—especially when planned ahead in the long-range regional context and coupled with progressive zoning controls.

Beyond the planned and fixed metropolitan limits no further urbanization will be permitted within a designated open space preserve—except within the adjusted boundaries of existing urban centers. Nonconforming uses are to be gradually eliminated until the integrity of the agricultural, forest, and conservation lands has been wholly restored.

Undefined boundaries

There are those who object to the imposition of boundary limitations. They make some good points—noting the difficulty of predetermining the future area requirements. It is held by them that new modes of transportation will shrink distances and new forms of communication will eliminate the barriers to free audiovisual interchange between people, wherever they may be. Constricting limits, it is argued, would be artificial and without meaning. Opponents of the fixed boundary option propose instead, as a recommended

Largely a U.S. phenomenon, *urban sprawl* is the unplanned proliferation throughout the countryside of various types of unrelated land uses or structures. It disrupts natural systems, and discombobulates established communities. It has few, if any, redeeming features.

———————

Scatteration is wasteful. It increases and duplicates services for which the unserved public must pay. It spins an ever-widening web of roads and utility lines far beyond the limits of reasonable need. It destroys the integrity of the farm-forest countryside. It trashes our landscape heritage.

———————

Scatteration leads only to chaos.

———————

There is no reason that sound regional planning should continue to be stymied by a patchwork of obsolete political boundaries that have no valid reason for being—and no relationship whatsoever to the underlying topography.

———————

The perimeter should be clearly delineated. That can both strengthen the inner life and create careful connections with the society around it.

Diana Balmori

A city succeeds, not more by what happens within it than by what is done to protect the integrity of its surrounding countryside.

Most new American development continues to take the form of suburban sprawl. Nonetheless, a growing number of designers believe that as traffic congestion grows, as environmental degradation worsens, and as interest in walking increases, there will be a growing demand for more compact, functionally integrated developments, often with a pedestrian-oriented community center.

JANE HOLTZ KAY

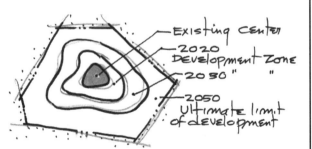

Contour zoning (A Means Of Growth Management)
Where activity centers have been planned for a receptive locality, they are to be developed from the center outward, to assure infill and avoid scatteration. This suggests the designation of concentric growth bands with tentative dates as to when the first construction will be permitted.

planning modus operandi, the formulation of "alternative strategies" to be applied as appropriate. This, they suggest, would provide a greater degree of flexibility. They fail, however, to suggest the nature of such proposed alternative strategies.

Proliferation

Certain it is that flexibility will be essential to phase-by-phase urban restructuring over the course of the years. The question arises, however, as to the best means of ensuring a receptive land-water base when such strategies are applied. For if the increasing proliferation of uncontrolled scatteration is not curtailed, cities will continue to disintegrate, and the dwindling supply of open space will have been usurped by more of the same scatteration. In such a case the workable planning alternatives would be few, politically costly, and painful. Clearly, a continuation of the megalopolitan sprawl would provide little latitude. Far better, whatever and whenever alternative strategies are applied, that there be a receptive land-banked reserve within and surrounding the evolving metropolitan centers. And better that within the metro galaxy the urban center satellites be compact and efficient entities.

Only by tightening and consolidating the urban centers, only by reestablishing a metropolitan open space framework—and freeing the surrounding farm and forest land of

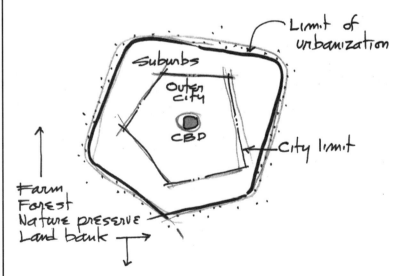

Urban expansion district
An alternative to contour zoning, sometimes a supplement, is the establishment of a fixed boundary within which urbanization is confined. The outlying areas are then designated as permanent open space lands—except in the case of a few predefined exceptions.

scattered intrusion—can sustained agricultural productivity be assured. Only thus can the intensity of unified cities be restored and maintained. Only thus can there be provided a receptive matrix for future urban development and revival.

Other problems

Within the dispersed and disarrayed cities there is also the problem of moving people and goods from one place to another. Transportation and transit systems fail because of gridlock traffic and lack of concentrated centers. Automobiles are everywhere yet seem to be getting nowhere. Interstate trucks and delivery vans plough through busy streets to deliver freight and parcels at on-grade loading docks in cram-jammed city alleys. The storage and distribution of goods is equally cumbersome.

Water, energy, and fuels are supplied by an uncoordinated maze of underground or overhead pipes and wires—the locations of which are often unrecorded. There is also the vexing problem of removing the sewage, garbage, and trash. Refuse is stashed here, piled there, or heaped in boxes and cans along the streetsides curbs until hauled away by clanking 10-ton stinkpots. It is hard to imagine a less efficient means of getting to and from, or taking to and away, than is provided under the misnomer "urban systems."

Population pressures

A further problem with threatening implications is the population explosion. For not only are cities overcrowded; much of the nation is overpeopled as well. In the United States within this century our population has doubled, redoubled, and redoubled again. There are limits. The time is fast approaching when this critical fact of life must be addressed and brought to a sensible resolution. In these pages we can only note the seriousness of the population onslaught and its crushing impact on cities.

Coupled with population pressures are the problems of housing the homeless, of giving help to the hungry, the stricken, and indigent. Directly related is the increasing menace of drug use and abuse and violence in the streets. These are social issues—but like those of economics and politics they are key factors in physical planning and the urban dilemma. They are not to be ignored. They must be "factored in."

The intruder

If ever there were a counterpart to the fabled "camel's nose," it's the hood of an automobile.

In one way or another the plight of contemporary cities can be blamed largely on the automobile. The fact that the

There is general agreement among urbanists that our cities should be planned for living and working as close together as is compatible with other requirements of the good, full life. The vision is for denser and more compact cities—and far more open countryside.

———————————

Despite the recent national decline in birth rates, the best projections of our demographers show an anticipated increase of approximately 100 million people in the next decade. By then more than 8 of 10 Americans will have gravitated to urbanizing regions.

———————————

There are more people alive today than have ever died in the the history of the world.

ANDY ROONEY

———————————

Even now, if the total food supply were to be equally divided among the people of the world we would all be undernourished.

———————————

The facts all lead to the certain conclusion that world population limitation is fundamental to human survival.

———————————

Main street was based on a precarious equilibrium, a balance of movement and stillness. Embodied in its simple plan—the wide street walled by shops and services—was a design that allowed permanence for the shopper, socializer, and worker, and transit for the traveller. The romance with the automobile ended that equity. From the 1920's the balance between the wheel and the foot tilted toward the automobile.

After World War II, it catapulted to disaster. Destruction and dispersal characterized the unraveling of downtowns large and small.

Jane Holtz Kay

––––––––––––––

The compulsion to drive our automobiles to and through the city has destroyed the very qualities that made them worth driving to.

––––––––––––––

Virtually every city in America is now facing the consequences of its failure to reconcile the imperatives of the automobile culture with those of urban design.

William D. Rieley

Europe is doing the same miserable thing we did—disintegrating their cities to accommodate automobile circulation.

Richard Galehouse

The automobile has to be accommodated, but not allowed to dominate the pedestrian environment.

George Pillorge

Average families spend more than half as much money on their cars as they spend to eat, and almost two thirds as much as they spend to own or rent their homes.

Nation's Cities

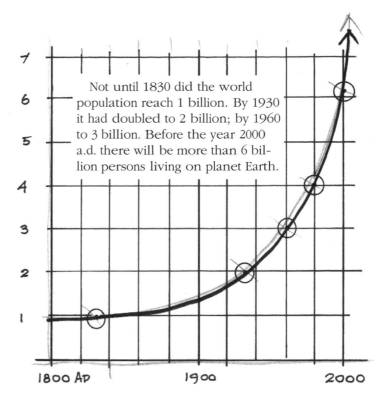

Not until 1830 did the world population reach 1 billion. By 1930 it had doubled to 2 billion; by 1960 to 3 billion. Before the year 2000 a.d. there will be more than 6 billion persons living on planet Earth.

Population out of control (World Population in Billions)
There are limits to sustainable growth. Clearly, within the next several decades one of the most critical problems facing humanity will be that of stemming human proliferation.

streets and parking lots usurp such a huge sector of urban land would be enough—for they rob the center city of its essential intensity. Their construction and upkeep at public expense is draining the city coffers. As life-threatening thoroughfares the trafficways separate people from people, shops from shops, and office buildings from office buildings. In addition streets and parking lots impose the noise and fumes, the frictions and hazards, of stop-and-go traffic. Like a dread fungus with its mycelium growth they have infiltrated the urban body and sapped its vital strength.

The grand compromise

There has long been a shameless love affair between Americans and their coveted automobiles. Since it is unlikely that this proclivity is soon to change—and since the effects on our urban areas have been so devastating—it is time to reassess the relationship and come to workable terms.

Reason suggests a compromise. The personal automobile serves best and most pleasurably when moving at exhilarating speeds over an unimpeded course. Further, since they are least efficient, least pleasurable, and most bothersome when churning through traffic-clogged city streets, it is proposed that they be stopped or diverted at the center city limits, while given free rein through 90 percent of the surrounding territory. This would seem a fair trade-off. As *interurban,* rather than *intraurban* vehicles, they could swish around and through suburbia and the open countryside on freewheeling parkways and freeways—and the city centers, or large portions thereof, could then be converted to lively pedestrian enclaves.

No doubt the downtown will always need streets and avenues—but *not* through streets or transecting freeways. The avenues of the future city will be designed as looping transit portals and distributor trafficways for cabs, buses, new forms of people conveyors, and emergency vehicles. The entrance loops will give off to lesser local streets to provide for the pickup and discharge of passengers at convenient points throughout the center city. Surface parking, except for transit vehicles, will be a thing of the past within the downtown core.

What would happen then at the critical boundary of the center city? There, at a delimiting *traffic distributor ring,* or roundabout, drivers could circle to the most convenient peripheral garage—or, if willing to pay for the privilege—could be admitted to exclusive parking levels beneath the pedestrian plazas. From outlying parking compounds rapid transit vehicles would speed one to the city center. On-grade vehicular traffic within the CBD would in time be limited to well-spaced nonfrontage avenues giving access to and around the in-city activity nuclei.

That such an obviously desirable arrangement has been so long in coming is a gauge of our reluctance to let loose the steering wheel until the very last moment. Now, with our cities under such stress, the moment is at hand. For too long urban traffic-transportation routes have slashed our cities apart and all but destroyed their primary function as centers of business and cultural interchange. New patterns of land use and transportation are needed to reverse the sorry trend of degradation in the urban centers and restore their dynamism.

Vital urban centers

The center city is at best the nucleus of regional government, business, and cultural activity. Those that have proved more successful are compact, easily accessible by automobile and rapid transit and provide for the efficient distribution of goods and services. Many now include traffic-free pedestrian realms of exceptional interest and appeal.

Perhaps the best way to visualize the future downtown is

When land values get high enough, parking can be structured, it can be underground, it can be part of the site. You can solve the problem.

ROBERT C. KETTLER

———————————

Faced with the doubling of metropolitan concentrations within the next several decades the contemporary U.S. city will of necessity be restructured around a radically different transportation system.

———————————

We have to tame the car, get it into the urban fabric, and make it behave.

ALAN L. WARD

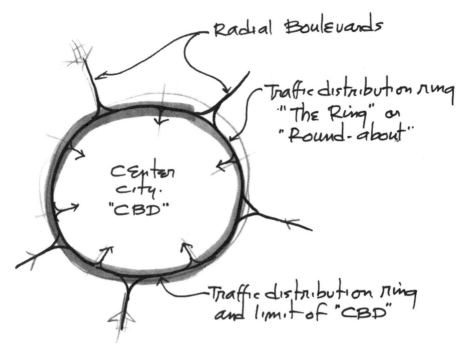

Center city traffic distributor ring ("The Ring" or "Round-about")
It is foreseen that in future urban centers, through automobile traffic will be intercepted at an external distributor ring. Destination vehicles will be directed to peripheral garages, parking decks, or local vehicular portals. Separate freightways will ramp to subsurface terminals for mechanized distribution.

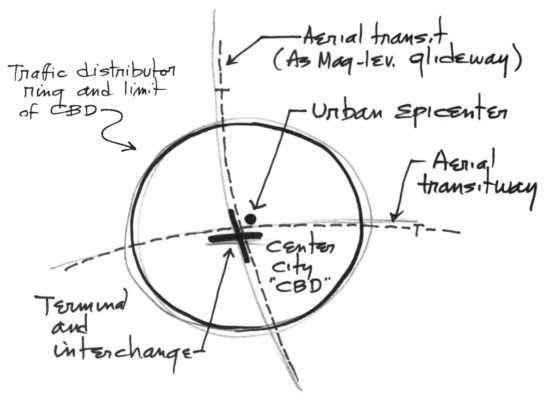

Center city interchange
Here at the hub of the regional rapid transit system will be found the city's greatest concentration—"the highest and best" of the urban metropolis.

to think of it as an aggregation of traffic-free malls surrounding and interconnected with the regional transit interchange. Each mall or compound will be devoted to one or more centers of government, finance, trade, culture, or entertainment—together with adjunct hotels, clubs, restaurants, and shopping. Towered and terraced, each varilevel complex will be formed around plazas, courts and passageways—a pedestrian realm of intensive activity.

People places

Lest density and centrality be equated with the monumental, architectonic, or the austere, however, let us hasten to dispel the notion. With the severe through-traffic checkerboard and abutting sidewalks replaced by a sequence of gardened spaces, these will be well-peopled, for here will be found those things to see and do that crowds so much enjoy.

The city centers must have their fashion shops, restaurants and cafes—their bookstalls, flower stands and all other conveniences. But *not* in the all-too-familiar form of the regional shopping extravaganza. Let there be no mistake. Such vast and sprawling single-purpose behemoths, with their acres of surface parking, would disperse and hopelessly diffuse the primary functions of the intensive urban cores. The simplest way to forestall their intrusion is to constrict and fix the center boundaries. The resultant rise in real estate values will "price out" the large-area, low-cost land users and ensure the vital concentration. Only the high-rent, multilevel office towers and department stores served by rapid transit can stand on their own as anchors to centered trade and commercial districts. High-bracket specialty shops will nestle in around them.

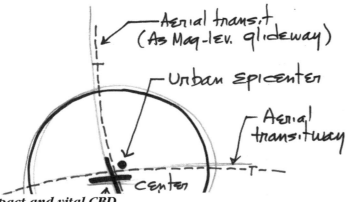

Compact and vital CBD
Within this theoretical CBD the circles represent major components such as city hall, the courthouse, stock exchange, department stores, business office complex, sports arena, civic auditorium or convention center. The connecting lines represent paths of pedestrian circulation. A compact center makes for convenient and pleasant interconnection—without the danger of trafficway crossings.

...a strong, simple concept for the public spaces (in a town or city center) will allow flexibility; it will allow change to occur over time.

ALAN L. WARD

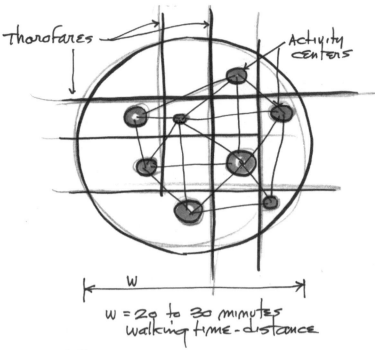

Thorofares

Activity centers

W

W = 20 to 30 minutes
walking time-distance

Fractured CBD
**Here the components are separated by major trafficways
and related parking deserts. The sundered city center has
lost its dynamic intensity—and reason for being.**

Other center city shops and service suppliers are to be
interlaced and supportive. There is as yet no better model
than that of Europe and Latin America—where shops of all
types occupy the first and second levels, with residential
apartments and offices above.

An experienced and keen observer of the urban scene
has provided useful guidelines for the design of downtown
congregating places.* Many of his findings and recommendations run counter to established suppositions. He found,
for example, it is not enough that urban parks and plazas
be spacious, leafy, quiet, or afford privacy. It is not necessary that they be handsomely furnished. Foliage, water, and
color help but are not essential.

What counts most is their location—a nearness to crowds
of the people who might use them. The best meeting and
gathering places are well-peopled and sociable. As spaces
they have a feeling of implied detachment, but open viewing, and nearness to the passersby, who give interest and
safety in numbers. People like to watch people and be with
people, especially with friends.

Some of the most used in-city places are small. They are
often no more than nooks or byways. In the downtown
ways and places, people expect a bit of crowding and
they even enjoy it. Area shapes do not seem to matter and

*William H. Whyte, Jr.

they may vary from the linear or geometric to free-form.

Seating is an attractor—perhaps the most appealing feature of all. Even a ledge, or broad steps, or the coping of a planter or pool will suffice—or a grassy slope or panel. Benches are always welcome provided they are comfortable and well-placed for those who will use them. For, although "loners" may seek out an isolated spot in the sun or shade, couples prefer to sit facing each other, close across, or better when seated side by side at the inside angle of an L-shaped bench or intersecting steps. Groups of three or more like to "bunch up," which is hard to do with fixed benches in a row. Movable chairs are often the answer. When they can be stored and brought out, they are used and appreciated.

The three most telling requisites of downtown, outdoor gathering places are location, people, and "sittability." A modicum of sunlit paving, overhead tracery of foliage, and the summertime splash of a fountain are welcome attributes.

Here again, downtown, as in former times will be open store fronts and window displays, the flower stalls, the news stands, the clustered shops and kiosks with posters, banners, and waving flags. Here in the open courts and passageways will be found the strolling musicians, the vendors of hot sausage buns, roasted chestnuts, popcorn, pretzels, cookies, and frozen custard. Here the racks of flamboyant T-shirts, the puppets, dancing dolls, whirring windmills, spinning tops, and floating balloons. Here the African, Indian, Latin American, and Chinese traders with outspread offerings of carvings, beads, amulets, and pendants of garnet, jade, and turquoise. With congregations of office workers, clients, and visitors moving through such intriguing spaces—indoors and out—cities will come alive.

Such urban centers of the future will provide a milieu of safety, expedience, and delight.

Overpass-underpass

The trans-trafficway skywalk or sublevel passageway can be an unfortunate plan device or, if well-conceived, an important attribute. Such passageways are least effective where user densities are low, where an underground labyrinth leads to disorientation, or where they draw users away from areas where pedestrians want to be. They are especially effective when connecting points of high people-concentration. This is even more so in climates where temperatures are severe or the weather inclement. The better walkways at any level are those interspersed with interesting things to see and do en route.

In landscape planning there is a useful analogy between streams of moving people and streams of flowing water. In either case, when the channel is narrow and smooth, the

The most-used people-gathering-places of the inner city are not the large, green, "go-to" kind, but instead fragmented bits and patches tucked in around the edges of well-traveled walks and ways.

_____

First level shops will come to line the pedestrian ways and plazas when and where they are made a requirement of inner city development.

_____

Shopping has evolved as perhaps the premier pedestrian activity. It's emerged as a much more recreational, leisure-time activity that requires a pedestrian environment.

GEORGE PILLORGE

The pedestrian experience

The separation of cars and people on foot is essential to the revitalization of cities. Where made a planning objective, separation can be accomplished by many means, including:

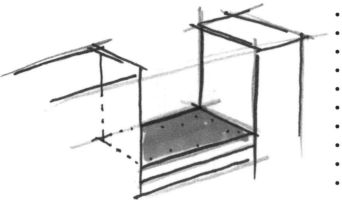

Interconnecting Plaza over Garage Decks

- The consolidation of small blocks into superblocks
- Street closings
- Elevated or depressed vehicular trafficways
- The creation of elevated plazas over the trafficways
- Midblock plazas and passageways
- Sublevel pedestrian places and ways
- Interconnecting plazas between buildings
- Utilization of garage decks and rooftops
- Flying walkways or skywalks
- A shop-lined overpass (as the Rialto of Venice)
- The alignment of roadways around, not through, shopping, office and other activity centers

Superimposed Levels over Existing Street

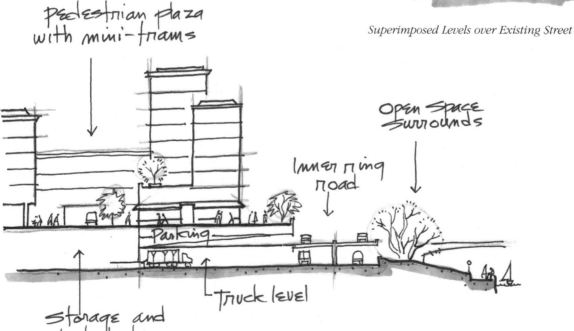

People, Automobiles, and Trucks—Together But Apart

Peripheral office towers and apartments over garaging. Truckway affords direct access to subsurface storage and distribution center.

The pedestrian experience (Continued)

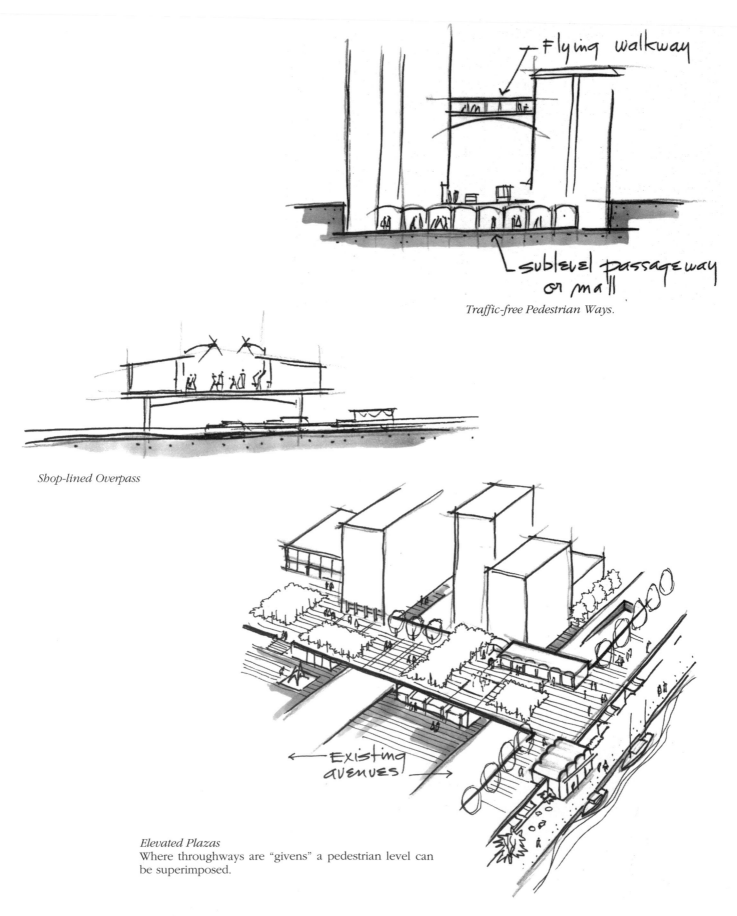

Flying walkway

sublevel passageway or mall

Traffic-free Pedestrian Ways.

Shop-lined Overpass

Existing avenues

Elevated Plazas
Where throughways are "givens" a pedestrian level can
be superimposed.

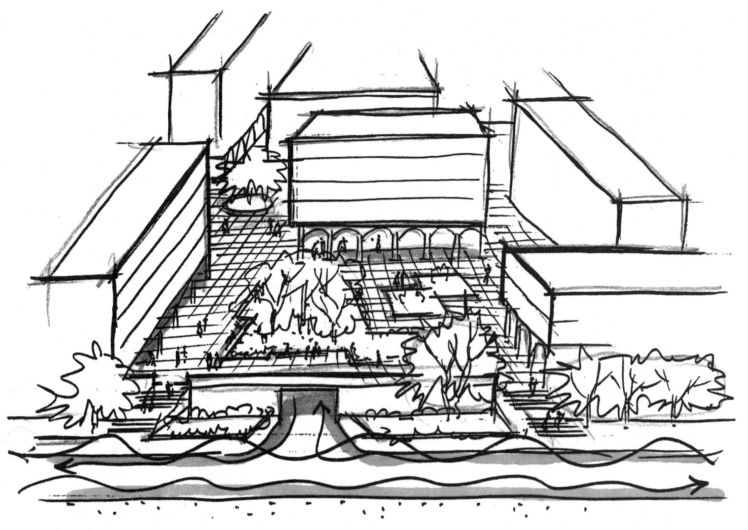

Midblock Plaza

A through-block plaza over garaging. Such interweaving spaces create traffic-free congregating places and valuable building frontage—with shops and restaurants at the pedestrian level. Upper levels are prime locations for offices and apartments.

In order for people on foot—shoppers, workers, and visitors—to fully experience the richness and delight of cities, they must be freed of the automobile's disruptive intrusion. With downtown redevelopment and new town planning, much of the inner city will be devoted solely to pedestrian use.

flows are swift and unimpeded. When the stream or river channel is wider, the velocity slows. If there are projections or recesses along the channel, or in-stream obstacles, there is turbulence. The flow then takes on patterns of animation—rushing water, riffles, swirls, eddies, and quiet pools. Such a stream is exciting to see or otherwise experience. So it is also with streams of moving people afoot. The straighter and less varied the channel and edges the more rapid is the passage. Meandering and eventful passageways afford less haste but increased interest in things experienced along the way. Animation is heightened by in-stream objects around which one must move, by bends and deflections in the course, by receptive bays and coves, and by edge attractions. As, on shopping ways, by projecting show cases, open storefronts, outside sales counters and displays and alfresco cafes or dining. All such walkway enhancers add pleasure to the experience of ambulatory movement.

Orientation

Where am I? Which way to the transit station, the civic center, the cathedral, the arena? The efficacy of a city plan can almost be judged by the number of times such questions need be asked. Ease of finding one's way around—so important in all land planning—can be achieved in a number of ways. First and foremost by the clarity and simplicity of the plan.

Aha! What could be more simple and clear than the familiar checkerboard layout of blocks and streets? *Clear,* it is indeed. It is clear that wherever one might wish to go on a crosstown sortie, by car or on foot, it must be done on a zig-zag course. This requires half again the diagonal distance, and the crossing of traffic at 300- to 500-foot intervals. And *simple?* Whoever would apply such an illogical diagram to a new community in the motor age must be simple indeed—for it separates people from where they are and where they want to go by streams of moving traffic. Why then is the grid used so often? For the same mindless reason that men still wear binding jackets with rain flaps over the pockets, useless buttons sewn onto the sleeves, and with flopping lapels that serve no purpose except to provide the slit (now stitched closed) that used to hold boutonnieres. Men wear coats rather than comfortable blouses simply because that's the way it's been done and because they don't know better. We know better now than to use the grid except in unusual circumstances. The grid-block pattern imposed on even mild topography is more costly in construction, in maintenance, and in the disruption or total destruction of the natural landscape.

Clarity in diagram instead implies the use of fewer streets and avenues—ways that flow with the land forms and

Most skywalks and concourses should not have been built. They rob from, instead of contributing to, normal pedestrian flows.

———————

The answer to heightened downtown activity is not to force it aloft or to subterranean concourses. The answer is to take through traffic off the ground level and give it back to pedestrians. Let *cars and service vehicles* move below or around the edges—where they can "do their thing" unimpeded.

———————

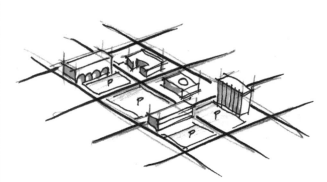

Typical grid street layout
Civic center buildings stand isolated by trafficways and parking.

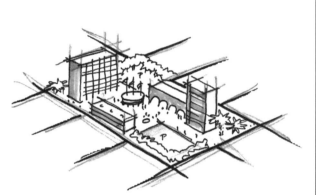

Blocks consolidated
By such superblock "campus" planning, building relationships, vehicular, and pedestrian access can all be improved.

define more usable traffic-free building sites. Clarity in plan implies the creation of directional and variformed pedestrian passageways between and around the structures and lined with the shops and sights and sounds of the teeming, livable, far more workable city.

Orientation can also be aided by the planning of larger, more self-sustaining superblocks, with access streets looping in from the periphery. Or by the meandering spine with feeder streets. Or by the trunk-branch-twig order of trafficways reaching inward to let-off points. The design of interconnected focal centers and variform plazas is also a proven plan device, as is the modified radial. Dominant landmarks such as the spire, the tower, the flag, the beacon—all serve as useful guide-ons, whereas off-site surroundings such as hills, peaks, valleys, and rivers give one a sense of place and direction.

To orient a city in the typical north-south, east-west checkerboard not only violates the topographical setting at huge, needless expense, it also ignores the sweep of the beneficent sun as well as the force and effect of prevailing storm winds and the play of the summer breezes. How could it be that in "backward" Malaysia, the simplest village, and every building within it, is designed with meticulous care in response to all such natural features? We have much to learn, or relearn, of such matters.

Safety

Statistics show that if longevity is a goal of life the average city of today is not the place to spend it. If a cab or truck doesn't get you, a mugger very well might. In many "inversion" cities, even breathing the air can be fatal, so charged it is with smog and the fumes of exhaust pipes. Again, crime on the streets in some cities has reached such alarming proportions that secretaries are afraid to accept employment. Isolated restaurants are forced to close because patrons fear for their lives in getting to and from them. After dark, parks, parking compounds, alleys, vacant streets, even some plazas and boulevards become a no-man's-land.

Can such conditions be changed by planning? Without question. With urban renewal and redevelopment many areas have experienced a near cessation of serious crime. The elimination of lurking places, vacant buildings, and the installation of lighting help, but even more positive is the provision of those uses and features that attract people out in the evening to shops, cafes, bookstalls, restaurants, artist studios and to attractive sitting areas under up-lighted trees or beside an illuminated fountain. As in the old cities of Europe so famed for their strollers and their charm—as in contemporary Montreal, Palm Beach, Carmel, and San

Francisco—the new pedestrian cities will provide in-town housing on upper apartment levels to bring life out of doors and down to the streets in the evening.

By far the most telling factor of safety in the pedestrian city will be the elimination of high-speed, high-volume vehicular traffic. With the wide throughways replaced by busways and minitransit loops the whole scale of downtown will be changed from that of the automobile to that of people afoot.

Expedience

Expedience equates with fitness. Expedience connotes the best kind of place for doing those kinds of things that one came to the place to do. It means the ease of coming together—of things being close at hand.

With this in mind, if we focus our thoughts on the average present center city as an ideal place in which to live, work, and trade, we can only wonder what all the cars are doing there. It becomes all too clear that we have sacrificed the desirable qualities of *place* to the means of driving through it.

To envision centers truly conducive to human interaction, one must conceive of an urban assemblage without the divisive intrusion of vehicular trafficways. Here, relationships can be close. Buildings will no longer stand haughty and set apart but will instead be commingled with inviting congregating places. There will be weather-protected passageways lined with shops and exhibits. There will be climate-controlled translucent domes, multidecked concourses, and flying balconies. There will be rooftop gardens and patios open to the sun and sky. There will be a multiplicity of courts and plazas of all shapes and sizes.

How does one get from the outer environs to this urban Eden? By regional rapid transit of a new high order, with tiered interchanges at the heart of the complex. They too will be light, airy, colorful, and alive.

Automobiles? Through vehicular traffic will be bypassed via the center city trafficway ring, while destination vehicles will be ramped to garages or subsurface parking decks at the periphery. Some, together with service and emergency units, may be consigned to internal subsurface levels. All transport trucks and delivery vans will be kept to the lower levels also, with direct access from the outside. Busses, cabs, and other forms of surface transit will be welcomed in town to loop between and around the pedestrian compounds for passenger discharge or pickup.

Delight

It is hard to think of our contemporary cities in terms of

A city of busy shop-lined streets and ways, clustered courtyards, close-knit neighborhoods, and focalized communities tends to be self-patroling. Local surveillance affords more and better protection than steel guard fences or walls.

Business offices, apartments, and shopping are all interdependent. They belong and work best together. The richer the mix, the better. The time-tested formula for success—worldwide—is that of shops lining the pedestrian walkways with offices and apartments above. Shops and restaurants thrive, residents walk to work and lunch, and the streets, with strolling people, tend to be much safer.

The more people who come to the city by car, the more who decide to stay out because of the congestion.

In stratified urban structures the lower strata are best reserved for parking and freight handling; the pedestrian levels for fronting stores, restaurants and places of assembly. The upper levels are most desirable for offices and apartments (the higher the level the higher the probable rent). Interior or rooftop spaces can accommodate theatres, bars, cafes, health clubs, and such recreation features as bowling, pools, and game courts.

The plaza's been broken into little pieces and dispersed over a variety of settings, some of them indoors, some of them outdoors, some of them public, some of them not so public; there's a much more complex structure to public life.

MARK CHIDISTER

We're seeing the development of a more truly American form of plaza or public space. It's part European square, part park, and it's even part garden.

MARK FRANCIS

Access avenues and boulevards within the center city will be designed as surface transit portals to the island subcenters.

For many folks cities have lost their attraction; cities seem inhumane, overpowering, and sometimes even frightening.

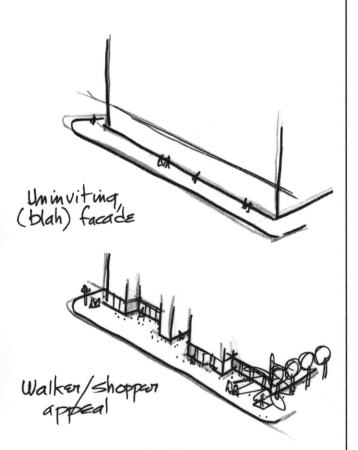

Uninviting (blah) facade

Walker/shopper appeal

Pedestrian level building frontage

delight. There are delightful events of course, many delightful things to see, and some delightful places. But for the most part, the downtown environs are dreary, sordid places—often they are forbidding deserts of asphalt paving and stacked masonry cubes. The yawning canyon streets are cold with gusting winter winds and stifling in the summer. Block after block of the business district is interrupted at the pedestrian level by the blank walls of parking garages or by ostentatious banks and imposing office buildings. There are occasional stretches of inviting shops, outdoor dining places, book or flower stalls, or fruit markets, and there are areas of animated street life. But then, too, there are the raunchy porno parlors, the vacant store fronts with boarded windows, the heaped garbage, and pollution in all its unsavory forms. And always the honking and roar of traffic.

Can this be improved? Can it possibly be that we may some day experience clean, comfortable, *delightful,* traffic-free cities? Although to some this thought may seem far-fetched, it is little more than replacing the usual auto-poxed "downtown" with a combination of highly successful examples of urban development that presently exist.

Suppose, for instance, that one were to redesign a center city incorporating the best features of, let us say:

The Galleria of Houston
Lincoln Center of the Performing Arts
Atlanta's Peach Tree Plaza
L'Enfant Plaza of Washington
The Embarcadero of San Francisco
Century City in Los Angeles
The St. Louis Climatron
Chicago's Oakdale or Old Orchard shopping centers
The San Antonio Riverfront
Plaza del Sol of Montecito
Plus a generous swath of internal Epcot Center

What a super delightful pedestrian realm such a center city could be!

Center city

The center city of each metropolitan area is its dynamo. It houses the regional generators of governmental, financial, and commercial energy. Just as a generating plant is designed for utmost efficiency, so, too, by all reason must our urban centers be designed and constantly adjusted to yield peak performance. This implies not only the selection of those elements best suited for inclusion but also the planning of their most favorable relationships.

Critical mass

An understanding of urban dynamics begins and ends with the concept of intensity. The planners of commercial developments are well aware of the term *critical mass*. Without it there can be no hope for success. A favorable critical mass implies an adequate base of potential clients or customers, which is a function of population area, density, and ease of getting around. Critical mass implies also a sufficient concentration of goods and services, of building mass and supporting open space, to provide a strong attractor. It connotes a centralized aggregation of compatible elements. It bespeaks polarity, activity, nodes of high interest—and people.

Relationships

Intensity is essential, but it alone is not enough. Much depends upon the elements to be associated. To illustrate the point, one might imagine a compact grouping of a trade center, a hospital, and a produce terminal. The resulting melee would, of course, become predictable. Frictions, disturbances, and complaints would soon be the general rule. Clearly, not even two of such incompatible uses

An extension of the residential *cluster* concept is being applied to many other uses as well. Shopping centers, industrial parks, business office, space and institutional campuses, for example, may be improved by the closer building grouping, which yields additional common space.

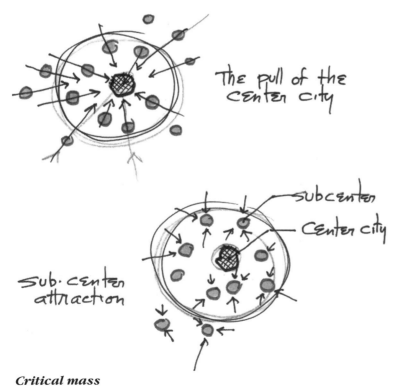

The pull of the center city

subcenter
center city

Sub. center attraction

Critical mass
Not only the city needs critical mass, but also every subcenter within it.

should ever be juxtaposed. Not that it hasn't happened.

But take a more favorable grouping—of, say, the governmental—city, county, and federal offices and courtrooms. For the public, the payment of taxes, securing of licenses and permits, title searches, hearings, appeals, and the obtaining of information and forms would be facilitated. For the various officials and staff members daily tasks would be conducted more efficiently and pleasantly than if crosstown travel were required. The grouping in its entirety would comprise an impressive civic symbol and, if well-designed, could instill in citizens a much higher regard for government than that imparted by the customary morgue, grim county jail, or often dismal city hall.

Or take a consolidated hospital complex. Formed by itself as an integrated grouping within parklike surroundings, a complex can bring together in a well-organized assemblage all related elements of health care and medical treatment. Here at close hand will be available the best of medical minds, skills, and equipment. Clearly, the quality of treatment, surgery, and nursing care will benefit. The arrival and processing of patients will be simplified also—as in admittance, record keeping, diagnosis, and billing. Patient transfer from place to place by ambulance with sirens screaming will no longer be required. Food storage will be facilitated with automated freezer and locker rooms. Food preparation will also be centralized. The immense daily volume of laundry will be handled far more efficiently, as will be the multitudinous tasks of maintenance and the operation of combined mechanical systems. In an era of soaring hospital costs and increasing needs, the planning of such efficient medical centers has now become crucial.

The close relationship of financial institutions has its benefits also. Centralized communication systems, reduced interoffice travel time, and shared services will all have their positive effects. Fine restaurants, bars, clubs, and specialty shops fitted in and around will add convenience and vitality.

Reason suggests a reorganized, restructured, more compartmentalized, and far more workable center city

Humanizing the city

The traditional urban centers of many metropolitan regions have fallen upon bad times. Slashed apart by ever more crowded trafficways, they have been robbed of their essential intensity and human interactions. Without confining boundaries city centers have spread outward along the feeder arteries, often leaving behind at the core a desolation of vacancies and obsolescence. Even in the surviving districts of towering banks, office buildings, and midtown parking structures, there is little of appeal at street level. It

The center city

THE CENTER CITY (CBD)
As a Dynamic Entity
Our fragmented cities are woefully inefficient. If they are to regain their historic role as centers of power and activity, they must be replanned and reconstructed to better serve their purpose in contemporary times. Their purpose is that of concentrated centrality—of intensive commercial, civic, and cultural interaction.

Each component part is to be reanalyzed and so designed as to best fulfill its own particular function. Then all parts are to be brought together in such a way as to provide the best possible interrelationships. This is an easier task than at first it might seem—at least in the conceptual stage—for all cities have similar working components.

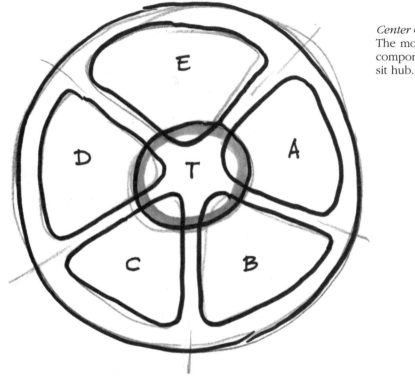

Center City—"CBD" (A Hypothetical Example)
The most successful city centers are those in which the major components are grouped compactly around the regional transit hub.

The Idealized Center City
(A Conceptual Model)
Components:

A *Governmental:* Federal, state, metro, and city offices, postal, customs, and consular services.

B *Corporate Office Center.* Corporate headquarters and subsidiary offices.

C *Financial District.* Stock exchange, brokerage houses, banking, insurance, and investments.

D *Cultural Center.* Civic auditorium, conference center, performing arts, library, museums, exhibitions, religious and educational institutions.

E *Entertainment.* Sports, theatres, music halls, restaurants, and bars.

T *Regional Transit Interchange.* An Omni-Galleria type complex. Prime commercial, department stores, hotels, convention center, fashion shopping, trade fair, and professional offices.

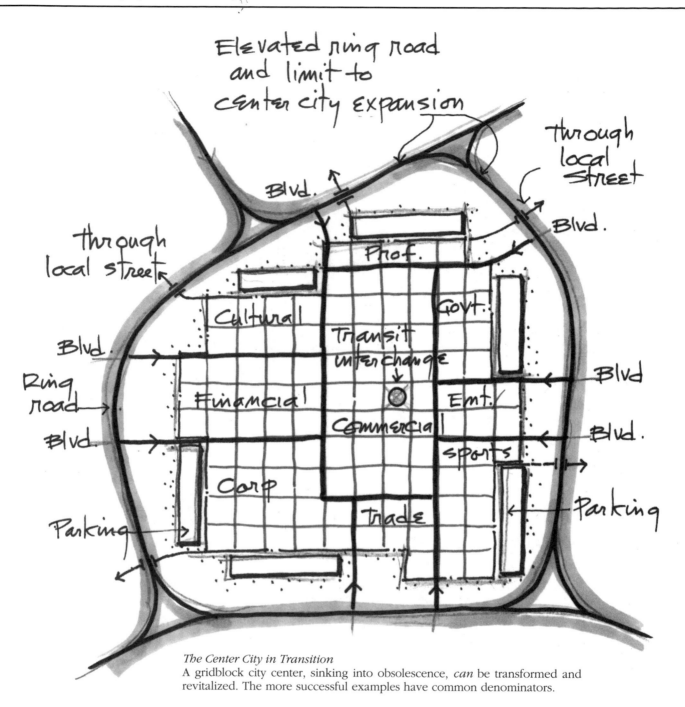

Elevated ring road and limit to center city expansion

through local street

through local street

Blvd.

Blvd.

Blvd.

Blvd.

Blvd.

Blvd

Blvd.

Ring road

Parking

Parking

Parking

Prof.

Cultural

Govt.

Transit interchange

Financial

Commercial

Emt.

Corp

Sports

Trade

The Center City in Transition
A gridblock city center, sinking into obsolescence, *can* be transformed and revitalized. The more successful examples have common denominators.

- *Compactness.* Area efficiency and dynamic throb are attained by grouping *like* types of enterprises around a central complex of interconnected plazas of open spaces. It helps, too, if they are surrounded with complementary uses. Overall compactness also increases the convenience of moving from place to place within the center.

- *Definition.* It is essential to the preclusion of urban sprawl and the resulting deterioration of the center city that fixed limits to expansion be established and controlled. Within these confining limits property will be kept at a premium, marginal uses will be squeezed out, and true urbanity will become a hallmark.

- *Automobile Access.* Regional travelers with no reason to enter the center will be intercepted and bypassed at the trafficway ring and center city boundary. The "ring" will also serve as the distributor for destination motorists wishing to enter the peripheral parking decks, internal access drives, or garage-office-apartment towers. During the transition period, at least, local traffic may move at low speeds through streets which bypass the pedestrian plazas.

- *Access by Rapid Transit.* The city centers of the future will be tiered above and around the regional transit hub, with convenient people-mover connections to all of downtown.

The center city (Continued)

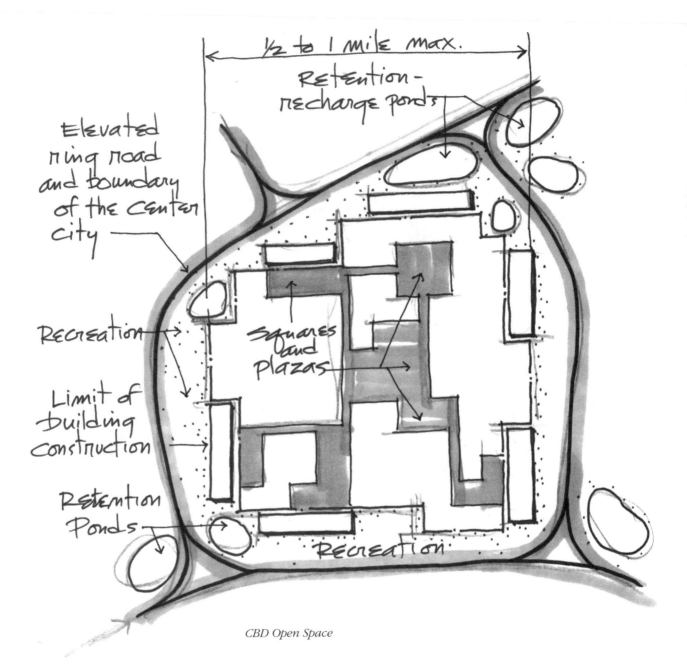

CBD Open Space

- *Pedestrian Enclaves.* Traffic-free plazas or super-blocks will be created and expanded throughout the center city As experience has demonstrated, the success of such freely organized pedestrian places soon results in the consolidation and conversion of other isolated blocks.

- *Circulation.* Circulation within the urban centers will be greatly enhanced by the elimination of the wide through trafficways and on-grade parking. All surface decks and terraces not occupied by approach loops or buildings will be designed as vari-formed garden courts and passageway—with shoppers, office workers, and new types of mini-vehicles moving freely about.

- *Open Space.* Within the terraced platforms of the center city the interconnected square and courts may share their space with compatible groupings of shops, restaurants and pavilions in a garden-like setting of fountains, sculpture and plantings. The extensive area of unbuilt-upon land between the trafficway ring and parking structures will serve as a welcome park-forest surround—with ample room for many types of recreation. Here, too, will be located the lakes and ponds to receive and filter the center's storm water run-off, and replenish the freshwater aquifers.

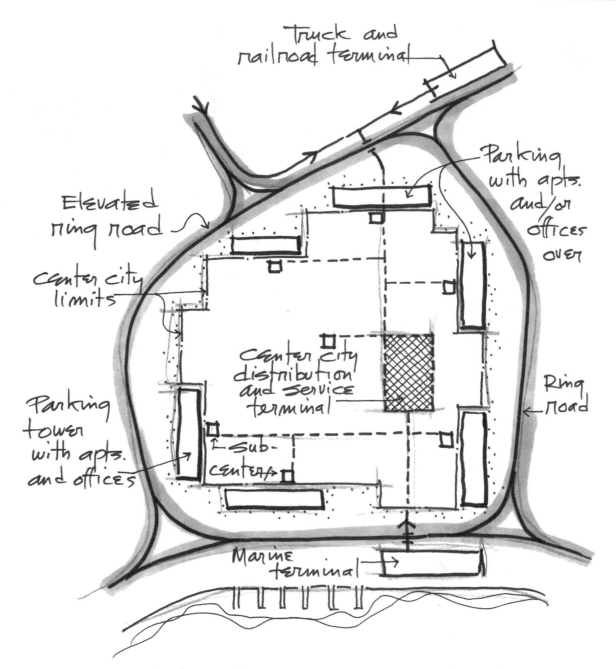

Goods and Services

Distribution. Goods and supplies will be received, sorted, and transported from a vast subsurface terminal with mechanized conveyance to strategically located subterminals for direct building to building delivery. Utilities in separate chases will be aligned through the same illuminated tunnels. On-grade street delivery by truck or van will in time be phased out entirely.

Urban Distribution Terminal
This computerized storage and distribution system is but a mini-prototype of the sub-level installations that will serve the city centers of the future. (*Photo by Cameron Davidson.*)

is no wonder that given the choice, investors and clients opt for the outlying shopping plazas, malls, and office parks where the daily experience is far more agreeable.

To most urbanites and visitors the typical U.S. city is intimidating. Its streaming trafficways, unlike the narrow, meandering streets of European cities, extend in straight lines to the far horizons—interrupted only by senseless crossings at the end of every block. Wide and menacing, the streets are flanked with monolithic buildings crowding in upon concrete sidewalks.

Starkly geometric in layout, our older city areas particularly seem endless stretches of monotony. Clearly, such a sprawling, conglomerate mass would be better subdivided by swaths of verdant open space, traversed by free-flowing parkways or freeways. If each such cohesive "island" were thus formed of a size suited to its principal use—such as a civic, commercial, or business office center—both traffic flow and uses would be better served. People would feel

How to kill a CBD:

• Separate the subcenters, block from block, with roaring vehicular trafficways.

• Line the peripheral walks of each block with the imposing nothingness of granite walls or cliffs of glass that face upon two- and three-story entrance lobbies.

• Squeeze out the last of the downtown walkside shops. Drive them along with the restaurants and cafes to the pedestrian courts of suburban shopping malls. Trade and business will follow.

The Ten Commandments of Urban Design

1. Thou shalt consider places before buildings.
2. Thou shalt have the humility to learn from the past and respect thy context.
3. Thou shalt encourage the mixing of uses in towns and cities.
4. Thou shalt design on a human scale.
5. Thou shalt encourage freedom to walk about.
6. Thou shalt cater for all sections of the community and consult with them.
7. Thou shalt build legible environments.
8. Thou shalt build to last and adapt.
9. Thou shalt avoid change on too great a scale at the same time.
10. Thou shalt, with all the means available, promote intricacy, joy and visual delight in the built environment.

FRANCIS TIBBALDS

more at home in their surroundings, more comfortable and secure. Moreover, identification with their own locale would develop a sense of belonging and community pride.

Such a conversion is now entirely possible with our newly evolving techniques of urban renewal and redevelopment. These, coupled with comprehensive planning by the agencies, are specific to the phased evolution and area-by-area transformation of obsolete cities or districts. Among the tested procedures many have been highly successful and hold much of promise.

The question arises, "Can the revitalized center city compete with an outlying shopping mall or office park?" Many examples give an affirmative answer. The downtown location has a number of clear advantages. It is centralized. It is positioned at the hub of the regional transit network. It has a wide circumferential trade area and sphere of influence. By association it connotes the highest and the best, urbanity, and the superlatives of city living.

Human scale

It has been well said that to restore their magnetism cities must regain their human scale.

What is meant by "human scale"? It has to do with the apparent size and shape of things—the way things *feel* to the human participant. Scale is a matter of perceived relationships—of that which is right and good, of that which is appealing. It equates with that elusive quality, charm.

How fortunate the urban center that has rediscovered the charm of diminutive places and ways—of narrow, meandering walkways, alcoves, patios, or balcony overhangs, and the inviting recessed entrance! Such appealing features, too, are the walkside cafes and immediacy of the timeless bazaar and the marketplace—where wares and produce are brought out to greet and tempt the customer. As by the sidewalk display cases of Unter den Linden in Berlin; the eye-catching kiosks of the Geneva lakeside; the booths of Stockholm's bustling market square; the bookstalls along the Paris Seine; the wine, cheese, and pastry shops that line the narrow winding streets of Venice; or the fruit, vegetable, and seafood stands of Lisbon's teeming waterfront. With this same personal enticement the more popular of U.S. urban places will offer a visual and olfactory feast.

Goal

Those experienced in urban resuscitation have found that there can be no simple solution. Change requires a sustained, well-organized campaign joining civic action groups, astute political leadership, and private enterprise—all coupled with advanced planning at the highest level of creativity. For starters, a worthy *goal* for the center city might be the creation or re-creation of a superlative and integrated metropolitan business, cultural and civic center, and a specialty shoppers' paradise.

The case for compaction

The central business districts of metro areas are smaller than most people think.

The whole of Chicago's CBD—from the Wacker Drive loop to Eisenhower Boulevard and Michigan Avenue—is about one square mile in area. Pittsburgh's "Golden Triangle" extends less than a mile from the Point, in its longest dimension. The present "downtown" of Dallas could be contained within a circle of no more than half-a-mile radius, with ample room to spare.

In each example city over a fourth of the area is presently usurped by divisive through trafficways which were better eliminated. The average height of occupied space in the buildings is less than three floors. With centrality at a premium and convenient access and interaction so desirable and feasible by elevators, it is only logical that the doubling of the usable office and apartment space required should be *up* instead of *out*. Those who best know urban function and form foresee a much higher and far more intensive core.

The new center city

The center city of the future will be stepped and rise here and there to soaring heights. Not row upon row of aloof monumental towers ranged along through trafficways—but rather integrated groupings of multistory, multifaceted megastructures interspersed with courts, patios, plazas, and piazzas. It will be light and lively. The new city center will be laced with saunas, exercise rooms, solariums, flower, book, gourmet and specialty shops, and with child care and personal services facilities.

The new center city's commercial, governmental, and cultural subcenters will be bounded by broad-boulevard access portals crossed by aerial and subsurface passageways from point of concentration to point of concentration. It will be ringed with an open space buffer and traffic distributor parkway. It will be alive with *pedestrians*—a true metropolitan center.

Inner city

If the new center cities are to be compressed within the confining trafficway ring, thus increasing intensity—but also land values and rentals—where are the workers to live? Where will the suppliers have their stores? Where will one find the trade schools, repair shops, and other support facil-

The idea is not to create grand open spaces, but to create usable pedestrian space where people will actually want to be.

JOHN KALISKI

Much of the attractiveness of future cities will be centered in found spaces—once-neglected nooks and slivers discovered and brought to life with a bench, fountain, sculpture…or planting.

If we lack a clear sense of direction in city planning, we need only to look to history. The great cities of the past were great because their leaders knew what they wanted to achieve and set out to achieve it.

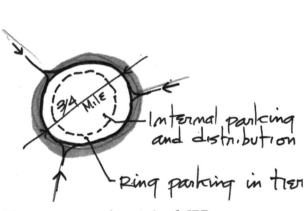

The compact and contained CBD

Municipal costs are increased by distance and reduced by reducing distance.

Making today's urban area twice as big horizontally for tomorrow's twice-as-big urban population would be impossibly costly in dollars, intolerably costly in wasted land, unbearably costly in added travel time to and from work and to and from open-space recreation. Doubling their area by growing up instead of out would cost far less and add only seconds instead of minutes to everyone's travel time.

NATION'S CITIES

The future city center will be less a collection of independent buildings and more a grouping of tiered and articulated megastructures of open and closed spaces and interconnecting passageways.

The extensive use of air rights—the multiple uses of ground surface area—can put parking and services out of sight and mind and intensify urban activity.

In stratified urban structures the lower strata are best reserved for parking and freight handling; the pedestrian levels for fronting stores, restaurants and places of assembly. The upper levels are most desirable for offices and apartments (the higher the level the higher the probable rent). Interior or rooftop spaces can accommodate theatres, bars, cafes, health clubs, and such recreation features as bowling, pools, and game courts.

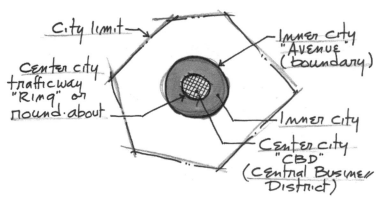

The inner city
The inner city, immediately adjacent to the center city, or central business district, is the area lying between the trafficway "ring" on the inside and the outer "avenue." With the ring road elevated (or depressed) those of the inner city will have free on-grade access to the CBD.

ities? With logic they should be close at hand, within the adjacent inner city.

With a strengthened, consolidated city center core, the surrounding inner city will take on renewed vitality. *Renewal* is the key. For here, close to the regional hub is a mother lode of old and renewable structures of all types and sizes—ready and waiting for improvement as housing or conversion to other uses. As in the old European towns crowded around the forum, castle, or cathedral, the buildings often face upon narrow local streets and ways. This can be the mixed-use haven—the "Jane Jacobs country" of the contemporary United States—with a rich and lively blend of the old, the remodeled and the new—all with lingering ethnic overtones.

Granted, at present the inner city may be threadbare and shabby in places, sometimes decrepit beyond the point of repair, for it has fallen upon bad times. Compounding the loss of its employment base, many families have moved away, to be replaced by a new influx of immigrants—some seeking asylum and all a better way of life. The city has lost much of its cohesiveness and sense of pride—but much remains ready for regeneration. With the pressing metropolitan need for lower-cost working space and housing, the inner cities can blossom again. Available here are vacant lofts, row houses, duplexes, flats, single family homes, and mansions in variety. Here are reusable shops, stores, garages, plants, factories, warehouses, waiting for repair and remodeling. Here are the touchdowns needed for thousands of start-up enterprises, workshops, supply, appliance, repair and service centers—and for offices, studios, shoemakers, tailors, bake-kitchens, leather, pottery and flower stalls, and corner grocery marts. Here, too, are job opportunities galore—in the demolition of too-far-gone structures, clean-up, repair, rebuilding, and refurbishing.

What will it take to start the regeneration? From whence will come the energy? It is there, and as renewal comes, more will be attracted.

It will take start-up and roll-over financing. Not huge subsidies for the development of more FHA-type apartment cliffs with their minimum standards and minimum appeal.

Not funding for massive displacement, clearing, and construction of more PHA public housing cantonments. Nor for sterilized replacement communities somewhere "out beyond."

Not reliance upon loans from the established banking community to self-help improvers or entrepreneurs. Banks have no time for such as these when immense profits are to be reaped from secured loans to bail out fellow S&L barons or for regional shopping malls, subsidized Toyota or Volvo factories, or for the construction of new highways and factories to replace the rain forests of Latin America.

Not more juice squeezed from the overstressed cities, for there's little more juice to squeeze.

The problems—and *possibilities*—of the inner cities are of *national* scope. By all rights and reason they are to be addressed by the federal government which by its founders was chartered to represent and work for the well-being of *all* segments of society. But particularly, the inner cities are to be "off limits" to further "ministrations" by HUD, the Department of Housing and Urban Renewal, which has destroyed more of cities than it has saved and failed so abysmally. It will take a whole new federal rethinking and a whole new focused commitment.

To crank up inner city renewal, two programs will be essential. One will encourage and facilitate home and business place *ownership*—through conditioned bargain sales of reclaimed properties, self-help, or other incentives. The second is a federally guaranteed, locally administered, small loan program for home and property rehabilitation. When home and building users feel secure in the prospects of ownership—and when they can borrow enough fix-up money for boards, glass, paint and other materials—the renovation process will start to roll. It almost always has, and with remarkably good results.

Function

The inner city—providing the supporting services and much of the work force for both the CBD and outer city—will be made up of neighborhood groupings and service clusters. The makeup of the neighborhoods will vary widely in character to reflect the location and the income levels

Fewer jobs are created in the glistening new office towers than in the older and lower buildings of the surrounding inner city, where lower rents attract new enterprises.

M. Paul Friedberg & Partners

Garrett Eckbo

EPD: Environmental Planning and Design

Garrett Eckbo

Theodore Osmundson & Assoc.

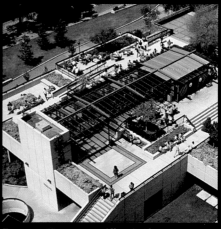

Garrett Eckbo

Royston Hanamoto Alley & Abey

CITY

M. Paul Friedberg & Partners   *Sasaki Associates (Alan Ward)*

EPD: Environmental Planning and Design   *M. Paul Friedberg & Partners*   *Peridian*

Sasaki Associates (Susan Duca)   *Sasaki Associates (Michael Houghton)*   *© The Walt Disney Company*

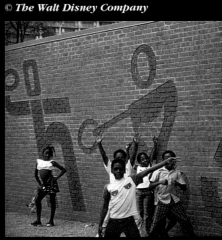

Johnson Johnson & Roy   *EPD: Environmental Planning and Design*

Oehme, van Sweden & Assoc.

Lawrence Halprin

Int'l Swimming Hall of Fame (J.E. Clark)

Garrett Eckbo

Theodore Osmundson & Assoc.

M. Paul Friedberg & Partners

Robinson Fisher Associates

Wallace Roberts & Todd

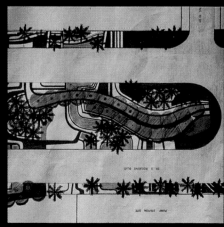

Roberto Burle Marx

CITY

EPD: Environmental Planning and Design

Wallace Roberts & Todd

GWSM (William Swain)

Peridian (Ron Izumita)

Garrett Eckbo

Peridian

Peridian (Ron Izumita)

Vollmer Associates

Oehme, van Sweden & Assoc.

Rich Haag Assoc. (Felice Frankel)

Small enclaves of people with the same background and about the same income are perfectly natural—no problem at all. But there are many good reasons why rich and poor, white and non-white should live close enough to know how the other half lives—and to share the community life and openness of opportunity whose sharing is the first essential of urbanism.

NATION'S CITIES

There is also likely to be an increase in the number of middle class professionals living in the city. Considering the reclamation of old neighborhoods they have achieved without government help, it is staggering to think what might be accomplished.

WILLIAM H. WHYTE, JR.

At the urban densities that command the highest rents from those best able to afford to live as they like (i.e. on New York's Park Avenue, Chicago's Gold Coast or San Francisco's Nob Hill) there are only three U.S. cities whose entire population could not live, work, shop, swim, worship, and attend concerts on the 18,000 acres within three miles of the center.

NATION'S CITIES

of residents. There will be those in need of aided and self-help housing. In response to expanded employment opportunities the inner city will draw an influx of skilled and retrained workers, office staff, and supervisory personnel. There will be need, too, for design professionals to help plan and guide the extensive inner city conversion. As the center city attractions are increased and land values rise, many residents in upper income brackets will also opt for homes and life in the inner city band.

Here in the inner city—section by section, and in good time—the rigid grid street pattern will be relaxed into freer-form tracts conforming to the topography. Some will be planned as residential neighborhoods, others as centers of supply, fabrication, or service.

Because of the need for higher densities and more affordable rentals, new inner city housing will tend toward off-street townhouse clusters and low to midrise apartments. All are to be combined into unified neighborhoods with their own convenience shopping and recreation. Within the expanded redevelopment tracts all other uses as well can be consolidated into compatible compounds which will be more or less complete within themselves. In their function the future inner cities will fill much the same role as at present—that of support for the CBD and the outer city. But the cities will have a far different mien, with traffic-free neighborhoods, far more efficient centers, and a trafficway system that works. If the watchword of the center city is *concentration*, that of the inner city will be *convenience*.

Here in the inner city it could be hoped that the thriving neighborhoods will hold their cohesive identity, largely unchanged. In good time other amorphous scatterings will be reformed and consolidated around their upgraded convenience and community centers and transit stops. Some areas will require little more than repair and repainting. Others will be in need of extensive renewal and remodeling. Still others may be so far gone—so deteriorated—that replanning and phased redevelopment is prescribed.

Whatever is done in the nature of inner city aid and replanning, let it be done only after thorough on-site reconnaissance of the good and the negative features that exist and only with the community leaders, groups, and citizens consulted and fully involved.

Access

To give definition to the inner city and preclude its outward sprawl there is need here also for a permanent outer boundary. This might well be provided by a circumferential avenue giving direct automobile access to both the inner and outer city bands and to the surrounding region. Within the inner city, selected streets will be widened to include walkways, bikeways, busways, and room for other types of transit vehicles that will penetrate the center city trafficway ring at upper or lower levels, to loop freely throughout the CBD between the pedestrian enclaves. For most residents of the inner city an automobile would be unneeded.

Outer city

The outer city is that area of the municipality lying between the inner city and the official city limits. This broad expanse of real estate is commonly subject to the full range of conflicting uses and abuses. There are handsome homes and estates, golf courses, village shopping compounds, institutional grounds, streams, and patches of woodland. But intermixed are such unlikely neighbors as the used car lot, laundromat, animal control shelter, forge, sanitary fill, and assembly plant. How do they all fit together? Quite obviously, they don't. Without the benefit of an overall plan and regulation, the mix has become so impacted and so fraught with frictions that it desperately needs sorting out.

In the sorting out and restructuring process are several promising possibilities. First, here again is a felicitous opportunity to apply the relatively new and highly effective techniques of comprehensive planning and urban redevelopment. They have been designed, in fact, for this very purpose. With phased implementation they can accomplish seeming miracles. Second, in the aggregation of similar and complementary uses into unified centers all participants stand to gain. Further, most of the grinding conflicts of unfortunate juxtaposition can thus be resolved. Finally, as the dispersed uses are in time reconsolidated, the vacated lands can be reassembled bit by parcel and restored as an open space frame.

Before setting about to redo the outer city, however, it would seem wise to know—*in the urban context*—just what it might better be. The "urban context" is important, for in relation to the inner city and the whole of the metropolitan region, the outer city plays a critical role. Only if the outer city works well can the center work at all. For, although the CBD is the focal core of the metropolis, the CBD depends on its various urban subcenters.

Urba-centers

Urban subcenters, aptly called "urba-centers," are outlying nodes of various types of activity such as those of education, research, health care, sports, or manufacturing. In some cases elements of each are of a size or nature to stand alone when dispersed throughout the region. More often, however, nodes of activity benefit when brought

The poor are not hurt or driven out by well-conceived neighborhood improvement; they stand to gain and participate.

Urban redevelopment works best when phased into being by slow, empathic stages, preserving the best of that which exists. Extensive, indiscriminate clearing can kill off the very community that it sets out to help.

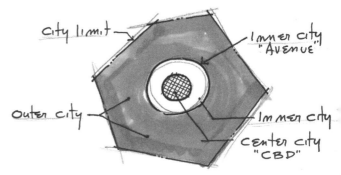

The outer city
The outer city, defined on the inside by the bounding inner city "avenue," extends outward to the official city limits.

———————

A typical "urba-center," or satellite "new town," as seen throughout Europe in various forms is built around a central transit plaza and office-apartment complex with shops at the lower level. It is usually home as well to one or more concentrations of regional activity such as health care, education, or research. Compact, intensive, and with fixed boundaries, it functions as a complete and balanced community. It features linked and extensive pedestrian islands with external access by automobile.

———————

Satellite urba-centers will combine high-intensity activity and high-density housing around the transit center—with low-density living around and between satellites. The land at the core will be devoted to multilevel, multipurpose use with all the shopping, services, and amenities that its area can support.

———————

It is our patterns of development that need serious revision. Single-use districts, be they downtown office clusters or office parks in the suburbs, cul-de-sac residential developments of attached or detached homes, vast segregated apartment complexes, commercial centers where one has to drive from one side of the street to the other, parks that require huge parking lots—each of these patterns encourages the exclusive and multiple use of automobiles for transport by a great majority of citizens. But if one makes the mental switch from physical segregation and isolation to integration and interconnection, then it becomes possible to imagine paths as meaningful and pleasant as the new places they will connect.

BENJAMIN FORGEY

together in a unified grouping—as when scattered shops or stores are gathered into a well-planned mall. By consolidating similar elements, each gains strength from the whole. Together these elements attract other supporting uses such as housing, suppliers, and recreation to form a balanced synergistic community. Major urba-centers, planned with highway and transit linkage, are well located as basic elements of the evolving outer city.

The list of typical urban subcenters might well include the following.

An industrial park.   On line with the freightway between the cargo airport and central distribution terminal, a light manufacturing and assembly complex can draw upon the resources of the whole metropolitan region.

A science/research center.   A high-tech research-and-development community can well be located outside the center city provided it has direct access and linkage to the universities, business offices, and other regional nodes.

An educational campus.   Depending upon the nature of the universities, colleges, and other institutions of learning to be brought together, they might benefit by the addition of such other components as a museum or a communications, computer, or conference center.

A health care complex.   Hospitals, clinics, laboratories, nursing homes, and retirement villages are often grouped to their mutual advantage. The benefits can be even greater if all are planned concurrently with residential neighborhoods, as a complete community.

A sports center.   Sports draw not only from the CBD and inner city but as well from a regionwide horde of enthusiasts. The gravitational pull of fans will be increased by combining into one complex the football/baseball stadium, soccer field, hockey rink, basketball arena, swimming pavilion, and perhaps even the race track. With staggered seasons and schedules the required parking areas and concessions can be shared and kept busy.

Other urban subcenters can focalize such activities as those of a corporate office grouping, a marina, resort, festival park, or zoological garden. No urba-center can stand alone. All depend on convenient interconnection with the others and center city. All benefit also by a close relationship with supplementary and supporting services, shopping, and housing.

The lands between

What of the lands around and between the new urba-centers? Much of the development already there will remain and benefit from the fact of proximity. Other construction

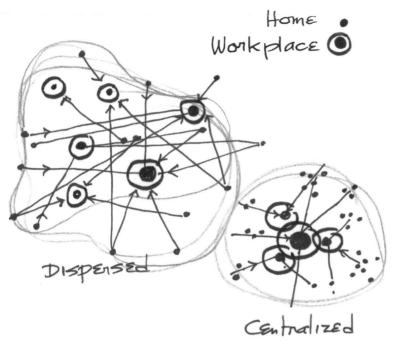

Home •
Workplace ◉

DISPERSED

CENTRALIZED

Mixed use communities encourage a diversification of uses within a unified setting. They promote the location of employment centers, shopping, schools, and recreation near high density housing. They provide a variety of dwelling types and stimulate innovative, energy-conscious design.

The advantages of the planned transit-community are manifold. Not only are all systems more efficient—the conduct of business is more direct, and living is more agreeable. Less energy is consumed and less land is used to provide the same usable floor area and number of dwellings.

The case for centralization

The gathering of dispersed workplaces, housing, and shopping into convenient subcenters at transit nodes reduces travel and transport time and increases efficiency.

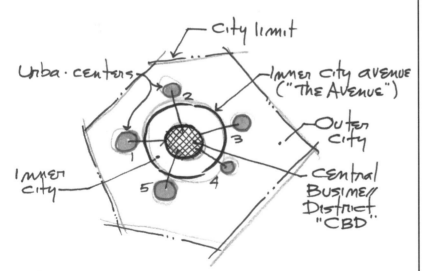

Urban subcenters

Urban activity subcenters, or "urba-centers," are ideally located in the outer city. With direct highway access from the bounding inner city avenue—and with interconnection to the central business district they give promise of a superior urban structure.

Typical urba-centers:

1. Sports
2. Industrial
3. Science
4. Education
5. Health Care

CITY

Planned communities function best within the orbit of established population centers.

———————

The exodus of corporate headquarters to the suburbs and beyond has slowed to the point of reversal. It is found that the gains of spacious and leafy tranquility are often outweighed by the isolation from the contacts, interactions, and animation of concentrated urban centers.

———————

The tide of the exodus will turn when the city, not the suburb, offers the most advantage.

———————

considered to be deleterious will be eliminated, with the properties land-banked or put to some better use. New proposals and projects will be welcomed provided they conform to the spirit and guidelines of the outer city transformation program.

Urban subcenter access

Except in the cases of major redevelopment, specialized activity centers should be newly sited and created along a projected circumferential avenue or parkway. They are best designed together with, over, and/or around a transit mall.

External automobile approaches will lead to and around the pedestrian enclaves, with convenient on-and-off ramps to parking, office, and apartment structures. Service and transport vehicles, together with a limited number of personal automobiles, will be parked at lower levels where all incoming goods and supplies will be received for lateral distribution.

Workers, clients, and customers will have access by free-flowing parkways, or rapid transit from all parts of the region. Upon arrival they will be within a short walking distance of destinations via garden plazas or covered passageways.

Transformation

In time, as transformation progresses, the outer city will come to be that urban zone of highest productivity and greatest diversity. People with special interest in any one subcenter community can live within it or nearby. Access to other urba-centers and circulation throughout the region will be facilitated by the new highway and transit loops. All types of outer city activity will be centralized and thus intensified, while contributing to the restoration of the natural landscape. The restructured outer city will relate more directly to the CBD and to the inner city from which it will gain—and to which it will give—support.

Satellite centers

Since the time of Sir Ebenezer the practice of city and regional planning has come a long, long way. Back then there was no such thing as zoning. Condominiums, the high rise, and even garden apartments were all as yet to come—as were such then inconceivable ideas as the environmental impact statement. The freeway and parkway were unknown; in truth the automobile itself seemed an unlikely, somewhat ridiculous gadget—hardly one to be reckoned with.

Yes, we have come a long way since Sir Ebenezer Howard and his garden city concepts. Some have been adopted with modifications, and many of our cities and communities are much the better for that. But his main idea never got off the ground. No doubt he was ahead of his time, but it could be that times have caught up with him. For what he proposed was the concentration of various types of urban activities—such as those of government, trade, research—into compact and unified groupings, each quite complete in itself. Some would be given a place within the center city. Others would be planned from the start as urban satellites.

Unlike our contemporary corporation villas, automotive plants or other single-use developments, the outlying garden city communities would be an assemblage of like and complementary enterprises planned together with their ancillary service and residential neighborhoods. Each would be planned for utmost efficiency. Each would be linked directly with other urba-centers, and so planned as to strengthen the center city to which it related.

The total city

Having suggested a number of possible regional activity groupings and the benefits of their unification, the question arises, "How are they best organized in relation one to the other and the center city?" Perhaps we should check with Sir Ebenezer. It was he who advocated, as did Leonardo da Vinci before him, a constellation of urban satellites around the city core. It is an idea hard to refute, for it consolidates into unified groupings those of the city's activities which gain from togetherness.

Land use allocation

A key aspect of urban and regional planning is the allocation of areas of the right size, shape, and location for each of the major activity centers to be accommodated. Whereas the actual and proportional sizes will vary from instance to instance, the optimum *relationships* are more easily determined. It is proposed that the optimum relationships will be those that for the most people provide the most convenient and reasonable access and interconnection.

Typical of urban activity centers are the following:

1. Commercial (the central business district, or CBD)
2. Governmental
3. Institutional (educational, cultural, health care)
4. Residential (worker and executive housing)
5. Recreational (sports and entertainment)
6. Manufacturing
7. Corporate (headquarters and offices)

Leonardo da Vinci proposed to abate the congestion and disorder of Milan by building a group of ten (out-lying) cities of five thousand houses, limited to thirty thousand inhabitants each.

LEWIS MUMFORD

Most city centers are plagued with lack of adequate housing and with unemployment. It might seem reasonable to encourage private enterprise (by tax incentives and subsidies) to build more housing and thus to stimulate business and industry. Experience has shown this to be counterproductive.

Since the center city land area is *finite* (and desirably so) the construction of further housing attracts more workers without ready employment and takes land that might better be devoted to the essential business, governmental and cultural functions of a polarized CBD. This suggests that the intensive regional activities of the center be given priority on the available land, and consolidated. That worker housing and services are better provided close at hand in the surrounding inner city band. It further suggests that, as needed, satellite activity centers of various types be established in the outer city and ringed with housing for those to be employed.

It is important that each be consolidated into an efficiently organized subcenter. It is also important that each subcenter be located in a logical relationship one to the other and to the CBD.

What of the city as a whole—the core and the satellites? Together they and their environs comprise the official municipality within the nominal city bounds. Let the bounds, as amended by topographic logic, be made permanent—fixed and inviolate. Let all scattered and unplanned development cease within the limits of established cities, towns, and communities. Let all new activity centers and subcenters together with their paths of interconnection be fitted to each other and the underlying topography. Let the infiltrated areas of scatteration be reclaimed and put to better use. It will take time, but with long-range planning it can be done, with gratifying results.

Putting the city together

As with spokes fitted into the hub of a wheel, radial access highways converge on the center city. Traditionally these trafficways have been progressively widened as increased roadway capacity has been needed—at the same time, inexplicably, "strip highway" uses that so constrict free traffic flow have been permitted to coagulate along the arteries. Where might these roadside enterprises of a thousand varieties be better located?

Some belong in the replanned center cities. Some in the commercial courts or malls set off to the sides of arterial roadways. Some in neighborhood or community convenience centers with a built-in clientele. Others, of regional attraction, might best be incorporated in a satellite transit node or urba-center. Located along the rim of the inner city avenue, each will emulate at a lesser scale the characteristics of the center city. Intensive activity will be induced by the ease of access, compact convenience, and favorable interrelationships. They will be working models of gestalt.

In such diagrams it can be seen that each component is freed of the chaotic urban hodgepodge and permitted to take its own best form in more favorable surroundings. Such plans are clearly superior to the status quo from the standpoint of sheer efficiency—no small consideration in these times of energy crisis, budget shortfalls, and fierce trade competition.

So far, in considering the city we have looked mainly to its structure—to the diagrammatic relationship of its working parts. This is important, for if the structural mechanism is faulty the city fails to perform. But there is more to the city than an operating mechanism. The city not only works or fails to work, it has its own appealing character and

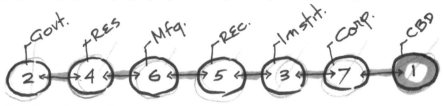

Irrational grouping

In this diagram, as an example, seven representative components of an urban metropolis have been aligned in a row without regard for interrelationships. It can be seen that movement from one area to another, as from the residential to the commercial (CBD), would be difficult in the extreme.

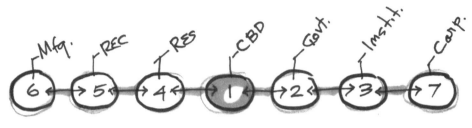

A more reasonable sequence

This linear plan arrangement shows a more logical sequence of movement from place to place.

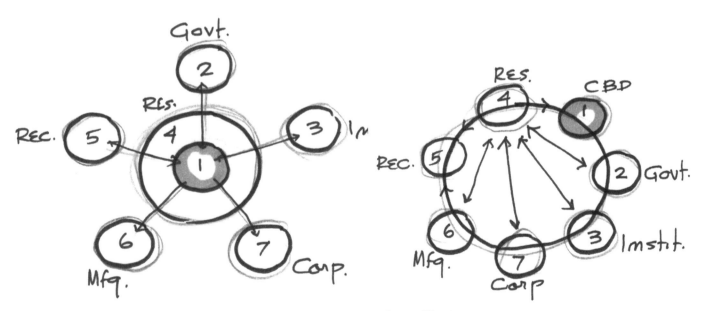

Circular arrangement

With a circular disposition of the selected land uses the lines of interarea travel are improved but through-area traffic presents problems of friction and disruption.

A satellite arrangement

Here the major business district has been centrally located, surrounded by housing for the work force. Access from the outlying subcenters is more direct and agreeable, as is their external boulevard interconnection. A more workable land use pattern for cities has yet to be devised. In even such simple diagrams one can sense the possibilities of more rational approaches to the planning of the urban metropolis.

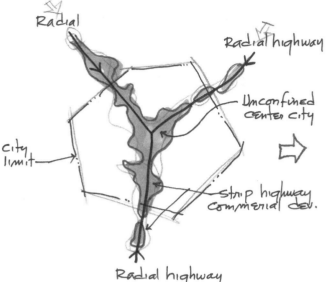

Clogged strip highway development

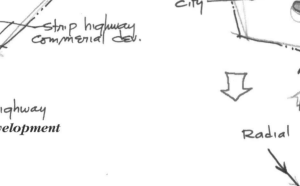

Non-frontage radial access

Combined with circumferential parkways

Automobile access
Unimpeded regional access to and from the central business district and outlying urba-centers is afforded by free-flowing radial and circumferential trafficways.

Throughout history the purpose of cities remains unchanged—to bring people together for ease of access and variety of contacts. All history thus refutes the logic of urban sprawl.

---

ambience. Or else it doesn't. Each city is perceived as a good place to be, or the tendency is to avoid it.

Topography

But should not topography be a governing factor in the plan layout of a city? Yes, clearly. The abstract diagrams described have validity only as a means by which to suggest and compare alternative relationships. Selected diagrams may then be superimposed in turn on a scaled topographic map of the city site to determine their feasibility and the degree of modification required to bring them, if possible, into harmony.

Often it is evident that a proposed diagram cannot

possibly work in the given terrain and must be discarded. Again, the fit may work but only with undue cost or stress—and the clarity of the plan and power of the landscape are both thereby diminished. At times, however, the exercise produces plan forms that sing in the landscape and sing in harmony. A compatible diagram evokes and dramatizes the full splendor of a landscape setting. Such is the case in such memorable cities as Kyoto, Geneva, and Bogota. But how often do urban planners have the opportunity to so diagram the ideal city for a given locality? More often than one might suppose. In the long-term planning of every new or existing city it is essential to explore and re-explore continually the optimum possibilities and to develop a program of phased transition toward the desirable goal.

Once a best-case conceptual plan has been determined for the city and region, then, and only then, can the more detailed design process be initiated for each specific activity center. Here again one must beware of the rigid master plan to which all that follows must strictly adhere. The best plan concept for any type of urban complex or subcomplex within it is that which provides a compelling design theme and guidelines, allows room for the exercise of individual choice and freedom of expression, and provides the flexibility required for adjustment to changing conditions.

Overview

Whatever its composition, whatever its underlying topography, the overall city within its official limits is comprised of three general districts—each quite different in function. Too often the district limits are lost or blurred. Too often their parts are scattered or intermixed. Too seldom does a city take form from a guiding plan by which the *CBD, inner city,* and *outer city* are well defined and work together as an harmonious entity.

It may be said of the center city, or CBD, that it serves as the regional command post—a concentration of governmental, financial, and administrative power. As such it is to be kept compact as by a bounding access/distribution ring. The encompassing inner city is by precedent an area of directly accessible housing and service facilities. This zone, too, is best confined to preclude its creeping outward expansion. Within an encircling avenue or natural boundary it is to be planned for livability and convenience.

Beyond, the outer city extending to the municipal boundary, is the logical location of the urban activity and production subcenters. Why? Because so located they can be interconnected by both the inner city avenue and outer city circumferential parkways, providing excellent regional access. And because here there is ample room to accom-

The design of a racing sloop is complicated beyond most people's comprehension. Yet to the practiced eye it takes but a glance to know that the craft is "yar." It's the sensed relationship of the sails to the mast, the masts to the hull, and that of the hull to the water. Only if in simple diagram the relationships are right does the rest of construction matter. So it is with any work of design—a structure, a community, or a city. The essence lies in the *conceptual diagram,* the diagram of fitting relationships.

The landscape must shape urban form....

MICHAEL HOUGH

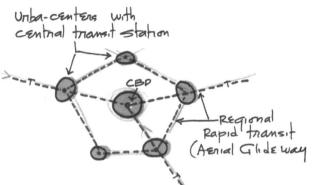

Rapid transit access to city centers
Rapid transit, as by Maglev or other aerial glideway, will link the CBD and outlying subcenters to each other and the regional environs.

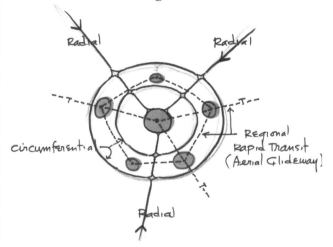

Combined roadway and transit access
Wide radial and circumferential boulevards, parkways, and avenues, within open space corridors, will speed motorists to and throughout the city. Transit by aerial glideway will provide rapid center to center interconnection.

People should not be mastered by a plan.

WILLIAM JOHNSON

modate a diversity of dispersed urba-centers, each with its own surrounding community and all within a spacious natural landscape frame.

The creation of well-ordered production and activity centers within the outer city will siphon off the many extraneous uses that now plague the suburban fringe. The "freed-up" suburbs will afford an open space setting for such compatible uses as new communities, resorts, music camps, and many types of outdoor recreation. Important, they will buffer adjacent agricultural lands from the pressures of urbanization.

How will this restructured city of the future fit into the greater urban metropolis? To postulate, we must expand our horizons

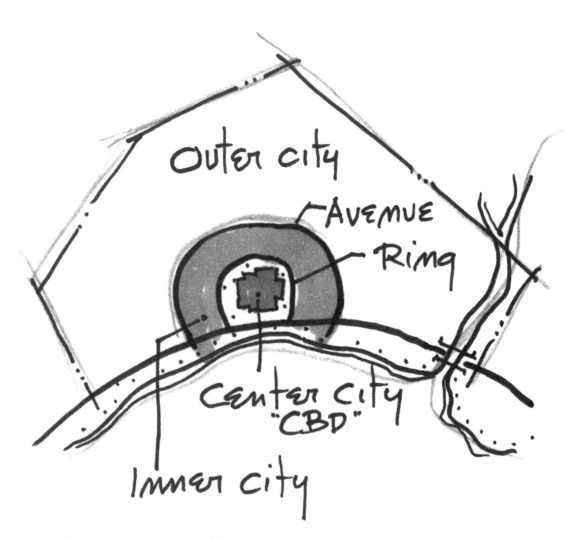

The three districts of a model city
1. **The CBD bounded by a traffic distribution ring**
2. **The inner city bounded by its delimiting avenue**
3. **The outer city extending from "avenue" to the municipal boundary**

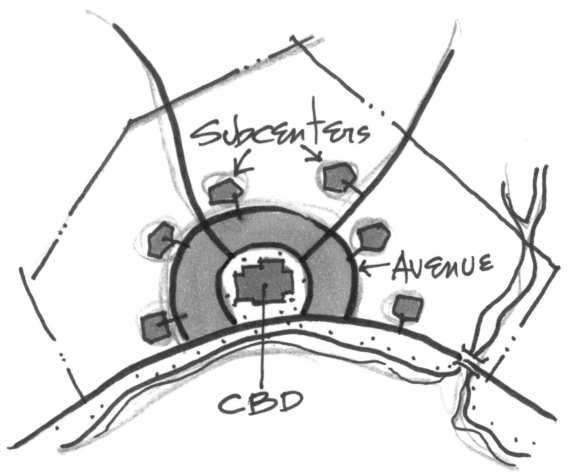

Satellite activity centers
In this diagrammatic plan layout the concept of satellite urban subcenters
is exemplified. With the central business district as a dynamic core, the
various urba-centers are ranged around the broad connecting "avenue."

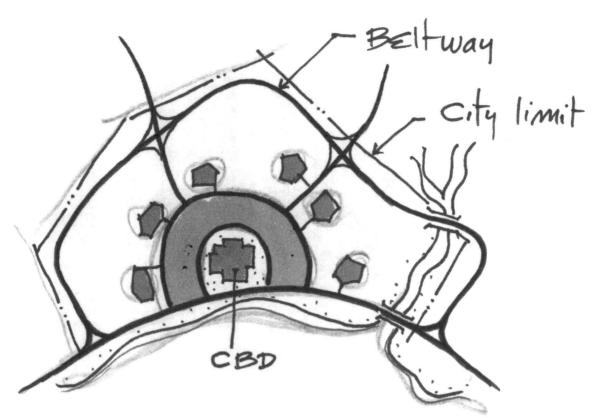

Outer beltway
The addition of a circumferential beltway at the approximate city limit completes the basic land use/highway digram.

The Basic City Components

Unfortunately,
nobody has ever seen or experienced
a city that comes anywhere close
to measuring up to today's potential.
Nobody has ever seen or experienced
a really good city—
a city that takes full advantage
of today's better technology, design, and planning.

NATION'S CITIES

5
The urban metropolis

A city in its structure might be likened to a sun (the center city) with its satellite planets, the urba-centers. In this context the greater urban metropolis resembles a constellation. This could comprise such supplementary "heavenly bodies" as suburban communities, villages, smaller cities, and lesser activity clusters— all more or less held together in dynamic equilibrium.

Ideally, an urban metropolis is organized in terms of *systems*. These include those of *land use, transportation, transit, transmission,* and *open space*. Ecologically, such natural systems include river basins and drainageways, wetlands, dunes, plant and animal communities, etc. There are also commercial systems and those of education, health care, welfare, justice, communications, governance, and so forth. With all systems in place and operating smoothly, the entire metropolitan region tends to function well.

Land use planning

Each city will differ in character according to the nature of the metropolitan region served. A maritime city will hardly resemble that of an agricultural or industrial area. Regions aren't static, however, and are difficult to define. For example, one "region" could be that in which the majority of residents are subscribers to the daily newspaper or regular viewers of the television channels. Another could be described as that in which most sports fans are loyal to one or more of the city teams. Yet another, of differing size and shape, would comprise that general district in which the majority of telephone calls are made to or from the central exchange. Again, the "commuter region" would be that in which the origin or destination of most daily trips lies somewhere within the city. There are geographic regions, political

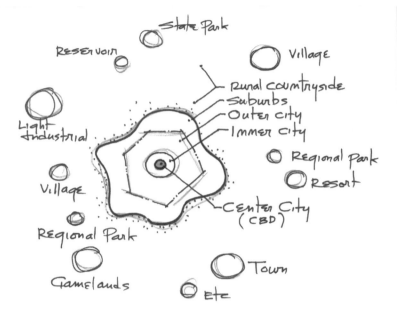

The urban metropolis
There are no fixed boundaries to a metropolitan region since its limits expand or contract depending upon the strength of the city's polar attraction.

regions, marketing regions, and those providing clients and patrons to the city's financial, religious, cultural, or entertainment districts. All, in their varied ways, pay allegiance to the center city.

Polar attraction

This recital of some of the various categories of metropolitan regions gives a clue as to the multitudinous elements that are to be crowded into the focal cities. There must be the housing, also, and all the required amenities. Then, too, there are the highways, streets, and parking lots that together take up from a fourth to a third of all the usable land available. How can it all be fitted in?

Fitted, in truth, is hardly the word. *Jammed* would be more like it—for reasoned fitting has seldom been part of the urban location equation. There has been, rather, free competition among the contenders to get as close as possible to the bull's-eye of concentration—the center city, or CBD. Why this compulsion to centralize? No doubt it is largely a matter of gravitational attraction—the more dense the mass, the greater the pull. Moreover, an accepted law of real estate economics is that the entrepreneur will pay as much as can be reasonably afforded to gain the most favorable location. Until recently this has been measured in terms of centrality. In a more competitive world the term *best* is coming to mean the more accessible, the more agreeable, the more efficient, and, in most cases, the more

System implies a variety of units combined as an operating whole, with common control and balance.

———————————

We tend to set natural and man-made systems as opposites, when we ought to seek harmonious integrations of the two.

ROBERT HANNA

———————————

Urban design is the crystallization of possibilities.

———————————

When a city loses its polar magnetic attraction, the strength of its regional "field" is likewise diminished.

———————————

Dependent on the automobile and on the always over-burdened highway system, most urban regions lack boundaries, a core, and that contrast between town and country that gave the old cities their identity.

Robert Fishman

———————————

profitable. It is not just a matter of prestige. It is a matter of all-round successful performance.

Containment

Every city and town has its own prescribed and official limits. They are set by law and may be changed only by legislation. These boundaries determine official jurisdictions, local politics, ordinances, regulations, and taxes.

In Europe such boundaries are the limits of well-defined settlements—for like the old town and city walls, they are considered to be the unyielding and dividing edge between "urbs" and farmland. They are nearly inviolate. As a result, the European countryside is to a large measure preserved as a landscape of gardens, vineyards, orchards, farm fields, and forest. Within the constricting town and city bounds each building site retains its high value and is utilized to the full. There are few if any vacancies and little obsolescence, for space is at a premium. In the compact settlements there is a lively mix of people and interchange of goods. Such towns and cities prosper.

Back in the United States, city boundaries provide little constraint to scattered development. Cities bleed out into

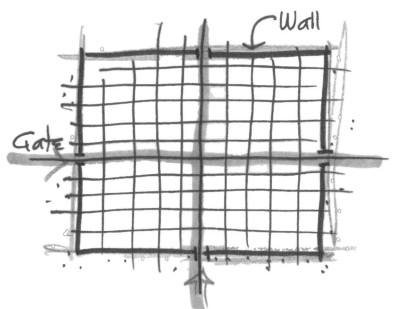

Roman town plan
The military cities and towns of the Romans were expressive of a predilection for order. The grid plan worked because, and only because, of the absence of high-speed traffic.

The walled boundaries of these and other medieval cities kept population, markets, water supply, and all else in balance. The surrounding lands were kept free for gardens, vineyards, pasture, and groves. These compact cities and open farmlands thrived. The principle of containment and the preclusion of sprawl is even more valid today.

the countryside until in time the suburbs, then the farm-lands, are infiltrated to the point that they can no longer function as cohesive entities. The name of this U.S. phenomenon, and curse, is *urban sprawl*. Over the years it has resulted in the jumbled coagulation of whole regions of "megalopolis"—such as the coastlands that stretch along the Atlantic seaboard from Boston to Baltimore and beyond. Compared to the coastal regions of Europe, such a trashed and blatantly commercialized environment is, in the main, a sorry place in which to live, to work, or even visit.

In the broad perspective—one that includes a view of the past and vision of the future—one of the great and challenging tasks in the United States is to restructure the towns and cities as largely self-contained entities. Concurrently, the surrounding countryside is to be reconsolidated and restored as a productive base and environs. This will take time, funds, ingenuity, and patience. It will entail the proven techniques of reclamation, mitigation, reforestation, resource conservation, growth management—and other techniques yet to come. It can and will be accomplished, for the alternatives are grim beyond tolerance. We look ahead, and plan ahead, to a whole new concept of true community living—in the well-conceived, well-planned urban metropolis.

Process

If a new town or city were to be planned from scratch in the open countryside—a supposition that in fact occurs not infrequently—how could its layout be improved over that of established cities? It is proposed that the planning for a new town should be the same as for a garden, a park, a campus, or community. The objectives in each case are identical—to accommodate and express all proposed uses in best relationship to each other, the site, and its environs.

With major component uses described, the approximate area requirements can be assigned for each. These can be designated by circles of relative size and the diagrammatic layout put aside for future reference. As in all landscape planning, the proposed site is then carefully analyzed. The natural topographic forms—the hills, valleys, water bodies, streams, and drainageways—are to be preserved insofar as feasible. Also preserved are the outstanding natural features such as waterfalls, dunes, ponds, wetlands, the best of the soils, and vegetative covers. Within and around this natural open space matrix the urban land use components are then located and their shapes adjusted for optimum fit and function. Insofar as possible the routes of vehicular and pedestrian movement are aligned to follow the natural ravines, valleys, and broad ridges—thus requiring a minimum of grading construction and landscape disruption. With such

As long as we think of the city and suburbs as separate entities they will remain separate entities.

——————————————

Traditionally, the ties between the city and its supporting region have been largely ignored. The time is at hand in the United States when they can only be planned together.

——————————————

In land use planning, generalized land use areas of various types are brought into the best possible relationship to each other, the trafficways and the underlying topography. With each area given bufferage to allow for limited change and adjustment over the years, the land use relationships are gradually refined.

The properly planned and planted urban street can become a linear arboretum.

Within the next 25 to 30 years for every two persons now residing or working within our crowded cities there will probably be three. It can well be imagined that to accommodate this massive influx, and to provide the essential mobility both between and within the urban centers, entirely new concepts of city and transportation must by then have been evolved.

The character of towns and cities springs in the main from their topographical settings.

Our way of life is characterized ... by this ambivalence: a misconception that nature can be "conquered," an ever-widening gap between corporate ambitions and nature's laws.

JAMES WINES

There are two conflicting attitudes toward life. One is to "grab all you can get—the Devil take the hindmost." The other is to "leave the world a better place because you've traveled through." The corollary in land usage suggests that over the past 500 years under these "beautiful-for-spacious-skies" the former type folk have prevailed.

For the past 300 years in America private land has been treated as a commodity. In the next 100 years (it may take that long) it will be recognized as the public resource that it is.

---

an approach, the land conformation, to a large extent, determines the urban form. We will have in effect garden-park cities and urban metropoli because they are so planned from the start.

But what of existing cities? How can they be opened up and refreshed? *Place by place and space by space!* By reclaiming existing streams and rivers. By renovating the waterfront. By creating, a segment at a time, a network of limited access parkways and interconnecting pedestrian paths and bicycle trails. By a citywide tree-planting program and reforestation. By the ready techniques of urban renewal and redevelopment.

Within the next 30 to 50 years—as in the past 30 to 50—most buildings, roads, and other structures in the United States will have been replaced as worn out or obsolete. We will thus have been given another chance. As a guideline in the reshaping-rebuilding process there is need by every jurisdiction for a comprehensive long-range plan. These, if they are worthy, will be designed *to* the underlying topography and *around* an open space frame.

Physical factors

For century after century the cities of the world were structured by the indigenous topography. Hills and slopes were maintained intact; rivers and drainageways were preserved to continue their vital functions. Further, such natural features as lakes, ponds, springs, rocks, groves, and venerable trees were protected as cherished, sometimes sacred, landmarks. This reverence for the land was to change abruptly with the advent of mechanized earth-moving equipment. In the United States, particularly, massive landscape destruction and leveling have become so prevalent that they seem to be a fixation. Perhaps because of our inherited pioneer compulsion to "clear the land, drain the swamp, level the rise, and fill the ravine," we have set about to tame the land and exert control over nature.

In urban areas the destruction has been so complete that for the most part only the major land forms and waterways remain. The landscape has been neutralized, homogenized; the loss is painfully evident. With newly emerging attitudes toward the environment, the disruption has been somewhat lessened. With responsible legislation and firm enforcement it can be effectively stopped.

What, then, is the hope for the natural landscape? Are we destined to live out our lives on a barren, leveled, human-desecrated plain? Or will our children and grandchildren know the delight of forested hills, rushing streams, rolling plains, tranquil marsh, the cresting dune, and other such topographical splendors? They will if, and only if, we act while there is still time.

Preserve

Protect the best of existing features. Where development is planned, at any scale—from garden plot to new community—planners must analyze the site and environs; must ensure the integrity of the basic ground forms, the established drainage patterns, and the plant and animal communities. Design them into the composition; bring them into the lives of the users and the passers-by.

Restore

Rediscover and unearth those features which have been hidden by obsolescent constructions or buried beneath trash and fill. Streams are waiting to be reopened, reshaped, and replanted. Wetlands are there to be cleared and reflooded. Whole river basins and lakeshores lie ready for planned restoration. Especially within a defined urban open space system can a long-range program of landscape reclamation be effective in reestablishing the natural setting.

Reshape

Create a new landscape. Where the original land forms have been destroyed—as by grading, erosion, or mineral extraction—a whole new, often superior, landscape can be designed and brought into being. The one guiding rule: newly created land forms should tie into the surrounding natural systems—and belong.

Mother Nature is forgiving of the slight abuse but merciless to the serious offender. She is relentless in her resolve to restore, recleanse, and revegetate. Given the chance, she will soon heal the wound and obliterate the traces of humanity's unthinking transgressions. Those who refuse, however, to respect the laws and dynamics of nature in their constructions are destined to pay the penalty. When violations occur, hillsides give way, structures crumble, seawalls fail, and towns are flooded or blown to oblivion. In time, proud but cognizant creatures that we are, we will relearn the wisdom of protecting the natural landscape and building in full awareness of nature's immutable way.

Natural features

The planning of any landscape area starts with an understanding of the site. Each landscape type or feature will suggest a fitting plan layout or treatment to recognize, preserve, and accentuate the native quality.

If a prairie, so plan as to appreciate and "glorify" its prairie-ness. If a dune, leave it for all its tough fragility; build upward for viewing over and across. If a wetland, hold back to protect it for what it is and does. And so with the crag, the cliff, the slope, the undulating meadow, and the

---

Strip mining

Strip mining — as of coal, gravel, metals, and potash is being brought under control. Millions of acres of once prime farm, forage and forest lands, since despoiled, are being reclaimed by the blockage of acid mine seepage, regrading, and the reestablishment of vegetative covers.

The environment is no longer simply "a consideration" in our planning of projects. It is now a "go/no go" test.

Lt. General H. J. Hatch
Commander, U.S. Army Corps of Engineers

---

plain. Each will have its unique conformation and character, its constraints and possibilities. Fine, intuitive planning will respond to constraints and optimize all opportunities. It will borrow from and dramatize, the natural strength of the land.

Valleys

Valleys and the rich bottomlands with their accumulated strata of topsoil and nutrients are to be reserved for agriculture and life-sustaining vegetation. Once disturbed by other development, erosion is soon to follow. Better that valleys, narrow to broad, be devoted to farmland and forest, with feeding streams and tributaries left in their natural state.

Hilltops, ridges, and plateaus

These weather-tested and stable promontories are normally well suited to building and roadway construction. Here foundations are secure and drainage assured. Here, too, the home and apartment dwellers and users of roads are afforded sweeping views of the valleys and intervening slopes. There is in the human an atavistic instinct to attain and command the uplands—and to till and harvest the low.

Slopes

Steeply sloping land is generally thought to be unusable. For most purposes it is. In urban planning, however, it has been found to have many positive values. Green bluffs and slopes are highly visible in the cityscape and give welcome relief to the built-out horizontal and vertical planes. Slopes can serve as dividers and definers of cohesive communities and other unified districts. Forested, reforested, or rock-faced, they serve as magnificent backdrops and do much to enhance the city.

Steep land is not to be used for scattered residential development. The cost of constructing and maintaining access roads, utilities, and providing public services usually far outweighs the revenues recovered. Except for very special exceptions it is better that slope lands of 30 percent or greater be zoned as permanent open space.

For what other special purposes then can such slopes be used? They are often well-suited for use as paths of movement or as various types of overlooks. As routes they offer the rare opportunity for unimpeded lateral movement throughout the city and region. By innovative means they can be used for the conveyance of people or goods along the friction-free drives, transit lines, or beltways. Passengers can be treated to uninterrupted rides and often spectacular views. Goods can be transported from outlying terminals to in-city distribution points through invisible tunnels or low profile, weatherproof passageways.

Urban hillside use and protection has many dimensions. Some slopes are best preserved in their entirety as leafy walls of backdrop and enframement. Some are tunneled and terraced to give lateral routes of communication and vertical overlook terraces and structure where appropriate. Towered promontories give sweeping views of the city while preserving wide expanses of green. In every case where a use is proposed it is to be weighed against the long-term open space alternatives.

Slopes

From the undulating to the precipitous, slopes when treated as liabilities become liabilities. When welcomed as assets they can make a telling contribution to the appearance and function of a metropolitan region.

Mild slopes add topographical interest, define unified development areas, and provide natural surface drainage flow and channels. They serve:

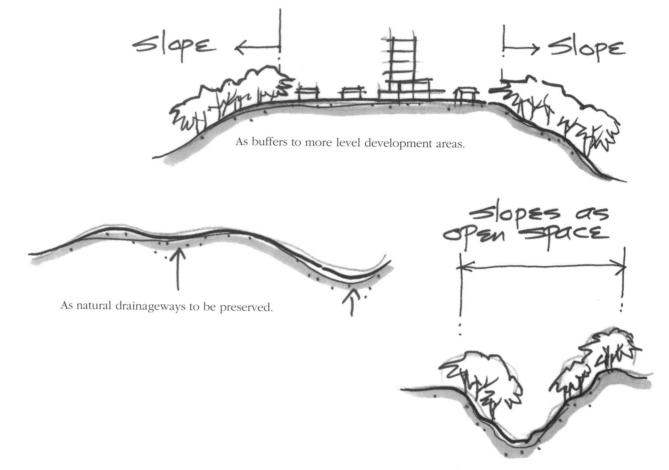

As buffers to more level development areas.

As natural drainageways to be preserved.

Ravines provide stable channels for storm water run-off.

Where the natural slopes can be maintained everyone benefits—including residents, hikers, bikers, and wee creatures.

Slopes (Continued)

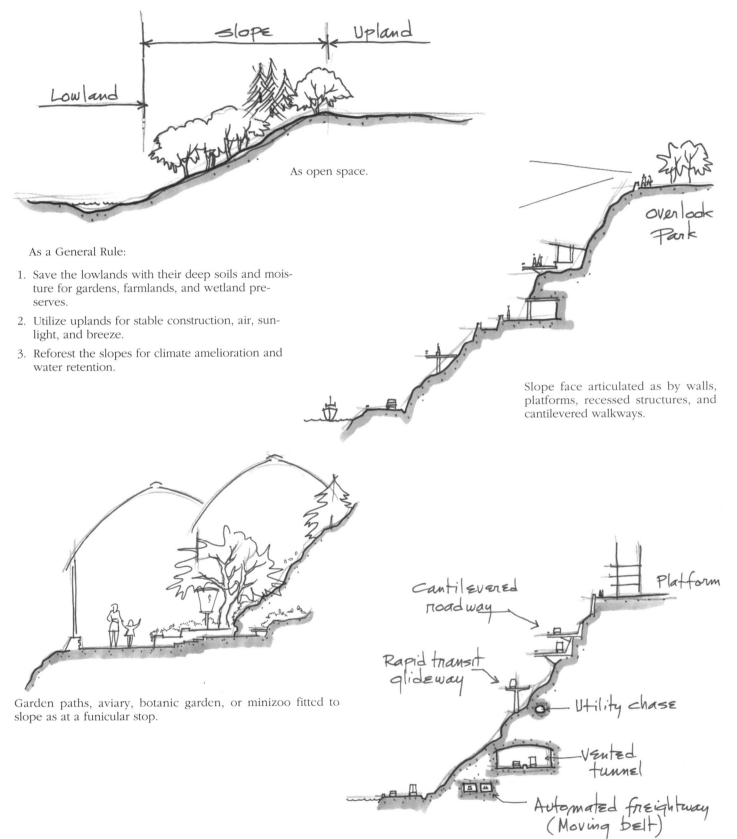

As open space.

As a General Rule:

1. Save the lowlands with their deep soils and moisture for gardens, farmlands, and wetland preserves.

2. Utilize uplands for stable construction, air, sunlight, and breeze.

3. Reforest the slopes for climate amelioration and water retention.

Slope face articulated as by walls, platforms, recessed structures, and cantilevered walkways.

Garden paths, aviary, botanic garden, or minizoo fitted to slope as at a funicular stop.

Paths of Lateral Movement
By tunnel, chase or cantilevered structures.

Slopes (Continued)

Steep slopes or bluffs have dramatic potential. Seen from below as rocky or wooded inclined planes they give a rich and powerful enframement. From above they afford magnificent views. The incline itself as a site and lateral passageway has many uses and viewing possibilities.

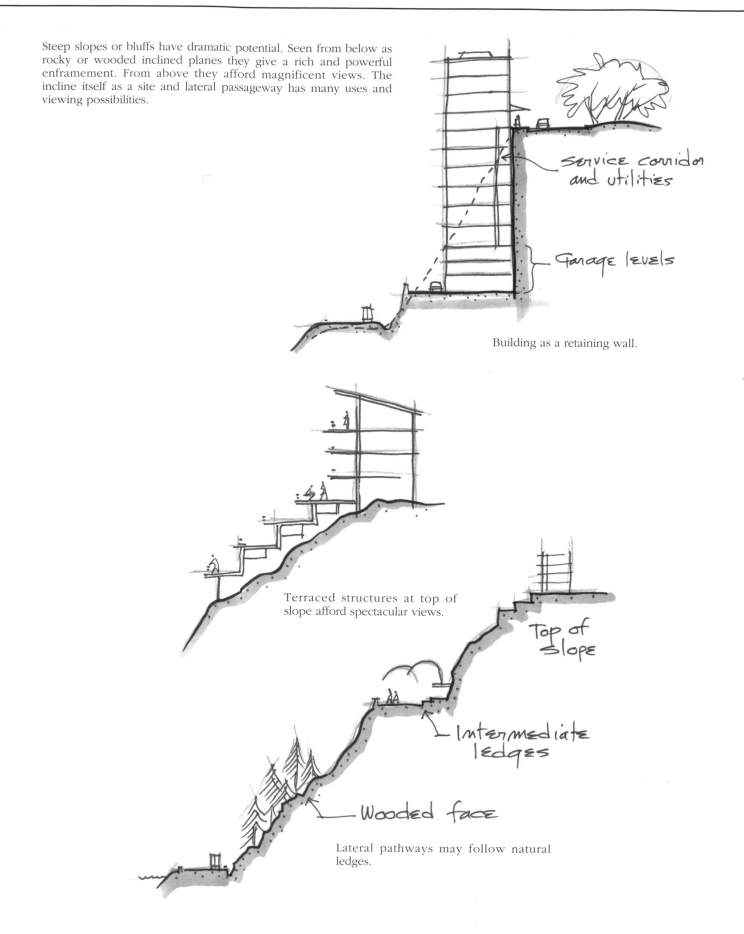

Building as a retaining wall.

Terraced structures at top of slope afford spectacular views.

Lateral pathways may follow natural ledges.

A popular trend in the planning/design of zoos, aviaries, and public gardens is that of dispersal. As supplements to the central installation, miniunits are located strategically throughout the metropolitan area and tended by mobile crews.

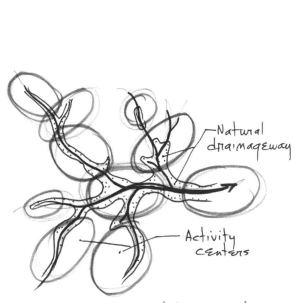

In this "how not to" example layout the natural watercourses divide and disrupt community centers and subcenters.

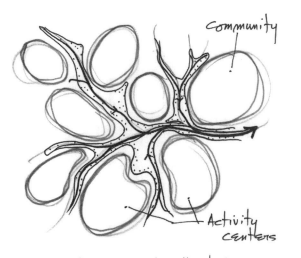

Here the sheathed drainageway: help define cohesive activity areas and provide unimpeded paths of interconnection between all areas of a city.

Urban blue and green

As sites for observation platforms and viewing structures they suggest the use of contour planning, retaining walls, flying decks, balconies, and pier and beam construction. In many cases a seemingly formidable slope is uniquely suited to a special public use—as in the case of tiered roadways, aerial tram, or terraced gardens. Where, for instance, could be found a better site for a zoological park or aviary, perhaps combined with all-weather escalators or a funicular? Or where better a contour jogging path or hillside overlook parkway?

Steep hillsides, and even precipitous mountain slopes, long considered development obstacles, will make their full contribution to the city and region when recognized instead as the attractive features that they are and as presenting new opportunities.

Wetlands

Wetlands, marshes, bogs, and ponds were once for draining and filling. It is only since we are beginning to learn of their value in water storage and replenishment that they are coming to be protected. We are learning also of their crucial role in wildlife management and the spawning of shell and finfish. Fully as important in urban areas is the contribution in climate amelioration—in raising air temperatures in winter and cooling them in the summer. Wetlands serve also to flush away traces of airborne soot and chemicals from foliage and soils—keeping air fresh and water clean. It has become obvious that waterbodies, streams, and their watersheds are to be defined and protected in the best interest of all citizens.

Lakes, bays, and tidal estuaries

Water-oriented cities such as Baltimore, Tampa, Chicago, Seattle, or San Francisco—or on a smaller scale St. Augustine, Petoskey, or Sausalito—are memorable in the relationship. The open water provides not only manifold commercial and recreational opportunities but also tempers the climate. Few natural attributes can do more to enhance the visual quality of the abutting communities and roadways.

Lakes and bays serve best when their beaches and shores are protected in the public ownership. The amenity and real estate value of the highly desirable frontage lands can be amplified if the bordering swaths are extended inland along the valleys and feeding streams. In time, by comprehensive planning and redevelopment procedures, even severely blighted waterfronts and backlands can be restored to highly attractive urban settings. As waterway and water-edge frontage they will draw the best of all types of development. The opportunities are not to be overlooked or wasted.

Tidal estuaries, with their brackish ebb and flow—so rich in their nourishment of the marine food chain—occur in lowlands bordering the coasts. Surrounded by marsh or mangrove, they are not to be crowded. They require wide building setbacks for protection and the interception and filtration of storm water runoff from adjacent development lands. When bordered at a distance by overlooking mid- to high-rise residential towers, estuaries afford some of the most beautiful natural scenery viewing in the world.

Rivers and streams

Streams and rivers are lineal. The fact of their directional flow provides remarkable opportunities in city and open space planning. First of all, if left uninterrupted they serve as natural drainageways, their natural water courses precluding the need for disruptive and costly storm sewer mains and outfalls. Paths, trails, or parkways that follow their alignment are not only scenic but provide ideal interconnection for the developments on their banks. Further, where streams intersect with other streams, or meet the river or shore, they provide direct water-edge linkage with all other waterways in the region. This being so, one of the best open space diagrams is one that moves along and embraces the streams and water edges. This suggests that wherever possible a protective stream/river corridor be defined and acquired in the long-range public interest.

Soils and vegetative covers

One of the most valuable assets of a land area is its mantle of topsoil and the grasses, trees, shrubs, and vines that hold it in place. A 1-foot layer of topsoil may take nature a millennium in its making. When exposed, it can be carried away with the first flash flood. With fertile topsoil being the basic wealth of a nation, it is no light matter that within the past decade alone more than 4 percent of our total supply has been washed down our rivers and lost irretrievably to the sea. This has been the result of clearing, overdraining, uncontrolled excavation, unregulated farming and grazing, and the unrestricted use of power equipment.

In our cities paving and buildings have replaced upward of half the once-vegetated land. This represents not only a waste of the precious topsoil substance (except in those rare cases where it was stockpiled and saved) but also a telling negative impact on our living environment—on climate, air quality, and water supply. Vegetated land absorbs the moisture of mists, rain, and snowfall. It tempers the air by transpiration, helps retain the moisture in the protected soils, and replenishes the underlying aquifers. Stripped of

Three of the dirtiest words in the vocabulary of earth defilement must be ditching, drilling, and dredging.

All forms of major earthwork — as by subsurface or strip mining, excavation, filling and grading — are to be permitted by license only when preplanned, officially approved, and backed by adequate bonding.

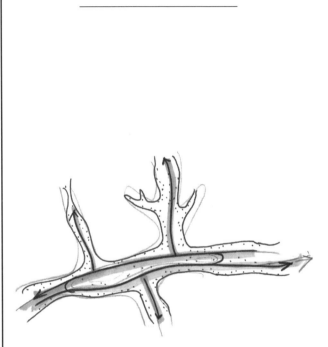

Open space corridors
An open space system that follows the streams and drainageways provides a free-flowing alignment for walkways, bikeways, and often scenic parkways.

We live on a layer of topsoil. All plant life is nourished by it. Below is rock. If the topsoil blows or is washed away, all vegetation will die. It if dies the animals will go. Including us. The earth will then again consist of saltwater seas and desert.

It is well known that certain levels of air pollution can be controlled by vegetation; that leaves absorb significant levels of ozone and sulphur dioxide; that soil micro-organisms are more effective than vegetation in removing carbon monoxide and assist in converting it to carbon dioxide; that vegetation collects heavy metals such as cadmium and lead....

Cities that have foxes, owls, natural woodlands, and regenerating fields are more interesting and pleasant to live in than those that don't.

MICHAEL HOUGH

(A reclaimed drainageway) brings a natural element into an urban environment. It takes people away from the hard edge of the city.

PHILIP HENDRICKS

———————————

Community: All plants and animals interrelating within a given habitat.

———————————

An *eco-system* is a system formed by the interaction of a community of living creatures and organisms with each other and their environment.

———————————

A landscape is the physical manifestation of an ecosystem.

The structure and function of ecosystems must pervade all landscape design and all urban design as a fundamental base.

JOHN LYLE

its soils and covers, the naked rock can no longer check the wind, cool and purify the air, absorb unwanted sound, retain and filter groundwater, or sustain the subsurface reservoirs. To comprehend the significance of the loss it is helpful to know that barren Spain, Greece, and Lebanon were once covered with grasses, herbaceous plants, and forests. One of the most significant prospects of the near future is that of converting the outpouring mountains of garbage, plastics, and other waste into fertile topsoil. Thus vast stretches of now barren land can be restored to productivity. By the same token, even grossly contaminated wastewater can be treated and purified for irrigation and to replenish our aquifers.

Our near-desert cities must, and in time will be, reshaped around open meadows, gardens, and urban forest groves. The forest preserves of Cook County that weave through suburban Chicago show what can be done with land rehabilitation. There, more than 100 square miles of depleted and eroded farmland and polluted swamp have been reclaimed, regraded, and reseeded or planted to native trees. These restored forest preserves, meadows, and waterways—prime recreational open space—have drawn to their sides the finest of new residential communities, institutions, and office parks to be built in the greater Chicago area. Cook County's preserves are but one example.

Wildlife

Cities aren't just for people. Ecologists tell us that all living things are interdependent—that the whole web of life is so finely spun that a tug on any one strand affects all others. It's a matter of checks and balances. Without the bee the apple blossom bears no fruit. Without the squirrel the unburied acorn sends no sprout; without the wren 10,000 caterpillars live to strip the leaves from overhanging foliage. Without the lark or mocking bird the evening air is hushed—a loss a city-dweller can't afford.

The existence of wildlife depends on suitable habitat. This equates largely with vegetative cover, not just in isolated patches, but in interrelated, plant and animal systems or "communities." These, in most urban areas, are rapidly disappearing. It is becoming all too evident, not only to ecologists, that the reduction in natural ground cover, waterways, and vegetation is harmful to the health and well-being of humans as well. There is ample proof of the need for conservation, restoration, and reforestation—to clear the air, to maintain fresh water supply, and to create a more salubrious living environment for *all* God's creatures.

Fortunately, the well-being of the native fauna and flora coincides with human well-being. Fortunately, too, the improvement of the urban living environment does not have to be achieved at economic or functional loss but rather at all-round gain. The restoration of the natural drainageways, the provision of an open space surrounding for the various city components, and the reestablishment of a cohesive farm-forest preserve around the city confines is in *all* ways desirable.

Transportation

The in-city movement of people from place to place is discussed elsewhere in these pages. Deserving separate attention is the larger-scale, longer-range transport of people and goods by trains, ships, planes, or automobiles. The corridors of these mass carriers form the vast transportation network that circumscribes the globe. Closely allied and sometimes, but too seldom, combined are the routes utilized for the transmission of fuels, energy, and signals. The location and function of these lines have much to do with what happens in the intervening areas. The transportation plan alone would tell much of the urban metropolis—for if the types, alignments, and capacities of the lines were noted, the plan layout and nature of the region would be evident.

Trains

It was the railroads even more than the highways that set the pattern and pace of our national development. Where the tracks led, farming, mining, and lumbering followed. Where the tracks crossed other tracks, roadways, or rivers, towns or cities sprang up. In the main, railway alignments, and thus patterns of urbanization, were accidents of topography. It was a matter of the easiest way to get through or across or the most convenient place to build a station.

American passenger train service faltered with the advent of interstate highways and air travel as faster, more convenient, and more agreeable alternatives. There were several contributing reasons. First, our passenger and freight trains have used the same clickety-clackity tracks to the detriment of both services. Such travel has become for the most part a dismal slumming excursion. Also, local commuter and through express trains have had conflicts of use and schedules. Cars were allowed to become outmoded, food service deteriorated, and maintenance became shoddy. With air lanes and highways now reaching the point of saturation, however, and with the restructuring of cities under way, it is entirely conceivable that high speed interstate and intercity trains may soon regain their popularity. It will require new magnetically levitated cars with superlative sleeping arrangements and dining. It will require a means of consoli-

The movement of goods and materials by rail, ships, airways and highways must be coordinated, or the entire transport system will break down.

The Intermodal Surface Transportation Efficiency Act of 1991:

"conceives of transportation planning as a system of complementary modes; regional railroads, high-speed magnetic-levitation trains, trolleys, busses and bike paths;

"requires states to support a broad range of transportation enhancement activities such as building scenic highways and trails, preserving historic roads and canals, acquiring scenic easements and recycling rail corridors; and

"requires that transportation policy be coordinated with regional and urban planning...."

NANCY LEVINSON

---

dating networks to provide fast through service to cities anywhere and everywhere. It will require separate and scenic routes and attractive centralized stations with transit interchange.

In theory the fixed-path passenger express should provide a near-ideal mode of mid- to long-distance travel. With new trackage, tunnels, and bridges in place, sleek cars should stream through the countryside unimpeded and at swishing speeds. The "TGV" or Très Grande Vitesse, of France and the bullet trains of Japan are good examples. Many trains of Europe, Canada, and India, too, are exemplary in their appointments, immaculate care, food service, and the scenic beauty to be enjoyed from comfortable cars with sparkling clean windows.

Rail transport of freight is expanding, especially where bulk and weight are telling factors. It is expanding because it has moved with the times. When trucking threatened as a competitor, the railroads offered "piggy-back" service for the long hauls. Container and palletized shipping has vastly improved loading and unloading efficiency. And a wide variety of specialized cars has attracted many new shippers. It is foreseen that freight transport by train will long be with us and in many new forms.

Ships

The history of civilization is closely allied with the history of shipping. From the earliest raft or dugout to the monstrous modern tankers, cargo vessels have plied the rivers, lakes, and seas incessantly. Bustling port towns and cities have formed along the landings and harbors worldwide. The overall impact of shipping today has been lessened by railways, highways, and airways, but piers and terminals and the efficient movement of ships and cargo are of major importance in many cities. Storage and transshipment have become increasing concerns, since all types of transport and distribution have yet to be integrated into a coordinated transportation *system*.

A complicating maritime consideration is that a polluted harbor with floating dunnage, battered docks, and tumbledown warehouses is no longer acceptable. In an era of improving environmental standards, city leaders have come to realize the dramatic possibilities of reorienting the downtown to the waterfront. A further complication is the diversity of boats in any harbor. There are military, commercial, and recreational craft ranging from battleships, barges, and ferries to speedboats, sailboats, and canoes. Confronted with such complexities, the prescribed planning procedure is to classify, group into the most compatible relationships, separate, and interconnect.

Planes

The airways have provided a new up-and-over dimension for the handling of freight and passengers. For longer distances and lighter loads they would seem the near-ultimate solution. An increasing problem, however, has been that of getting goods and people to and from the airports. Once again there is need for the coordination of routes and terminals. When, and only when, all modes of transportation can be planned together as an interrelated system can there be smooth and efficient flows.

As with rail transportation and transit it would seem that the transport of freight and passengers on the same plane—or even from the same port—works to the detriment of both, as does the intermix of private and commercial craft, or commercial and military. Diversification is in order, with ports of varying types spaced out with their own air envelopes and corridors.

Airports have two conflicting needs that must be reconciled. One is for extensive land area with abundant overhead air space. The second need is for direct and speedy connection to the urban activity centers, which are perforce some distance away. The solution lies in an advanced form of interconnecting rapid transit with radial linkage to the center city hub and circumferential beltways.

Highways

The most visible forms of transport are the vehicles that roll along our highways and into and out of our cities in diurnal tidal surges. Trucks, busses, vans, and personal automobiles roar night and day along the traffic networks—dispersing into the countryside or converging upon urban centers. Of all factors in urban planning, the automobile and highways are the hardest with which to reckon. They are assertive—as if demanding by some God-given right to be where they want to be and go where they want to go. Since it is the owners of automobiles who make the laws and draw the plans, the highways have been permitted to take over the run of most of our national landscape.

Cars have invaded the city centers, which historically throughout the world have been compact and of pedestrian scale. With ever-extending roadways and expanding parking compounds, cars have pried the city apart and all but precluded the close human interactions so vital to true urbanity. Our sprawling, traffic-crazed centers have lost their intensity and with it their reason for being. Obsolescence, vacancies, and rampant pollution are common. To many officials it seems impossible to stem the trend of degradation.

Now at last, however, there are those who realize that we must make the hard choice—increasing chaos or con-

Trafficways and parking compounds have usurped approximately one-third of the land area of our cities.

Where wide throughways divide otherwise unified city districts the latter may be reunited by rerouting or by roofing the trafficway fully or partially. The premium land regained will be valued for supporting uses, recreation, or greenway connectors.

Center cities are for driving to and around—not through. Surveys have shown that 8 of 10 drivers in big city downtowns have no reason or wish to be there.

———————————————

Until but very recently the design and location of U.S. highways has been based almost solely on the *cost-benefit ratio*—or the least cost per mile of travel from one point to another. "Costs" have included land acquisition, roadway and bridge construction, maintenance, etc. Although valid considerations, there are other neglected and important factors including impacts on the adjacent properties, historic, ecologic, and scenic considerations, and the use of the highway network to provide a sound land-use and transportation framework for the region served.

———————————————

A highly placed highway official has said that to his knowledge no federally aided highway has been located with the objective of helping "structure" a region. He averred that the time has come.

———————————————

A bridge is not for just crossing water. It is for knowing the glory of a river—for partaking of the wonder of a bay.

———————————————

trol. Workable cities, or more parking deserts and highway spaghetti-land.

Could there be a reasonable compromise? It is believed so. As a drastic but altogether feasible measure it is proposed that in time cars be banned from expanding pedestrian islands within our city centers. They will be intercepted and garaged at the edges or on subsurface levels. Eventually, within the distribution ring corridor there would be few surface streets or avenues. Outside the ring and throughout the surrounding countryside higher-speed traffic would move on controlled-access freeways and parkways, and lower-speed movement would be accommodated on circulation drives and local streets. By this plan the automobile would move more expeditiously throughout all but a small fraction of the territory—while within the tightly drawn urba-center rings the city cores could rebuild their essential strength.

To understand the reason for the fragmented pattern of our U.S. highways one must realize that for the most part they have been planned segment by segment, when and where additional capacity was needed—and then with the cost-benefit ratio as the accepted criterion. Seldom has even a small section of the roadway network been preplanned as an element of a total and balanced system or as part of an overall land use and trafficway plan.

By all logic, the roadways of the future will be classified and designed as an interrelated hierarchy. At the top of the list will be the interstate freeways and national parkways. There will follow controlled-access arterials and lesser circulation roads with parkway characteristics. Then will come the local frontage streets, loop drives, and cul-de-sacs. And finally, such specialized types as scenic-historic trails, private roads, and industrial truckways. Each has its own particular function and distinguishing characteristics. All are to be interconnected.

Street and highway adjuncts and hardware

Among the most visible elements of our cities and countryside are the bridges, retaining walls, lighting, signs and structures built into the nation's roadways. As with other construction, the "fit" is better if the improvement is suited to its site, if the design is suited specifically to its purpose, and if the materials, forms, and colors are suited to the locale. Again, *less* is usually better than *more*.

As to the street or highway user, clarity of vision and understanding of the signals and signs are essential to safety. Also to be considered is the quality of the driving experience and viewing. Billboards distract both from the signage and scenery and by all reason should have been outlawed long ago. Retaining walls and sound barriers are best blended into their surroundings, as inconspicuously as possible. Conversely, bridges are sculptural in form—usually handsome in themselves and made more so by the application of deep, rich metallic colors to the framing and steel spandrels. Often a bridge affords dramatic views which are to be unimpeded by the traditional, and inexplicable, solid side panels.

As important as that of the driver and riders is the experience of those who live beside, look to, or must cross the passing street or highway. Safety is a primary concern. Noise, glare, and visual distraction are to be eliminated or reduced insofar as feasible. Here the use of natural ground covers and the preserving or planting of native trees in groves or drifts can do much to soften the roadway intrusion.

Parking garages and compounds are extensions of motorways. When located at the periphery or in subsurface levels of the urban centers they are inconspicuous—out of sight and out of mind. On-grade parking compounds within the peripheral open space bands provide more affordable parking and if made attractive can be welcome attributes.

Freeways

One of the great highway construction programs of the world has recently taken place right before our eyes and with little fanfare. It has been the completion of the interstate highway system that links all major cities of the United States. It has provided not only rapid interconnection but the elimination along the way of all highway building frontage. Another mark of the later freeways is that they circumvent the city centers, affording access from well-placed external interchanges. In their free-flowing performance they provide the model for all future arterial and circulation roadways.

There is no rational reason that highways built at public expense should provide direct entranceways to roadside real estate. Strip highway development must go. It has blighted the roadside and clogged the traffic far too long and far too often. The function of all public highways is to move traffic freely and safely at optimum speeds—as on our U.S. freeways. It is not to line the pockets of realtors, lucky landowners, or opportunistic speculators with access to projected highway plans.

National parkways

To enter upon and drive along the Blue Ridge or Great Smokey national parkways, as examples, is to experience the sky, cloud shadows, forested slopes, and scenic mountain regions in a whole new, exhilarating way. These recreational roadways were conceived to make accessible to the

By the inclusion of mounded borders and planted islands—bleak, windswept parking compounds can be transformed into pleasant "motor garden" oases. Such paved and shaded spaces can double as settings for weekend markets, festivals, or fairs.

The intention to form beautiful roadways in concert with the lay of the land and to ensure that a motorist's experience of the roadway be enjoyable and fulfilling may seem naive, in the face of the pressures generated by raw traffic data. But they're rock-bottom essential to any and all attempts to build better roadways in-city and semi-city alike.

MICHAEL LECCESE

Vehicular movement is best experienced in a wide, sweeping, uninterrupted trajectory. Movement on foot is at a much slower, often leisurely, pace, sometimes meandering—and with distractions. It has taken too long for urban and traffic planners to recognize that the two types of movement are incompatible.

Successful parkways should include independent lane alignment, with each direction of pavement sculpted to follow the topography, leaving a median of varying width; a protected view-shed (the scenic vista created by the curvilinear alignment); the weaving of horizontal and vertical curves to create a sense of flow; and the incorporation of park areas or features such as scenic overlooks, bike paths, boat ramps, or hiking trails.

MICHAEL LECCESE

Beautiful highways do not result from a garnish of exotic plants installed along their edges. They are achieved, rather, by sensitive roadway alignment that preserves and reveals the best features of the natural terrain through which they pass.

Clarke + Rapuano

Peridian

Westinghouse Communities

The Crosby Arboretum

Westinghouse Communities

Clarke + Rapuano

Royston Hanamoto Alley & Abey

Clarke + Rapuano

Sasaki Associates (Alan Ward)

Oehme, van Sweden & Assoc.

Johnson Johnson & Roy

Peridian (Jeff Beals)

Peridian

Peridian

Clarke + Rapuano

Peridian

Wallace Roberts & Todd

Theodore Osmundson & Assoc.

Peridian

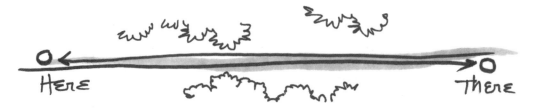

Nonfrontage roadway
Why build highways at public expense to get us quickly from here to there...?

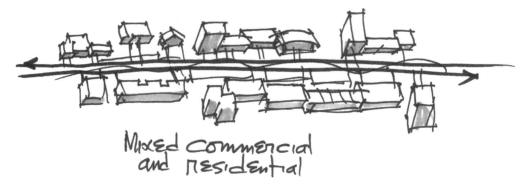

Strip highway development
Then allow speculators to buy the abutting properties to construct all types of structures with driveway access from the highway—which slows traffic and clogs the road?

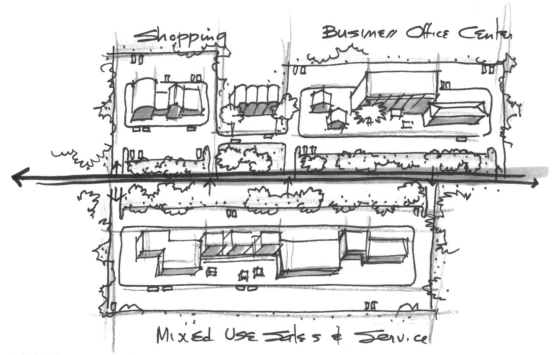

Off-highway groupings
Arterial highways are best designed for the free flow of vehicular traffic without direct building frontage. Off-highway frontage roads and/or ramp access to clustered residential-commercial groupings are better for all concerned. Area land values are thereby increased.

motoring public some of our country's most scenic superlatives, They are more works of landscape architecture than of engineering, for as lineal parks they were aligned and sculpted, station by station, to bring the view and viewer into the most favorable relationships. By curvature, section, edge treatment, foreground, and natural enframement, they extract the full beauty and power of the landscape.

There are many parkways of lesser magnitude but equal quality. There come to mind the Storm King and Taconic in upper New York State, the Palisades Parkway opposite Manhattan, the Garden State of New Jersey, Virginia's Yorktown-Jamestown, and Skyline Drive. Colorado has the breathtaking Trailridge Road, Wyoming its awesome drive through the Tetons. And then there are the scenic routes through the desert canyon country, the Cascades of Washington State and the Big Sur of California. In time there will no doubt be others—through Lake Superior territory, down the Missouri and Mississippi River valleys, and along the length of the Florida keys.

Such parkways avoid urban areas, traversing the heartlands in between, with connections to the side.

Arterial highways

Nominally, arterial highways are used primarily for through traffic, usually on a continuous route. U.S. 1 from Maine to Key West in Florida is an arterial highway, as is route 101 in California. Both examples and their counterparts, nationwide, reveal the plight of our basic highway nonplanning. Arterial highways, they smash through towns and cities dead center, discombobulating everything in their path. They are interrupted by myriad crossings and traffic signals. They are congested with stop-and-go traffic. They are flanked in the cities and suburbs with all manner of sleazy to elegant shops, stores, factories, eateries, bowling alleys, service stations, single family homes, motels, and apartments. In the open countryside strip development is replaced by a barrage of blatant billboards which obscure what might otherwise be a glimpse of the natural scenery.

Such obscene disasters are probably beyond salvage in the near future. For now, they can only be bypassed to decay amidst their own clutter—as glaring examples of never-to-be-repeated mistakes in the design of new trafficways and in their roadside planning.

What might arterials better be? It is anticipated that in the future they may be so aligned as to sweep between and around, not through, the activity centers. Their rights-of-way will be of variable widths and adjusted to the topography—sometimes with widened medians to embrace a stretch of wetland, an outcrop, a grove of trees, or a stream. Arterials will be lineal parks, providing no direct

... cities should be hung on a skeleton of parkways and landscaped arterials, laid out in advance....

JOSEPH PASSONNEAU

Variformed roadway corridors with undulating medians can preserve natural drainageways, vegetation, and wild bird habitat and bring nature into the city.

Since transportation is the life blood of commerce it would seem wise to sustain vital flows. Why is it, then, that most cities have a chronic case of hardening of the arteries?

Billboards, "pollution on poles," dominate the roadways and skyline of most U.S. cities—overshadowing homes and blighting whole neighborhoods.

As one drives the highways there are points or curves where the viewer's interest is focused inward to the community highlights or outward to scenic splendors. These are the very points at which billboards are concentrated. There can be no more obtrusive a form of visual pollution.

The "green wall" concept of draping urban roadways or other embankments in verdure—as in structural planting coffers or tiered trays—can convert barren slopes into hanging gardens.

... its vistas designed to facilitate something called "making pictures as you drive."

WILBUR SIMONSON

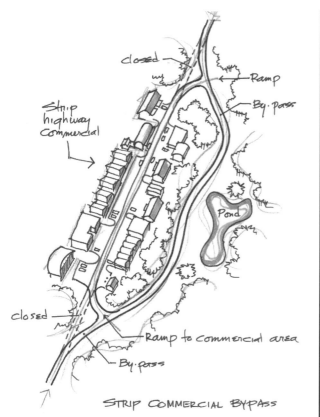

STRIP COMMERCIAL BYPASS

Strip commercial bypass
Where strip commercial districts exist they may be bypassed and screened by new non-frontage circulation drives—with optional ingress-egress ramps.

At times the roadway goes airborne on concrete piers to leave streams and wildlife migration paths untouched.

Michael Leccese

They should be tailored to the landscape and lie lightly on the land.

John J. Bright

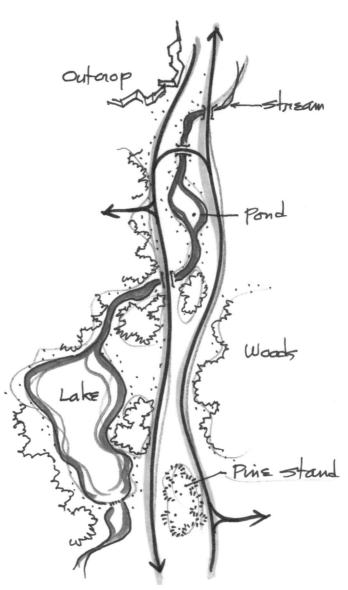

The arterial parkway
Arterial parkways with variable width medians can weave through the urban landscape—preserving and revealing to the travelling public the best of the regional features.

building frontage or curb cuts; rather, at intervals of no less than one-eighth of a mile, ramps to a perpendicular roadway will give access to the abutting land. They will be free of advertising signboards, and designed to fit harmoniously into the surrounding countryside or city, with appropriate planting.

Circulation drives

Circulation drives are what their name implies. As one nears one's destination on the throughways there will be a well-marked turnoff onto the circulation ways, which should lead from one neighborhood or community to another. With free movement an objective, the routes should be unimpeded. They will have parkway characteristics, without building frontage at the sides. Much of what one sees and knows of a region will depend upon the experience of driving to and through on such lineal motorways.

Frontage streets

Frontage streets are local, low-speed roadways running through or abutting residential neighborhoods and upon which homes or groups of homes may be faced.

By precedent, most Americans are street dwellers. The familiar residential pattern is that of streets upon which homes face at regular intervals. There are obvious dangers and disadvantages, but since habits are so hard to change, it can be expected that this housing pattern will persist in part for many years to come. In such a case it can only be proposed that high-speed through traffic be discouraged by law and plat plan and that the streets be made as safe and attractive as possible. Looped side streets and curvilinear cul-de-sacs provide the best direct street frontage, for by their very layout they ensure lower speeds and a certain degree of privacy.

A better arrangement by far, however, is that in which motor courts or parking compounds are designed at the sides of local streets, with homes clustered around or beyond.

Private drives

It is not uncommon in new developments for roads to be built and maintained by a private taxing district or home owners' association. The advantages may be those of gated control, reduced speed, privacy, and often less than outsized municipal rights-of-way and paving dimensions. A relaxation of prescribed geometric alignment and widths permits a more harmonious fit with the land forms and landscape features. Further, the lighting, signage, and level of maintenance may be far superior to the accepted municipal standard.

Scenic-historic byways

At the low end of the scale of magnitude is the off-highway local road or street preserved for its scenic or historic attributes. Many such byways are looped extensions of an urban or rural parkway and are identified by special trail markers as tourist attractions. Others lie within a designated historic district and may even be closed in some hours or seasons for pedestrian use and enjoyment.

The curvilinear street with cul-de-sacs is perfectly suited to residential development that puts a premium on privacy.

GEORGE PILLORGE

Highways, parkways and streets

Highways, as paths of vehicular movement, are to be designed for safe, efficient, uninhibited, and pleasurable travel. In order of magnitude they range from the high-capacity, high-speed interstate freeways to local frontage streets and the tenuous, meandering scenic-historic byways. Where traffic flow is a primary consideration interruptions or undue frictions are to be avoided. As lethal lines of force, thoroughfares should never cross at grade, nor should they transect cohesive activity areas.

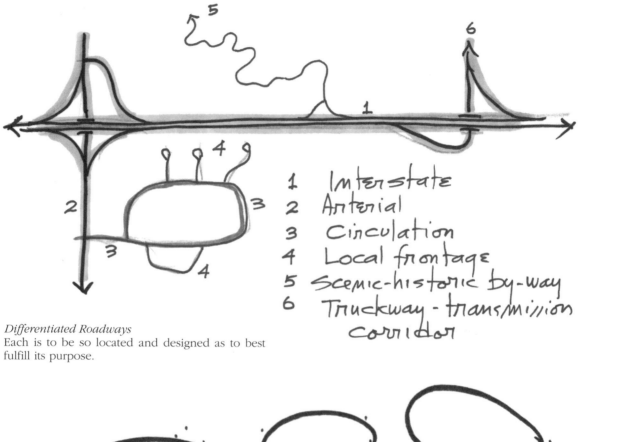

1 Interstate
2 Arterial
3 Circulation
4 Local frontage
5 Scenic-historic by-way
6 Truckway - transmission corridor

Differentiated Roadways
Each is to be so located and designed as to best fulfill its purpose.

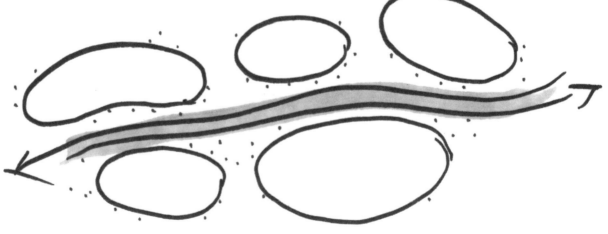

Highway Alignment
Future highways will weave between, not through, unified neighborhoods, communities, campuses, or commercial centers.

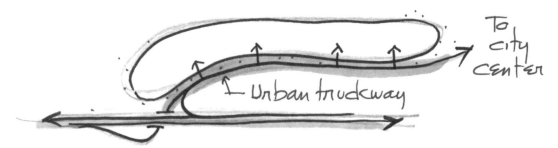

The Urban Truckway
Transportation and cargo vehicles will move on separate roadways as they approach industrial parks and distribution terminals.

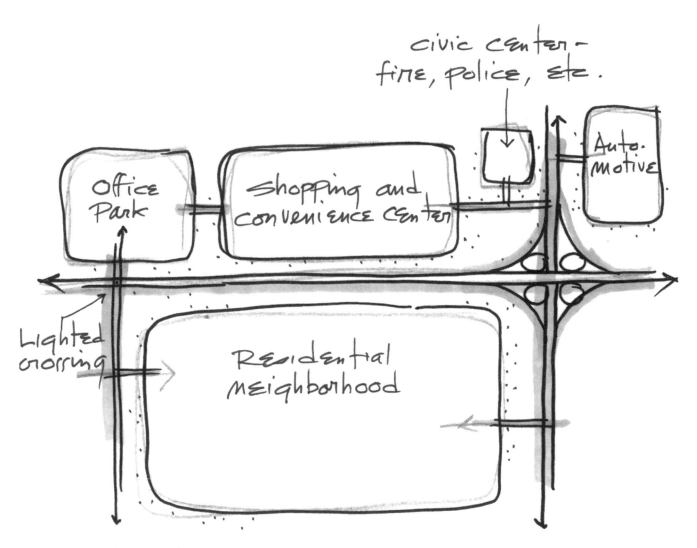

Limited Access Roadways
Freeways, parkways, and circulation drives are to be planned for free vehicular movement without direct building frontage.

The life style of Americans is based on the motor car.

_____

People will use automobiles until something better comes along.

_____

Mass transit works only if many thousands of people want to get to a reasonably small number of destinations from a reasonably small number of points of origin.

NATION'S CITIES

The densest and probably the most naturally evolving mixed use centers are those on the transit station stops—sub-nodes on a metropolitan scale.

GEORGE PILLORGE

Higher density is the only solution to our transportation problems.

RANDOLPH HESTER

Transport by highway
A single transport truck on a stretch of freeway can reduce its passenger car-carrying capacity to less than half. Reason suggests a specialized truckway.

Truckways

No discourse on transportation routes would be complete without mention of the logic of classified truckways. In a more reasonable scheme of things, as freight-carrying transport trucks on the interstate highways approach urban terminals or manufacturing areas they will be directed by off-ramp to specially designed truckway corridors. Such routes will carry also the massive energy transmission lines and will serve as the spine of more functional and efficient production and distribution centers.

Transit

Having regrouped urba-centers of intensive activity strategically throughout the metropolitan region, how are people to get to and from and around?

The most popular means of conveyance has long been, and will long continue to be, the personally operated motorized vehicle, or automobile. Suffice it to say at this point that no center can presently thrive, or even survive, without direct access by the urban highway system. As a telling adjunct, however, the revitalized centers will be served by various forms of transit, some traditional, some relatively new, and some not yet imagined. Together they will include a panoply of such options as magnetically levitated "Mag-lev" trains, monorail, minirail, trams, moving walks, and bicycles.

Rapid rail

Rapid rail transit has yet to come into its own. The regional and in-city movement of people by rail had a rather discouraging beginning. Horse-drawn then motorized street cars were clumsy and often little faster than walking. Suburban-to-urban commuter trains shared the tracks with through passenger express and freight trains, treating riders daily to the rear view of abatoirs, sidings, loading docks, and dumps—often to stop at grimy stations. Where rapid rail transit-ways have been planned to loop through the open countryside, and where cars and stations have been made appealing, they soon attract riders.

In the United States, most new rapid rail transit systems have made the error of attempting to connect *existing* population centers by plowing to and through them. The disruptions and consequent budgets have been devastating. Elsewhere, as in Canada and Scandinavia, rapid transit has been used instead to structure or restructure a developing region. From hived stations at the city center they radiate outward through forest and fields to various urban and suburban centers. These include newly planned educational, recreational, or manufacturing nodes, new communities, or entire new towns. Separate freeways with reserved bus lanes link them externally. Such coordination of land uses and routes of pleasant, high-speed interconnection is bound to become the norm in the future.

The essential requisite of the successful rapid rail transit system is that it provide rapid interconnection from *center to center*. The nature and magnitude of each center must be such as to make the stop worthwhile. This implies a concentration of passengers converging upon or dispersing from the various transit interchanges. Such concentrations seldom occur by happenstance. They must be astutely created. They are achieved by locating a regional node of high intensity—such as a trade, sports, convention, or educational center—at the site of each transit stop, or vice versa.

The multilevel stations are to be made as pleasant as possible—each with its own individuality and each alive with such attractions as convenience shopping, service centers, offices, bars, cafes, flower stalls, and colorful displays.

Passenger concentrations are further attained by so planning the transit system—routing, stations, cars, and operation—to ensure for the potential users the most convenient, economical, and pleasurable means of getting from one destination to another. When communities are designed from the start as transit communities—and when each urban center, whatever its type, is conceived as a transit-related complex—only then will the transit systems and centers realize their full potential.

Since the movement of people to and from urban centers is often sporadic—depending upon working hours, seasons, holidays, and special events—and since to be efficient trains must operate at near capacity, there is need for finely tuned coordination of passenger counts and available seating. With computerization there is now at hand the means of planning optimum schedules and the automated dispatching of trains with linked cars in response to surges in passenger demand.

Monorail

It wasn't all that long ago when the monorail was no more than a futuristic possibility. Now, for those who have been transported soundlessly from station to station as in the curving trajectory through the delightful Epcot landscape, travel by monorail has made the conventional commuter train or subway seem archaic.

The elevated glideway has many advantages. Aside from avoiding the hazard of on-grade obstacles and crossings, it can be aligned in the median of constructed or projected freeways with great savings in land acquisition and construction costs. Being raised on pedestals it can bridge highways, ravines, and streams. It can glide between com-

A rapid transit glideway can carry five times as many passengers, point to point, as an 8-lane freeway—at greater speeds, one-fourth the cost, and with far less disruption.

Rapid transit

Rapid transit now comes in many forms—from the minibus, articulated tram, and monorail, to the swooshing magnetically levitated zephyr trains that travel on grade or overhead. When elevated on graceful pedestals they can sweep freely into the very heart of urban centers. Or they may arrive and depart within the lobbies of multistory hotel, convention center, business office, or other structures planned with this in mind.

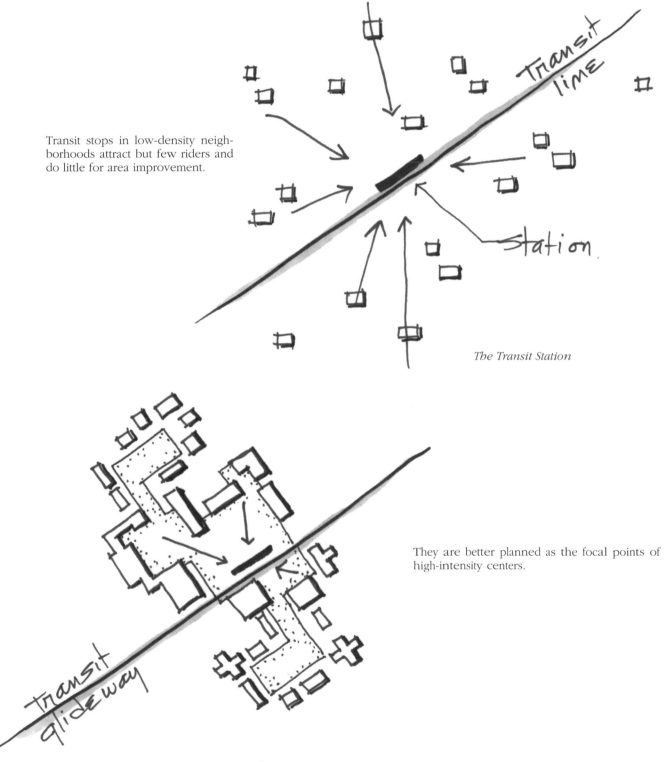

Transit stops in low-density neighborhoods attract but few riders and do little for area improvement.

The Transit Station

They are better planned as the focal points of high-intensity centers.

Urba-center Access

Rapid transit (*Continued*)

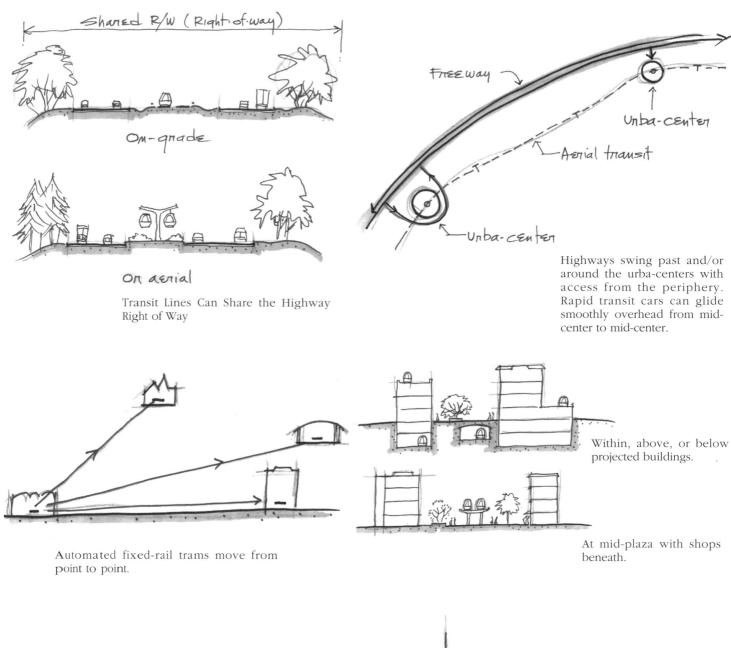

On-grade

On aerial

Transit Lines Can Share the Highway Right of Way

Highways swing past and/or around the urba-centers with access from the periphery. Rapid transit cars can glide smoothly overhead from mid-center to mid-center.

Automated fixed-rail trams move from point to point.

Within, above, or below projected buildings.

At mid-plaza with shops beneath.

Mini-busses, with or without linked cars are person-operated and move at moderate speeds through pedestrian areas.

Trams and Minibusses

Cars move freely about on aerial glideways.

Transitways at the City Core

munities along or within the buffer strips and can penetrate urba-centers with a minimum of disruption to discharge or pick up passengers at or within apartment or office plazas or within the building lobbies. The monorail bodes well to become a major means of in-city and regional transit. It is especially applicable on the circumferential transit beltway, with radial linkage to the center city.

Motorbus

The-in city bus has long been with us, threading from neighborhood to neighborhood and often stopping mid-street to load and unload while traffic backs up behind it. A tolerated nuisance, it has served the families of workers, school children, and the elderly as their only means of transit. It is needed and will be used increasingly with improvements now in the planning. The newer vehicles themselves will be improved—low-slung, streamlined, electronic, and in some cases articulated. Improved neighborhood plans will provide centralized, off-street bus shelters reached on foot or by bicycle through internal traffic-free greenways. On the highway, the bus will travel at make-up speeds along reserved bus lanes to center city transit plazas. Welcome aboard!

Minirail

We have seen them in major airports whisking from the gateway portals to the terminal lobby—the small single or coupled cars that move on narrow elevated or subsurface tracks. They are completely automated—doors, operating speeds, and even taped announcements. People stand or lean, for the distances are short; many can be transported comfortably and quickly.

Such minirail cars, with or without seating, are well suited for direct back and forth or looped point-to-point interconnection—as from the peripheral garages of the center city to the governmental trade, financial, or entertainment plazas, as from one such plaza to another, or as between two or more stops within an urba-center.

Trams

Trams, or trackless trains, come in many sizes and shapes. They are usually segmented, drawn by a motorized cab, and may be open or enclosed. Normally they have designated and posted routes, but since they are under the control of an operator as to speed and direction they may share walk paving where widths allow, and move about freely, even amidst a throng of pedestrians. Powered by energy cells and equipped with plastic-clad wheels, they will become as familiar in the compact new center cities as are now the prowling taxi cabs on our downtown city trafficways. As a contributing element of advanced transit systems, trams may be subsidized and provided without fares as another urban convenience.

Aerial cable cars

While floating down the River Rhine as one approaches Cologne in Germany, there passes before one's eyes high above the water a string of scintillating cable cars spanning the distance from the central city to the cross-river recreation park. What an exciting way this must be to start a family excursion! Again, the cable cars of Bogota and Caracas, like those of St. Moritz in Switzerland, treat passengers to some of the most spectacular urban views of the world. But beyond this, they make otherwise near-impossible access economical and pleasant.

The funicular

Cities of steep topography have other options. Long hillside or mountain slopes dividing metro districts may be well suited to the funicular with stations at top and bottom. Usually the ascending and descending cars are designed to be mechanically compensating.

It is said that for several decades the funiculars of Pittsburgh, with 5-cent fares, yielded the operating company one of the highest profits of any local enterprise, including the steel and rolling mills. Moreover, they allowed workers to live in the cleaner atmosphere of the hilltops while working in the riverside mills of the then smokey valleys. Today the historic "inclines" are still in use, a featured tourist attraction. Although their reasons for being have changed somewhat, they have contemporary applications. Streamlined versions, including dual- and monorailed lifts and lines, are being designed to traverse varying types of difficult terrain.

Bicycles

Have you been to Amsterdam lately? If so, you have seen what transit by bicycle can be and do. With fairly level topography, designated bikeways, and with provision for parking at destinations, the city is the scene of swooping cyclers that move about like flocks of birds. In the parks, suburbs, and open countryside they follow forested trails, town borders, and waterways to couple recreation and exercise with pleasurable access to all parts of the city.

In many U.S. cities—especially in newly planned communities and towns—we are learning the lesson well. With automobiles largely excluded at grade in the future urba-centers, bicycle transit will increase in popularity.

When bikeways are provided they are used. High-speed, high-volume, and motorbike cyclists belong in a paved strip at the edge of the roadway. Heavy bicycle traffic requires its own route. Light bicycle use and pedestrians can share a meandering path when there is width for passing.

As in Holland, Scandinavia, and Japan, the bicycle is coming to replace the automobile for much of local "getting around" in America. When secure bike parking compounds are provided at schools, shopping centers, and transit stops, fleets of bicycles soon begin to use them.

Pedal teguments

The most popular people-movers are attached to our ankles. Pedestrians (those who move about on foot) have instant mobility, can change direction at will, and shift into variable speeds. To walk or jog is natural. The greatest deterrent to pedestrian movement has come to be the automobile, along with its skein of trafficways. With the automobile confined to the edges and subsurface parking levels, our city centers will be far more compact, safe, and pedestrian-friendly.

Moving walks and escalators

Step aboard, and in but a few minutes you've been moved perhaps a thousand feet horizontally or up or down several levels. If the route is well lighted, exposed to attractive graphics, displays, or views upward, downward, or outward, it provides a delightful travel experience. Comfort is increased on moving walkways of any considerable length when modular benches are attached at one side, or across the entire width, for on-and-off seating. Pleasure is increased by converting the normal tunnel-like passageways into variform outdoor and indoor spaces. Weather-sheltered or climate-controlled, they can transport one through parklike squares, plazas, courts, a mini-botanic garden, aviary, zoolet, or across a festival ground. Indoors, they can move directly through a shopping mall or exhibition hall. While riding from in-city place to place one can visit the annual orchid or chrysanthemum show, move into and through a climatron with floral, sculptural, and fountain displays, or perhaps through a changeable exhibit of the historic society, natural history museum, or art gallery. Or one might even enjoy the fleeting strains of a wayside concert.

In such possibilities can be foreseen a truly exciting city. We have seen glimpses of the coming attractions. Wait 'til you see the show!

Transmission

Transmission lines, one might think, should pose few planning problems, for they are no more than cables and wires to be strung aloft, or conduits to be buried. In sum, however, the power transmission towers and transformer installations, the communication cables, and cross-country and in-city pipelines, utility mains and laterals together form an unbelievably scrambled network that may set or limit land use patterns for many years to come. Yet all are necessary. What does reason say to this? It says to consolidate!

New concepts of energy generation, transmission, and efficient use are transforming U.S. cities.

Overhead or subsurface

Installed a line at a time, the seemingly innocuous wires and cables have been added until the poles and arms are weighed down with the looping strands. What a pervasive web they weave—the whole overhead snarl that suburbanites and city dwellers have come to accept without question. With few exceptions these offending lines could be stripped away to give once again a clear view of the sky. They belong in shared underground conduits or utility ways where they would be out of the weather, easily available for repair and connection, and out of sight and mind. A persistent problem has been that each utility company has made its own plans, without regard for negative impacts, coordination, or the public good. The result has been the unending disruption of trafficways and relied-upon services.

Easements

Wires and pipes go where the easements lead them. Usually these follow the streets and roadways, which are then lined with unsightly poles and the familiar tangle. The paving must be torn up and patched each time a cross-road connection to a buried line is needed. Poles, wires, and the trenching for cables and pipelines all mutilate the roadside trees, existing or yet to be planted. Easements are therefore better aligned off-street, on sideyard or rear property lines where repairs and connections are less disruptive and where the open space swaths may double as intercommunity bicycle paths and walkways.

Where wider rights-of-way are required, as for trunk sewers, or for water, power, or fuel transmission, the cleared paths that presently move through the landscape present greater problems but also more opportunities. As to the problems, the invading strips are divisive and are usually poorly maintained and unsightly. Further, they represent a sizable acreage of valuable land, unused and removed from community use and the tax rolls. Recently many utility companies, increasingly aware of their image, have welcomed the opportunity to cooperate with public officials and private groups in offering to share their holdings for compatible uses. These may include playgrounds, parking areas, access driveways, vegetable gardens, and various types of paths or trails. A written agreement is required, describing the use and governing conditions. For many communities in which open space is at a premium and acquisition cost prohibitive, the joint use of utility easements presents a promising alternative.

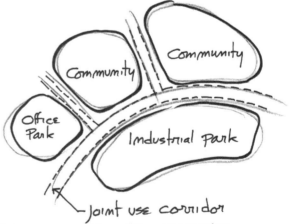

Joint-use corridors (Transportation, Transmission and Transit)
Preplanned corridors, acquired and administered by a public agency or Metro government can set the framework for orderly urbanization.

Energy Conservation
Questions:

- In the building/land planning process have the elements been grouped compactly for efficient interconnection?
- Have locations and orientation been responsive to prevailing wind and storm patterns, to the seasonal sweep and incidence of the sun?
- Has solar heating been considered—or the cooling effect of channeled breeze, moistened gravels and ground covers, shade and shadow, the transpiration of foliage, of ponding, the conservation of moisture in the soils, of xeriscape landscape planting...?

Combined corridors

To ride in a plane over a metropolitan region is to see below a criss-crossing of highway and utility right-of-way gashes that stretch to the horizon. For all this cleared land and landscape desecration the lines in place require but a fraction of the width usurped. A 100-foot cleared swath, for example, may hold only a single cable or buried gas main. In the interest of conserving land and reducing environmental despoliation it would seem evident that many single-use rights-of-way could be combined into a common corridor. Experience has shown this to be the case

A most promising arrangement, again to be worked out by a regional council, would be that of leased channels in a planned public right-of-way of sufficient overall dimension to meet foreseeable needs. This could accommodate not only future road and transitways but also all utility and transmission lines that might be aligned in the same general direction. Once acquired, the land area could be retained in its natural state until needed or leased to present or future users. It could be utilized in part to supplement the recreation and open space system, or its surface rights might be granted for interim gardening, wildlife management, storage, or other appropriate uses. The existing single-use holdings would then be incorporated or phased out. With astute long-range planning such publicly controlled corridors can yield great overall savings and other benefits.

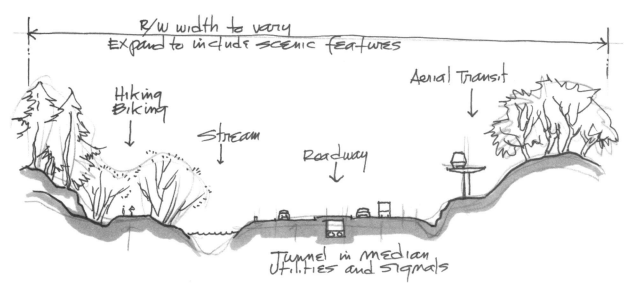

Joint use possibilities
Wide preplanned and publicly owned corridors can accommodate a wide range of transportation, transit, and transmission uses—many as yet unforeseen.

Regional councils

The time has come for the formulation of regional planning councils or authorities to coordinate the installation of all new utility and transmission lines. Such joint councils are to be empowered by enabling legislation to eliminate duplications, phase out deleterious uses and routing, and acquire and manage the multiple-use corridors. When coordinated with the long-range metro land use plans, such corridors will be a dominant factor in the reorganization and reshaping of the metropolitan regions.

Highly significant gains will be made throughout the regional countryside by the consolidation of transmission and utility rights-of-way and by their systemization. Joint corridors aligned as elements of the long-range regional plans will be of ample width to accommodate not only new transport, transit, and transmission ways but drainageways and other open space uses as well. Where will all this real estate come from? How can it be acquired? Most will be aggregated simply by the phased vacating of existing and underused easements and by the multiple use and widening of others. Much of it, following stream courses and narrow valleys, is presently open—often in public ownership. Other strips and parcels may be acquired by right of eminent domain and with funds from highway or other agency budgets, but mainly with revenues received by long-term leases of extremely valuable rights to the utility companies which are thereby relieved of costly right-of-way purchase and maintenance. For some needed properties the taxpaying public may have to knuckle down—after all, it is the people of the affected communities who will be the ultimate beneficiaries. By this approach, the preplanned corridors will serve to guide and support sound land development rather than prevent it.

Urban installations

It is in the restructured urban centers that the new systems of transmission and distribution will have the most telling effects. There they will go subsurface, where they belong—out of the weather, out of sight, and out of conflict with people and vehicles. One solution in downtown areas will be the construction and leasing of commodious joint-use tunnels beneath the public walk paving adjacent to the buildings served and to the overhead lighting and signals. The walk slab can serve as the top of the heated and lighted utility tunnels with access hatches at convenient intervals. Pipes and cables hung on the walls or formed into floor channels will be readily accessible without tearing up streets, and the heat will help keep the walkway paving dry where snow or ice might be factors.

Some transmission passageways may be formed as ser-

With midtown deliveries and distribution handled at subsurface levels, the vacated alleys, freight docks, and related storage areas can be converted to inviting pedestrian shopping ways.

Growth management (limitation, or guidance)

The five most effective means of growth management: 1. Concurrency. The requirement of all facilities in place prior to occupancy. 2. A surcharge on all new construction (per unit or floor area basis) in support of community schools, parks, trafficways and upkeep. 3. Steep (5 to 10%) building permit fees for new structures. Nominal fees for building rehabilitation or site improvements. 4. Fixed development boundaries and phased growth contours. 5 A jurisdictional P.C.D. (Preservation, Conservation and Development Plan) with environmental impact performance controls.

Effective growth management can only be achieved as an outgrowth of comprehensive planning and the uniform enforcement (no political favors) of protective regulations.

Urban transport and transmission

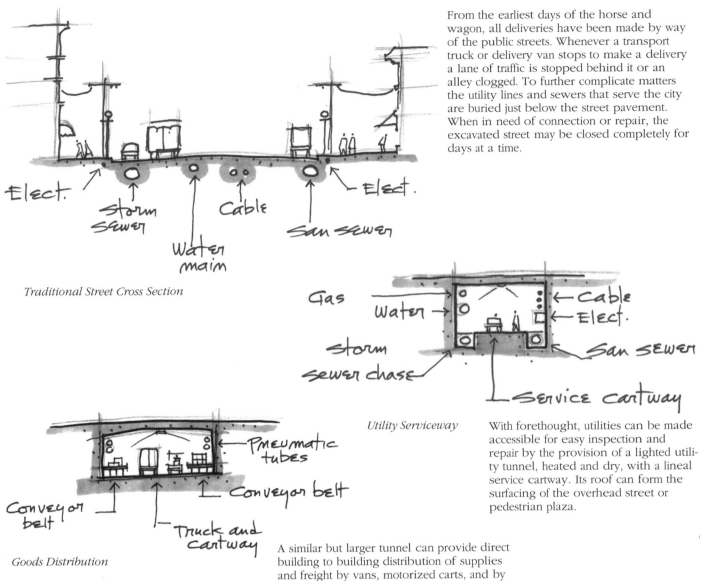

From the earliest days of the horse and wagon, all deliveries have been made by way of the public streets. Whenever a transport truck or delivery van stops to make a delivery a lane of traffic is stopped behind it or an alley clogged. To further complicate matters the utility lines and sewers that serve the city are buried just below the street pavement. When in need of connection or repair, the excavated street may be closed completely for days at a time.

Traditional Street Cross Section

Utility Serviceway

With forethought, utilities can be made accessible for easy inspection and repair by the provision of a lighted utility tunnel, heated and dry, with a lineal service cartway. Its roof can form the surfacing of the overhead street or pedestrian plaza.

Goods Distribution

A similar but larger tunnel can provide direct building to building distribution of supplies and freight by vans, motorized carts, and by beltways similar to those in use by airport terminals.

Utility chases beneath the pedestrian walkways and sewer chases built into the tunnel floor can be made integral parts of the transportation-transmission system. Utility lines and sewer mains are thus made accessible simply by lifting the cover plates—and the street-level delivery of goods by truck is precluded.

On-street pick-up and delivery by van or truck have for too long been a problem for inner cities. By the construction of a terminal with sublevel truck or rail access and distribution tunnels, direct transport and transmission can be accomplished with utmost efficiency.

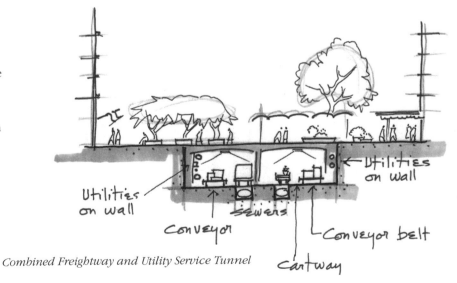

Combined Freightway and Utility Service Tunnel

Urban transport and transmission (Continued)

Goods destined for use within the center city are best received and processed by mechanized sublevel terminals. Building-to-building distribution and collection can be accomplished by a network of tunnels, chases, beltways, or pneumatic tubes.

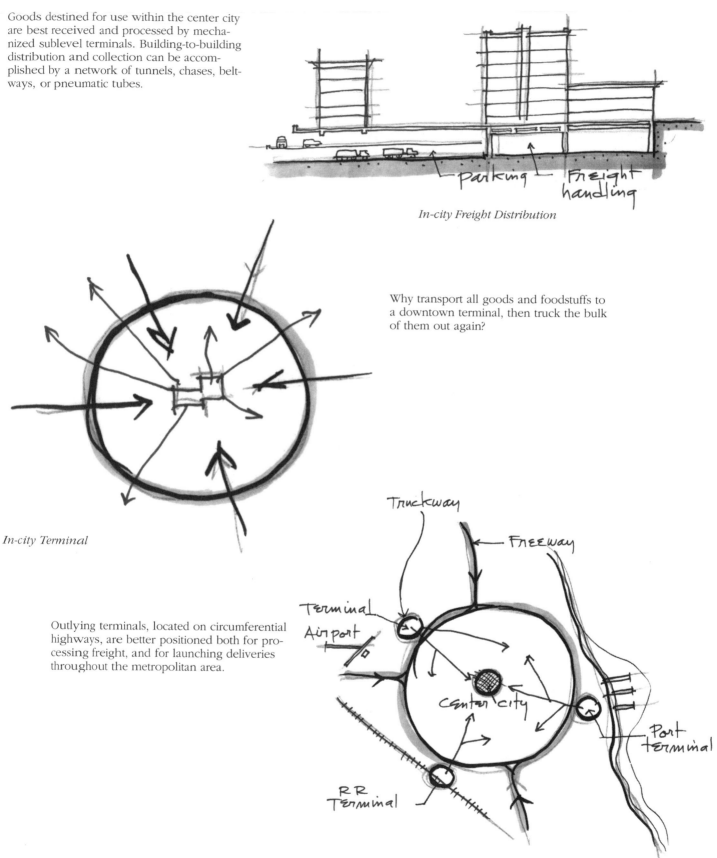

In-city Freight Distribution

Why transport all goods and foodstuffs to a downtown terminal, then truck the bulk of them out again?

In-city Terminal

Outlying terminals, located on circumferential highways, are better positioned both for processing freight, and for launching deliveries throughout the metropolitan area.

Dispersed Terminals

vice corridors within new building construction. Others may follow new street or walkway paving as part of the understructure. In the more compact urban areas the internal courts and plazas may be in effect the ceilings of underground storage and service depots and distribution centers, which will be computerized and mechanized to the limits of current technology. From these distribution-collector points will flow a system of service tunnels of varying types and dimensions depending upon their intended function.

Concurrency

All too often new communities or projects have been brought into being without adequate provision for power, waste removal, telephone service, or even water supply. It is not enough that these be "in the planning stage" to materialize sometime in the future. As new users tap into existing lines already under stress, local officials begin to feel the pressures of resentment. Responding to complaints both from within and outside the new developments they have come to the concept of "concurrency"—whereby all essential facilities must be in place and operable before the first occupancy permit is issued.

The concurrency premise has proven beneficial not only as a means of making new projects more welcome in the host localities but also as a key factor in the siting of all types of development—and in responsible growth management.

One of the chief reasons for comprehensive regional planning is that the various types of communities and the utility systems to serve them can be designed together and kept in balance from the start. Once the ultimate systems have been sized, they are best installed segment by segment in accordance with their predetermined capacities— not by frequent replacement and up-sizing but rather by extension of the established permanent mains.

Parks, recreation, and open space

One of the more remarkable features of the future urban metropolis will be the open space system. It will serve many functions. In time it will reestablish the natural drainageways which have all but disappeared. Restored and revegetated they will slow storm water run-off and erosion while contributing filtered fresh water to the overtaxed water tables. The system will provide defining buffers to reconsolidated and more compact communities. It will sheath uninterrupted corridors for parkways, bikeways, and pedestrian greenways. It will interconnect and embrace a wide variety of tot lots, playgrounds, game courts, athletic fields, picnic groves, and water-related recreation areas.

A city planned within and around an open space framework puts every neighborhood within a

The system will in effect make recreation in its many forms readily available to all citizens, part of the daily living experience. Parks and playgrounds will no longer be isolated or encapsulated, requiring the crossing of multiple trafficways to reach them. They will be contiguous to the living and working places which they will border or surround

The planning, development, and operation of a regional open space system directly affects the programs of many agencies—including those of community development, water management, forestry, highways, and environmental protection. These should be represented on a coordinating council or advisory committee. It would seem logical, however, that the actual management of the open space holdings be conducted by a reconstituted and expanded department of parks, recreation, and open space.

Parks

Parks, so long a cherished feature of U.S. towns and cities, are undergoing a period of rapid transformation. Many are shrinking, some disappearing completely. Yet again, they are being converted to other public uses or sold outright for revenue-producing development. This is due in part to the pressures on unbuilt-upon land, in part because of increasing demand for more active forms of recreation, closer to the people.

In retrospect, it is seen that many of the early parks came into being as community pasture lands or "commons." Being at the center of things these still do much to enhance their environs. Others have taken shape on leftover, unbuildable tracts, or on such outlying sites, ahead of development, as might yet be available. In few metropolitan areas were lands acquired in advance of immediate need or in accordance with a well-conceived plan.

A common problem with park and recreation lands has been that as scattered fragments they were neither well suited to their use nor well related to the people who would use them. Today, with far more progressive planning, they are being conceived as complete balanced and interrelated *systems*. The land acquired is selected to serve its purpose. The use or uses, in turn, are site-specific, designed to meet a particular need of the neighborhood or community. This might be no more than a bank of tennis courts, a spray hydrant and drain for summer cooling-off, or a link in a regional bikeway. Or, again, it might entail the construction of a whole new recreation complex.

With the need for exercise trails of various types urban recreation areas are often linear and interconnective. Route right-of-way may be obtained by easements or the multiple use of utility lines. They may share road rights-of-way. Or they may follow designated drainageways along streams,

The open spaces our cities need most are those that people can use and enjoy.

———————

The parks of the future will be an integral part of urban life—not an antidote to it.

———————

Mile upon mile of interconnecting urban "green ways" now trace abandoned (and active) canals, railway lines, and roadways. They are also beginning to find their way along streams, natural drainageways, and utility easements.

———————

You can look at a park primarily as a social tool, primarily as an asethetic element, or primarily as a practical and functional thing.

Paul Goldberger

In the city, *nature* need not imply the naturalistic. It can connote as well the use of natural elements in a new and refreshing way.

rivers, or the edges of flood plains and wetlands. Larger areas, as are required for playgrounds and athletic fields, may be planned into urban renewal or redevelopment projects. They may be available in vacated local streets, regraded landfills, or reclaimed industrial sites.

School parks are becoming popular. Here, together with the school buildings—playcourts, fields, picnic areas, and perhaps gardens or arboreta are combined in a year-round, daytime and evening community center. School gyms, dressing rooms, kitchens, library, and meeting rooms thus get double use—as do parking compounds and the park surroundings.

A further developing trend is that in which the city park and recreation departments provide the buildings, grounds, and equipment, and the actual recreation programs are devised and run by local school, civic, or other responsible groups. More and more, community representatives are being brought into the planning process to express needs and preferences. Yet another breakthrough is the increasing practice of holding interdepartmental sessions in which trafficways, drainageways, and recreation are considered together in conjunction with a metropolitan open space system which ties the whole city together. Such is true environmental planning at its best.

As our evolving U.S. cities assume more efficient and reasonable form, the *experience* of urban living will become a chief design factor. The emerging high-tech, mechanistic lifestyle requires new types of "soul nourishment" as an antidote to stress. This translates in part to the need for daily communion with nature. It suggests participation in a multiplicity of recreational experiences such as provided by traditional games and sports, new forms of exercise, travel viewing, and simply living and working in pleasant surroundings. It is no longer enough to plan parks within the city—but rather, with all means at hand—a city within a park.

Recreation

All cities have parks and a recreation program. In most, the park lands have been patched together a piece at a time as tax-delinquent properties were acquired—or more often at exorbitant cost as demands for recreation grew in developing communities where few suitable sites were still available. Such isolated and "make-do" holdings are seldom related to the best topographical features. They are incomplete, often less than pleasant to use, inefficient to operate, and difficult to maintain.

Other municipalities enjoy the many benefits of a complete and well-conceived park, recreation, and open space *system*. The Milwaukee area is one of these. Here from the start the needs and opportunities were described, the best land and water areas and interconnections acquired, and the total system developed an area at a time as a smoothly operating entity. With such foresight it is possible to create a whole parklike urban environment in which people enjoy each day the good full life in a beautiful open space setting. There is seldom, these days, the opportunity to plan a park system on virgin land—but in every evolving city there is the absolute necessity for a comprehensive long-range recreation and open space plan envisioning the utmost possibilities. Only with such a best-case plan at hand can it be phased into being.

Active

Active recreation areas, play courts, and athletic fields are to be designed with precision. There must be the right orientation to sun and air currents. There are precise dimensions, preferred gradients, and state-of-the-art materials and equipment. Lighting, if used, is to be carefully calibrated. The relationship to spectators is a matter of scientific study, as is the coordination of related vehicular and pedestrian movement and approaches. Attractive surroundings are of special meaning, and there is need to locate facilities close to the population centers and users.

These things being so, it is incumbent upon the recreation planner to prepare a detailed listing and general location of all foreseeable active recreation needs and to recommend preacquisition of the most suitable sites as they become available. This in most cases will require bond funding and new enabling legislation with the added powers of eminent domain.

Passive

Not so specific in their siting requirements are lands to be enjoyed in more passive pursuits such as picnicking, walking, riding, cycling, and nature appreciation. They tend to be more lineal and often follow ridges, valleys, stream banks, shores, and woodland edges. They are free in form and may vary in width from a narrow pathway to an intermittent flood plain several miles across. An obvious possibility in the creation of a recreation and open space system is that of interconnecting all or most areas into a combined pattern of ways and places having continuity. Where this is feasible, walking, jogging, or cycling through the park land from one area to another may be a highlight of the recreation experience.

Greenways and blueways

In considering continuity as a highly desirable feature of

We can tie this country together with threads of green that everywhere grant us access to the natural world.

THE PRESIDENT'S COMMISSION ON AMERICAN OUTDOORS

Mini and Mobile Parks
Mini-parks or dispersed recreational segments of the larger park system are becoming increasingly popular. Sometimes no more than pathside seating or a well-placed volleyball net — they may be as expansive as neighborhood allotment gardens, or as specialized as a zoological parklet. Roving mobile units take music and television into congested areas, as do showboats and music barges tied up to in-city river and harbor landings. Even Punch and Judy shows, display gardens, and pet-farms can be floated from place to place.

Linear open spaces can connect traditional parks and other activity centers such as schools and shopping centers. They can also accommodate popular recreational activities such as jogging, bicycling, and canoeing which may be incompatible with traditional urban parks.

WILLIAM FOURNAY

The green swaths of the future city will follow the natural drainageways. They will surround and contain, not intrude upon, intensive activity areas which work best when in compression.

Large empty tracts frequently occur over filled-in floodplains whose streams are buried in sewers. Together with the need for flood control and wastewater treatment, these low-lying, unused lands represent an opportunity to reshape the city.

ANNE WHISTON SPIRN

The development process is an incessant journey, and since nature was our beginning, should it not now be our guide?

BENJAMIN THOMPSON

It's open space that gives definition to a town, because it creates a structure you can hold in the mind, and at the same time gives people the very things that hold them in cities; what we now call "livability" and "quality of life."

BRUCE KELLY

Open spaces…are enabling us to sense our kinship with all of life, as well as with each other. A sense of urgency is also becoming universal— because almost everyone has already been touched by a sense of loss, as some place that has been much loved is redeveloped without any sensitivity for the experiences it has made available.

TONY HISS

recreational open space, one might look to the means by which this may be achieved. Foremost is interconnection by the roadways themselves—especially those of lower speeds, such as the local loop drives and parkways. These may have supplementary lanes marked for cyclers or pedestrians. Better yet, if the right-of-way is of ample width, there may be a separate, undulating walkway reserved for those on foot exclusively. Circulation drives, if of sufficient right-of-way dimension, offer an ideal opportunity for parklike planting and separated paths for automobiles, bicycles, and pedestrians.

As previously noted, cross-country utility easements may be made available for limited open space uses—especially if the local government accepts their maintenance as a condition of use. Pathways may thread through planned neighborhoods, communities, institutional grounds, office parks, and commercial malls. They may extend to and through the most intensive urban centers, adding interest as they go. Far and away the most desirable routing, however, and one so often overlooked, is one that follows the course of the drainageways and streams. Here the native vegetation is most generally undisturbed. Here the air seems fresher, the breezes cooler in the summertime, and even the song of the birds more lilting. Most stream and river valleys are subject to intermittent flooding. This poses some problems in their use but affords even more opportunities. Many municipalities no longer permit building construction within the limits of a projected 50-year flood, and federally supported insurance requirements are even more restrictive. Thus, by regulation, the drainageways are now protected as variformed green and blue swaths fairly begging to be acquired, leased, or otherwise incorporated in the regional open space system.

Greenbelts

The "greenbelt" is largely a U.S. planning device by which cohesive activity areas of various types are separated and buffered. Ideally, the green swaths are planned to form an interrelated nature preserve which follows the land forms and incorporates woodlands, streams, and the natural drainageways. They provide not only separation, but bird and animal habitat, and "breathing room" as well. Often there is sufficient area for agricultural lands, community gardens, many forms of recreation, and paths of interconnection.

Greenbelts bring nature into the city, and allow the citizens to live, work, and move about within a verdant setting. Often—in a lake, river, wetland, or forest environs the greenbelts may be expanded into sizable reservations within which urbanization is prohibited. These provide the best possible means of guiding and controlling development patterns.

Greenways, blueways

The metropolitan regions of tomorrow will be laced with verdant paths. These will thread through and interconnect the replanned urban centers, neighborhoods, parks, and open space preserves. They will trace the overlook ridges and follow the valleys and streams. For those myriad joggers, cyclers, and strollers now seen hugging the edges of trafficways city living will be more pleasant.

Essential. Superior greenway systems will provide:

1. *Safety.* They will avoid the crossing of high-speed vehicular trafficways. They will afford protection from falls, as from a precipice or into deep or swift water. Hazards such as sharp objects, electrical wiring, or unexpected obstructions will be removed or shielded. Adequate lighting, alarms, and surveillance are to be provided.

2. *Convenience.* They will be close to where people live and work—providing connection between neighborhoods, schools, shopping centers, parks, historic sites, outstanding natural and scenic features, and the countryside beyond. Continuity and convenience are always to be kept in mind.

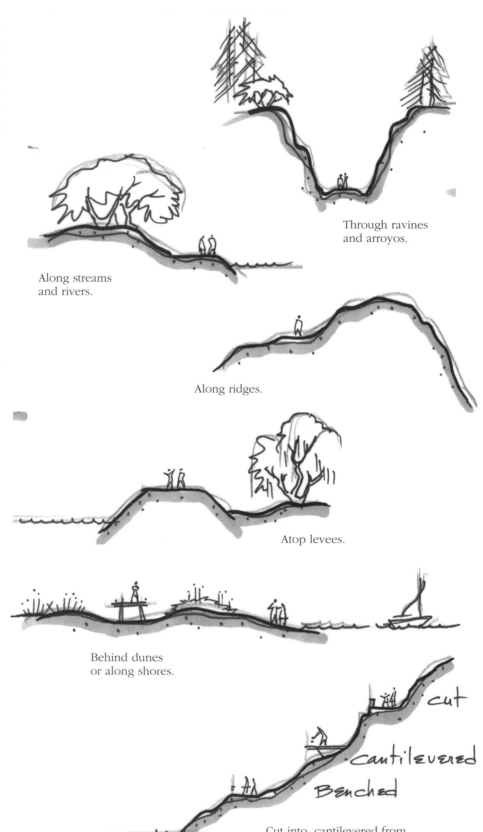

Through ravines and arroyos.

Along streams and rivers.

Along ridges.

Atop levees.

Behind dunes or along shores.

Cut into, cantilevered from, or across a slope face.

3. *Comfort and Pleasure.* A sweeping or meandering alignment, undulating profile, and variable widths add interest and enjoyment to a pathway. Suitable gradients and good footing contribute their measure of comfort.

On low walkways over wetlands.

Along a canal.

On abandoned railroad track (rails to trails).

4. *Alignment.* Greenways, and blueways which follow the shore or streams, may be routed through the urban and regional open space frame, its drainageways and floodplains. They may traverse state and national forest lands, parks, recreation areas, wildlife preserves, and conservation easements. They may follow abandoned roadbeds through farmland and forest. They may share highway rights-of-way and multiple-use transmission corridors which lead to and through city neighborhoods and urban activity centers.

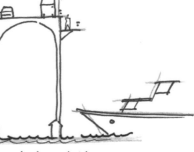

Within a utility R/W.

Attached to a bridge.

Such inviting ways will serve fleets of enthusiastic cyclers, files of joggers, and appreciative nature lovers for many years to come.

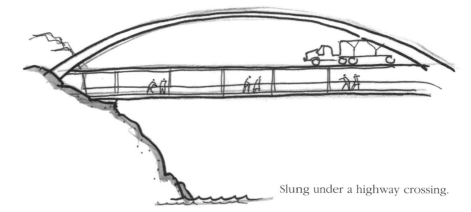

Slung under a highway crossing.

Livability is thereby increased, urban centers are more condensed and efficient, and travel throughout the metropolis is more rapid and free. In terms of sheer economics—construction costs are lowered, and overall land values zoom.

Open space

It might seem, with good reason, that *open space* is the very antithesis of *city*. For cities, by definition, are centers of concentration. Most are jam-packed. There is, however, a persuasive argument to be made for cities which might be both more compact and yet more open—for most present urban agglomerations provide neither intensive activity centers nor meaningful open space.

The problems can best be realized by study of any current city parcel map in which the principal use of each parcel—business, governmental, cultural, residential, and so forth—is indicated by coded color or symbols. The patchwork reveals at a glance that there is no conceivable logic to the helter-skelter, disorganized array. The various city components are seldom arranged as cohesive operating entities. The principal uses are neither grouped with, nor well related to, supply, service, or other support facilities. Nor are they well related to either adjacent or outlying concentrations of housing for users or workers. There is little apparent correlation of the loosely composed groupings with the transportation routes that should tie them together. In short, it is painfully evident that few of our present cities have a reasonable land use plan.

Were it possible to start all over again—to ignore the present patterns of ownership and existing construction—it would be an easy matter to regroup the centers more wisely and compactly. They might well be spaced around and within an open space environs. Such a parklike setting could envelop the best of the topographic features and provide both separation and routes of free-flowing interconnection between activity nodes.

Seldom—short of war, earthquake, or other disasters—is it possible to start entirely anew in the planned development of a whole metropolitan region. Over the course of a few decades, however, the aspect of most urban areas will have changed beyond recognition. It is therefore entirely feasible to move, phase by phase, toward, or in accordance with, a more desirable plan arrangement. As obsolescence sets in with time and change and as redevelopment occurs, improved land use relationships can and should be established. It only makes sense that they be transformed into a more workable pattern in general accordance with a guiding long-range, open space plan.

Such a conceptual plan will incorporate existing park and recreation lands, nature preserves, and conservation areas. It

From the evidence at hand it would be hard to conclude that the human being is a rational creature.

City planning is an exercise in effective correlation.

To heal the environment we must look to the transformation of urban liabilities into amenities.

ANGELA DANADJIEVA

Cities should take a closer look at what they already have. Most of them are sitting on a huge reservoir of space yet untapped by imagination. In their inefficiently used rights-of-way, their vast acreage of parking lots, there is more than enough space for broad walkways and small parks and pedestrian places—and at premium locations.

WILLIAM H. WHYTE, JR.

More and more, it's the left-over land, the problem sites, that become raw material for urban parks.

WILLIAM WENK

Reclamation has connotations of dealing with distressed landscapes. There is a broader issue—to look at the mining operation as being a creative part of shaping a new environment—an art form, a wildlife area, or a housing development.

ANTHONY BAUER

Design professionals have an opportunity to make a huge impact on urban landscapes that have been ignored—vacant lots and unused land, such as alleys, in low-income neighborhoods.

STAN JONES
as quoted by SALLY B. WOODBRIDGE

will borrow space from the unbuilt-upon institutional grounds and share utility easements and highway corridors. The plan will be aggregated from the vacating of grid street rights-of-way within more compactly designed urba-centers. It will gain from the consolidation of vacant and leftover parcels, eroded gullies, steep slopes and ravines, mandated 50- to 100-year flood plains, wetlands, reopened streambeds, and recleared river edges. It will reclaim obsolete housing districts, derelict industrial sites, extraction pits, and other deleterious properties. It will rid the city of much that is unwholesome and unsightly and create a landscape setting of increased recreational use and appeal.

Where essential for rational planning or continuity, critical lands may be acquired at public expense as a long-term investment. Again, for such a purpose, substantial gifts of land or funds may be donated by individuals or foundations. As the open space city begins to take form it will make its own persuasive case, on the basis of performance.

Urban contributors

Where else does open space come from? Once the best of the natural features have been recorded, preserved, or reclaimed and protected, how are these to be linked and supplemented?

Within any city limits are further open space contributors. Included will be the berms and swales of trafficways, which are lineal and connective. Intermittent watercourses or floodlands, too, are usually connective and must be kept open and free-flowing. By the reclamation of strip mines and extraction pits large areas of blight can be eliminated and replaced with welcome verdure. Sanitary fills are often utilized, as are salvaged public dumps. And, too, the awkward and bypassed vacant parcels and tax delinquent properties that pock the urban landscape.

Sometimes overlooked for their open space contributions are agricultural lands and those in public and private ownership.

Public agencies

Aside from the department of recreation and parks there are in every city numerous regional, state, and federal agencies with extensive land holdings. Among them, for instance, are waterworks and reservoirs, state forests, game lands, and wildlife management areas. There are utility easements and rights-of-way, experiment stations, water management holdings, and military reserves. Some are obsolete or unused and could well be vacated. Others are only partially used and could be leased in part on an interim basis as highly desirable open space for public use and enjoyment. Even if retained without public access, their open and vegetated land would enhance their surroundings.

Institutions

It is surprising to discover how much open space is provided by institutional grounds. Conservancies, as institutions of sorts, also make a highly significant contribution by acquiring, managing, or dedicating sites of historic, ecological, and scenic importance. University campuses needing room for future expansion are interlaced with undeveloped lands. Botanical gardens and zoological parks add their total sites to the open space aggregation. And then there are grounds surrounding the museums, institutes, and all manner of hospitals, libraries, churches, schools, and the like. In some cases a part of the grounds or the drives or walks may be open to public use. In any case there is benefit in just having the open land there and visible.

Private lands

In some areas of rugged or flood-prone topography it is conceivable that a major part of a metropolitan open space system could be assembled by lands donated by private owners for limited passive use. Marsh land, open water, ravines, or steep hillsides may be dedicated to the municipality or to an intervening conservancy. Covenants running with the land would restrict in perpetuity the uses to be permitted. These might range from more active recreation such as riding, cycling, or boating to bird-watching or merely off-site viewing. The conditions of donation may vary from public land and water management, to tax abatement, or the economic advantages of making an outright gift. Where the conveyance of land rights by deed is not attainable, the owners may be willing to grant scenic or conservation easements by which for some stated consideration the property will remain as permanent open space.

Easements

It might be assumed that in order to use land one must own it. This is usually the case except when a person or agency has by some means acquired certain rights in the land or an easement across it. Rights may be granted casually, as for example by verbal or written permission to plant a neighborhood garden or set up a volleyball court. Leases or easements are a more formal means of conveying property rights under agreed-upon terms and conditions. They may give the right of use or of passage across a property as by a road or utility main.

The leasing of land for short to long term construction—as for housing, commercial or other purposes—is effective where land values are high and where savings in site acquisition costs can be translated into lower apartment or floor area rents.

Land leasing, now rare in America, will become more prevalent as in-city populations grow and land values rise. Publicly owned open space—as from airfield borders, highway medians and shoulders, utility corridors, drainageways, and land banks will be leased for agricultural purposes. Increasingly building construction will take place on leased parcels and air rights.

Sometimes the easements held by a single utility company add up to the largest real estate holding in the region. Traditionally, most utility easements when acquired have been fenced off or otherwise jealously guarded against intrusion. The joint use of the property for other public or private purposes—even for emergency access—has been steadfastly denied. It has become more and more evident to the public, however, that to lock up so much land for such limited use is unreasonable. Moreover, the restricted swaths often cut across an otherwise unified landscape and interfere with sound community development.

As land values and needs have escalated, so have the pressures to open up the underused easements to various compatible uses. These are many—including, for instance, health trails, bicycle paths, local parkways, or alternative truckways to the plants served by the utilities. Such installations, being lineal also, would be ideally suited to the alignments of the utility ways. More localized joint uses might well include parking for the adjacent plants, offices, or apartments. Except in the case of high-voltage transmission lines with their potential danger, most easements are suited also for public parks, playgrounds, athletic fields, community gardens, or similar multiple uses. Where the more progressive utility companies have come to adopt a policy of sharing, the benefits are those of improved public relations and community betterment. Further, as an economic gain, they may transfer to the co-users, as a condition of joint use, the responsibility for ground surface upkeep.

Any planning for urban renewal or restructuring will by reason be done as an overlay to a map of the regional easement network. In a well conceived future land use plan the easements will continue to serve their primary purpose while accommodating a host of secondary uses. All concerned will stand to gain as the restrictive boundary lines are breached and one day disappear.

Easements may be devised to forestall land uses as well as permit them. By granting a conservation or scenic easement, for example, the landowner may either sell or donate certain of the rights of ownership. These may include the right to build additional structures, erect signs, cut trees, or otherwise significantly alter the topographic features. In the revitalization of cities, it can be seen, such easements can be of great value in the creation of a coherent drainageway, open space system, and the protection of scenic views.

The open space system

Open space of itself isn't much account. It can be only nothingness. Worse, it can be deleterious. Cluttered vacant lots, paved and unused plazas, abandoned factory sites, or polluted streams and marshes can drag a city down. Other

---

In the design of our new urban places and ways we may learn from sculptor Isamu Noguchi the power of the hollow or negative space—of vibrant city centers in which the spaces become the architecture, and buildings the enframement.

---

open space swatches, swaths, and sweeps contribute in useful, positive ways—especially when each in itself is well suited to its function. A colorful tot lot tumbling with kids, for example, can add sparkle and life to a neighborhood. A parking compound with easy turning movements, up-lighted trees, and planted islands can provide an inviting welcome to the community center. A bustling shopping complex with its appealing sights, sounds, and smells can make an agreeable setting for the offices and apartments crowded around.

Open space comes in larger sizes as well—as in sports fields, recreation centers, and riverfront parks. Then, too, there are the school and institutional grounds and business office campuses. Again, such spaces or groupings of spaces are to be designed to best serve their particular purpose, not in terms of area alone but volumetrically, with the appropriate degree and type of enframement and enclosure. Each open space in itself, if well conceived, adds its bit to the city. It lets the sunlight in and the breezes blow through. It complements the adjacent structures and enhances their use and appearance. It provides linkage to other buildings and other activity nodes.

Then too there are the linear open spaces—the paths, walkways, bikeways, the parkways, and the freeways. All, with their own spatial qualities, are best conceived as space-to-space connectors. Connection and sequential interconnection suggest an open space network or system. Outdoor space is by its very nature a system. As a continuum it flows, knows no bounds, and is a composite of many variable interacting subsystems which together are all-encompassing.

On what can an open space framework be based? One possibility is a tracing and expansion of the arterial highway network. This will be logical when such primary highways are planned (as they should be) as limited access roadways in corridors fitted to the topography. The enveloping spatial sheath could then reach out on either side to extend the open space system along the connecting roadways.

A second possibility is a system devised to follow the existing streams, rivers, and natural drainage channels. This has an advantage in that they exist—all by their very nature tributary and interconnecting. Moreover, with few exceptions they create their own open space passageways—especially where construction at their sides is kept back to the limits of a 50-year flood. In most metropolitan regions the best possible regional framework (and open space diagram) will be one that follows the course of the natural storm water flows. Fortuitously, this is also a natural alignment for most highway corridors, since they are thus assured of positive drainage and a reduced number of stream and valley crossings.

In U.S. cities with a population of 100,000 or over about 6.3 percent of the total area, on the average, is now devoted to parks and recreation.

For the *total* public open space system a desirable goal would be close to 30 percent. This would include park and recreation lands, school grounds and institutional campuses, lakes, streams, water management lands, bikeways, gardens, forest, and conservation areas.

Urban land policy, as a whole, must encourage the creation of both commercial and community gardens to make productive use of currently wasted resources.

MICHAEL HOUGH

The "greenbelt" concept of a protected rural, open space band surrounding defined urban areas is rapidly gaining advocates. It is seen as the only means of stemming decentralization, healing the land, and recreating cities that thrive.

The future of the Chicago metropolitan region would be grim beyond belief were it not for the (100+ square mile) Cook County Forest Preserves around which the best of our residential, cultural, and business office development is presently taking form.

IRA J. BACH

The average urban area is 30 percent forested, but experts believe that figure is declining.

The resulting situation leaves cities poorly positioned to battle air pollution, erosion, floods and, at worst, the trend toward global warming and drought.

Cities have been developing their municipal strategies. Whereas departments of urban forestry scarcely existed before 1970, they now thrive.

MICHAEL LECCESE

In the coming century there should be a growing shift in focus from cities as construction to cities as landscapes.

GARRETT ECKBO

———————

It is foreseen that the tailored landscape expanses of mown turf, shrub borders, and floral displays of traditional urbana will give way in large part to private and community produce gardens.

———————

Urban parks should serve productive as well as recreational functions. In Britain during World War II, cities produced more than 10 percent of the nation's food supply.

Studies on both sides of the Atlantic have shown that community gardens and urban farms in depressed neighborhoods can reinstate a sense of pride and social cohesion.

MICHAEL HOUGH

Community gardens are very important. You begin to establish a constituency that has vested interests....

LEE WEINTRAUB

Supplemental to the regional open space frame may be such extensive components as market garden lands, farms and forest preserves, wetlands, and water bodies.

To be meaningful, open spaces must serve a purpose. Each makes its own unique contribution to the urban environment. In sum, and in a very real sense, they *are* the urban environment.

The greening

A city without vegetation can be likened to a desert. Stacked with cubes of masonry, metal, plastic, or glass—and paved wall to wall with asphalt or concrete—the windswept canyons of our center cities weave and shimmer with summer's heat and in winter inflict bone-chilling cold. In the amelioration of such extremes nothing can be more effective than the preservation or planting of vegetation.

Wooded parks, urban forests, and grasslands are the most telling contributors. They serve not only to retain precipitation, recharge the water tables, cleanse the air, and provide wildlife habitat—they act also as wind breaks; they cool and refresh the summer breeze and temper the winter storms.

In the years ahead, the garden city envisioned by Ebenezer Howard may yet be realized, though in a different form. His concept, a forerunner of planned communities and new towns, was more than one of escape from the oppressive city to outlying home garden plots. Instead, he foresaw restructured and revitalized cities in which the city itself will become the garden. Within an overall parklike setting there will be allotted community gardens, hydroponic farms, orchards, vineyards, and solar-domed conservatories. City centers will be "hanging gardens," the main trafficways will be lineal parks, and local streets will be sheathed with canopies of foliage. With a broader brush the "greening" may result also in reforested hillsides and valley slopes, replanted streambeds, lakeshores, and stabilized beaches.

• • •

With an in-born affinity for the soil and plants, and with new-found leisure, city dwellers will turn increasingly to gardening as a favorite avocation. The rewards will be healthful exercise, freshly picked vegetables, fruit, and flowers—and visual delight. As our cities are made to leaf and bloom again, nature appreciation and outdoor recreation will become ever more a part of city living.

PGH. NOV. 1926.

6
Garden city
21

What will it look like? What will it be—this bright and shining lodestar urban metropolis of the twenty-first century? What do our best minds have to tell us of the ideal city?

Although few might agree on the ultimate form, one could expect a broad consensus as to the ultimate goal, for this has changed little down through the centuries. From Thebes to Babylon, from Constantinople to San Diego, that city has been most acclaimed which provided the *best experience of living*. The most renowned and agreeable have been those most expressive of and responsive to their *time, place,* and *culture*; those which are *functional,* which *afford convenience,* which are *rational and complete.*

The expressive city

It has long been recognized that to understand and appreciate any work of art one must first develop empathy for the time of its creation, the place, the cultural background, the materials and techniques available, the nature of the artist, and what he or she was trying to accomplish. So it is with all works of design—the fine arts and crafts, architecture, engineering, landscape architecture, and the plan layout of cities.

Time

The time of a city's creation, or being, has much to do with its nature. Pittsburgh, for example, was founded at the time of George Washington's explorations in the mid-1700s as a strategic fort at the confluence of two rivers and head of the Ohio. Its plan layout was an eloquent statement of its purpose.

One hundred years later defense had become secondary to developing trade and river transportation. Accordingly, the walls of the fort were dismantled, and new patterns of growth were formed along the river edges and transmountain approach roads. With materials at hand by mining and barge Pittsburgh was soon to become a center for glass, iron, and steel manufacturing—a "hell with the lid off" city at the time of James Parton's visit in the 1860s. The transition from the manufacturing to business office center took another 100 years. The next century will no doubt bring equal transformation in response to changing needs and opportunities.

Most cities, to a greater or lesser degree, evolve as responsively to time.

Place

A city's location is telling. Its position in relation to neighboring peoples may spell the difference between war, relative peace, isolated tranquility, poverty, or wealth. Proximity to routes of land or water transportation—to harbor, forest, agricultural lands, or minerals—has much to do with its character.

Such topographic features as hills (San Francisco), mountains (Denver), prairie (Chicago), rivers (New Orleans), or lakes (Milwaukee) leave their indelible mark.

Climate, too, is a function of place. Relative temperatures, precipitation, fog, frost, ice, and snow have a direct effect on sensitive plan layout as well as on architecture. The threat of flood, earthquake, hurricane, or roaring tornado is an obvious design consideration. Even such seemingly subtle factors as light quality and intensity, the direction of breezes, vegetative cover, and local coloration must be taken into account.

Nor are subsurface conditions of place to be ignored. Geologic structure and bearing may make the difference between a Venice and a Mont Saint Michel. Not as well understood are the tenets of geomancy—the tracing of subterranean lines of force and upwellings of energy that were key, for example, to the location of prehistoric Stonehenge, the Cathedral of Chartres, and the plan orientation of ancient Kyoto.

Often a glance is enough to reveal the design implications of place.

Culture

Each culture throughout history has shaped its cities not only to meet its physical needs but also to express the beliefs and ideals of its people. There have been, and are, restrictive taboos, demanding religious rites, and immutable in-born preferences and traditions. These deal with such matters as favored locations, plan organization, abstract forms, and symbolism.

The ultimate form of a city can never be predetermined—because it could never be imagined.

_____

"Change of course is the law of survival . . ."
MARY GRINNELL GORDON

Fort Pitt at the point
Fort Pitt, commanding the rivers, was expressive of its purpose, place, and time.

_____

Cities planned for the people who use them will satisfy the needs and desires of their citizens. They will reflect the thought and spirit of their times.

_____

Spengler has described the distinctive mindset of various ethnic groups and the effect on habitations and urban form. He notes, for example, that traditionally the Egyptians have been imbued with a compulsive religious drive to extend body and mind as far as possible along a sacred processional line—which accounts for their axial ceremonial avenues and the symmetrical plan arrangement of their homes and temples.

The democratic Greeks have cherished their privacy and individual freedom. Their homes, entered by unpretentious doorways along narrow winding streets, open upon a private domain for family living. With lives attuned to the pantheon of their gods—Zeus, Apollo, Venus, etc.—their temples have been given positions of prominence, to be viewed from a variety of approaches. The Greek agora or marketplace, the temple grounds, towns, and cities are freely disposed. Delight is taken in sequential progression and revealment—as in the changing prospects afforded in ascent to the Acropolis of Athens.

The medieval cultures of Europe produced compact walled and moated city-towns surrounded by open fields and forest. No precious measure of space was wasted in these lively, utilitarian warrens. Yet each was unique in character, as may be attested by visits to such vestigial cities as Amsterdam, Cologne, Geneva, Bruges, or Helsinki.

With the European Renaissance, free plan organization gave way to rigid geometry. Villas, palace grounds, and cities were designed to express the imperious dominance of the rulers of church and state. The powerful axis and cross-axis usurped the natural landscape and produced vast stretches of sterile nothingness, for no purpose but to impress. Versailles, the lavish pleasure ground of Louis XIV, the "Sun god," is but one example. The axial plan form, bilateral symmetry, and "wedding cake" architecture were to be adopted by the Western world as the ideal in urban and building design. Many believe that they have left their imprint on far too many U.S. cities.

Traditionally, however, the Asian cities of the Taoist and Zen-Buddhist cultures have revered and deified nature. Homes, temple grounds, and cities have been fitted to the natural topographic forms and features with infinite care. Streets are meandering, tracing the ridges, valleys, and receptive cross-slopes. Rocks, streams, ponds, and groves are preserved to provide a setting of often breathtaking beauty. Traditional Chinese and Japanese planning and city design have been axial only in those rare instances where the imperial will was to be made manifest—as in Peking's Temple of Heaven or the Forbidden City. Elsewhere, for long centuries, delightful asymmetry and refreshing natural beauty have for the most part prevailed. The new Western-style cities of China and Japan show little regard for natural features—or for clean air, clean water, or sunlight. Shops, factories, homes, and apartments are crowded haunch to haunch along traffic-laden streets amidst unprecedented pollution.

The traditional Moslem cities, with their Mecca-orientation, their symbolic domes and spires, their bazaars and narrow shaded streets; the Norwegian sea and forest towns; the Spanish courtyard cities; and the African kraal-city compounds of a herder way of life, all have deep underlying reasons for being what they are, and will largely continue to be.

. . .

These expressions of time, place, and culture are observable phenomena. What have they to tell of the city-planning art? Simply that such design criteria must be understood and applied if the city or any component thereof is to succeed as a meaningful unit.

The functional city

Cities come into being in response to human needs. Cities are judged according to the degree to which these needs are satisfied. In general terms the human requirements are those of protection; shelter; food, air, and water; a healthful environment; gainful employment; trade; social intercourse; and some form of governance.

Protection

Throughout history people have banded together for mutual protection and safety. The first cities were no doubt little more than armed camps. The site chosen would be that which was most defensible, which provided water for daily use and siege, and which afforded materials for building the walls or stockade.

Defense in present times has assumed new forms. The threat of nuclear attack would logically indicate the need for dispersed activity centers; low, stable building forms, extensive underground installations, and rapid point-to-point transport and transit. The consequences of warfare, however, have now become so utterly devastating that defense at the city level in fact seems almost futile. It has little apparent effect on urban design save in consideration of immediate shelter and ease of evacuation.

Protection also implies public safety from accident, crime, and contamination. There is new emphasis on safer trafficways, pollution control, the elimination of slums, and the creation of a more salutary living environment.

To understand the Oriental approach to landscape planning at any scale—from garden, to farmland, to city—we Americans must first put from our minds all thoughts of Nature as the enemy. This is harder for us than it might seem, for we are born with an anti-nature mind-set.

Ambassador Joseph Clark Grew

A city is more than steel and stone. The essence of city is life. ' Like a good city is where the fishmonger's cry is heard at dawn, where the evening gives way to music and laughter, and at noon on the streets one can feel the pulse of the crowd.

Dylan Simonds

———

Reduced to its essential—the aim of city building is the fulfillment of human needs.

———

In all probability people still have the same basic needs today as from time's beginning.

———

Landscape architecture is not primarily a visual art. Like architecture and engineering, it is basically functional. This is so when and only when the term *function* is correctly conceived to embrace the full range of human needs and aspirations. Included are the factors of safety, protection, comfort, productivity, and a sense of well-being. Function may also deal with such abstract considerations as philosophic integrity, perceived moral rectitude, and ecological fit.

———

Shelter

With cities soon to be the habitation of over three-fourths of the U.S. population, the need for improved types of shelter is evident. Yet in burgeoning cities housing is generally archaic, inadequate, and unaffordable. Clearly, new concepts of housing and community living are an unmet challenge of contemporary urban design. True modular construction, the application of innovative building materials, and advanced techniques of fabrication hold the promise of hived garden cities of a wholly new and delightful mien.

Food, air, and water

Food for the cities of history was for the most part produced in surrounding farm plots, orchards, and vineyards. With improved means of transportation, preservation, and refrigeration, the city can now import its food from around the world. Where possible, however, fresh produce from nearby farm fields and home gardens is clearly desirable. New types of geodesic growing houses, terraced roof gardens, and hydroponics give promise of garden cities far surpassing those that Ebenezer Howard envisioned.

The feeding of a city is no small entail. A visit to the stockyards of Chicago, the Fulton Street fish market of New York, or Pittsburgh's produce yards in the wee hours of the morning gives an inkling of the dimensions. If underscoring were to be needed, the grain elevators of Nebraska and Kansas should do it, the expanses of Florida citrus groves or of artichoke fields in Southern California.

With pollution control now taking effect, clean air for pleasurable breathing and healthful living seems again a reasonable possibility. Abundant fresh water, too—in our faucets, aquifers, streams, and lakes—is technically feasible. Soil and water conservation programs, reforestation and afforestation, new approaches to water use and waste treatment are all having their good effects.

The saga of civilization is that of the migrations of people in search of potable water and their battles to obtain and secure the rights to an adequate supply. What is an adequate supply? In water-abundant United States, where the draw-down of subsurface aquifers is finally being noted, "enough" has come to mean all that one could possibly use or squander. In many cultures the family's daily water supply can be carried home in a jar on the head. We have become so used to wasteful consumption that we think nothing of using some 10 gallons to bathe or a gallon in brushing one's teeth. It is said that the spill from a city's leaking hydrants and faucets could fulfill the essential water needs of its inhabitants.

It is foreseen that future cities will be amply supplied, using but a fraction of the water presently drawn from wellfields or reservoirs. This will result from the application of emerging techniques of sound water resource management.

Soon, water will be classified and supplied separately for household and industrial-agricultural uses. Potable water will be piped into habitations for drinking, cooking, and bathing purposes. Recycled and treated water will be used for irrigation and industrial washing and cooling purposes. With residential water rates based on a sliding scale, increasing with unit consumption, there will tend to be less waste. Xeriscape (water-conservative) gardens and parks will be the general rule. Further, by conducting surface runoff into sizable retention and recharge ponds, the underlying freshwater tables will be continually replenished.

Environment

In viewing the city as a desirable place in which to live, it seems reasonable to equate the term *environment* with those conditions most conducive to optimum human well-being. These not only must satisfy the physical needs discussed but also must provide the visual, social, cultural, educational, recreational, and inspirational amenities. And it is not enough that these be provided; they must also be made readily accessible.

The wonder and delight of Paris is in large part occasioned by the rich and tumultuous mix of people, goods, and amenities, all laced together by intriguing pedestrian walkways and pleasurable rapid transit. Montreal, too, in the Parisian tradition, and San Francisco, in its own way, provide such an exhilarating environment for urban living.

In these, as in all contemporary cities, there is always room for improvement, such as:

- The provision of an open space framework to separate and refresh the various districts
- More intensive urban activity centers of various types, complete with related housing, restaurants, shops, offices, and supporting services
- Effective pollution abatement—clean air and water, sanitation, and relief from excessive noise, glare, and other forms of stress
- Energy conservation. The very idea of energy conservation raises many questions, such as: In the land planning and building process have the elements been grouped compactly for efficient interconnection? Have locations and orientation been responsive to prevailing wind and storm patterns; to the seasonal sweep and incidence of the sun? Has solar heating been considered—or the cooling effect of channelized breeze, moistened gravels and ground covers, shade and shadow, the transpiration of

Using reclaimed water for landscape irrigation is important, but we need to go far beyond simply using water…and begin to treat and process water in the landscape.

John Lyle

The aesthetic you see is formed by the process at work.

Edward Blake

Engineered systems of wastewater processing can introduce clean ponds, lakes, and wetlands (beauty with utility) into the urban environs.

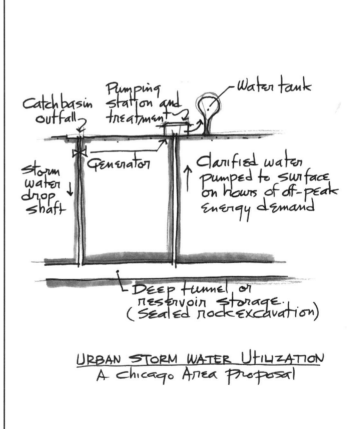

URBAN STORM WATER UTILIZATION
A Chicago Area Proposal

Cities of the industrial era have consciously excluded natural processes, substituting mechanical devices made possible by intensive use of fossil fuels. Rather than using the solar energy falling on their streets and buildings they dissipate it as excess heat. At the same time they import immense quantities of concentrated energy in various forms, most of it derived from petroleum coaxed from the ground in distant landscapes.

They rush the water falling upon their roofs and streets as rain out through concrete pipes and channels into the nearest bay or river and, at the same time, bring water in from distant landscape through similar channels. From outer landscapes, too, they import nutrients in the form of food, use it once, then send it out through pipes as sewage waste.

Thus, we might see our overwhelming problems of depletion and pollution as largely outgrowths of our ways of shaping the urban environment.

JOHN T. LYLE

foliage, of ponding, the conservation of moisture in the soils, of xeriscape landscape treatment...?

Employment

Most people work for a living. They are drawn to the city in search of opportunities to work at those occupations for which they have special aptitude. Urban areas are thus reservoirs of special skills and capabilities. Cities can draw upon a whole region, or worldwide sources, for materials and equipment. Cities are linked by air, land, and water transport networks for distribution.

We have seen that in the traditional town-city, home was the workplace. With garden plot or vineyard just beyond the city wall, the family would produce the needed cheese, bread, wine, leather, shoes, or woven fabric and sell the surplus. As certain products gained popularity, the first floor of the dwelling would be converted to a shop, and the family moved to the rear or to the overhead loft.

With the advent of mechanization and industrialization, the dairies, mills, factories, and industrial plants were centralized, and, except for the service trades, the workers were forced to commute or move to the industrial districts or company towns. Today things have changed again—as to types of employment, as to the nature of families, as to means of communication and travel, and as to the ways of living itself.

In contemporary times the types of skills in demand are as manifold and diverse as the profusion of new products. Families are smaller, less cohesive, more mobile, and multi-skilled. Their members are employed wherever opportunities and aptitudes lead and transportation will take them. Audio-visual-electronic communication now permits many to work from their homes and live where they will. The choice is usually one of lifestyle and amenity. The increasing trend is toward agreeable community living near major hubs of employment.

In any production center—from farm, to fishery, artist colony, university, research park, or assembly plant—certain optimum conditions are conducive to successful operation. Such centers are in themselves designed with care to provide the best possible facilities and relationships. Is it less than reasonable that a city, the most complex and potent production center of all, be organized with as much thought?

Trade

Commerce and trade are the city's dynamos. From time immemorial the barter or sale of such commodities as salt, provisions, cotton, grain, livestock, furs, silk, pearls, or fabricated products has sustained or brought wealth to the cities of the world. Often the tendency is to associate cities with their articles of commerce.

What has trade to do with city planning? Much. Each center of commercial activity is, ideally, given the location, area, form, and supporting features to make it attractive and efficient. In this regard the planners of U.S. cities have many lessons to learn.

From the department store one may learn the importance of plan layout, routing, display, receiving, storage, delivery, customer comfort, and appeal. Industry can give instruction in the design of efficient *systems*.

European trade centers demonstrate the desirability of maintaining the integrity of the commercial street, of shops side by side on narrow ways without interruption at street level by uses or structures that destroy the continuity or dilute the intensity of the shopping experience.

Again, from the near-East bazaars and those of the Orient can be learned the value of compression; of generating excitement; of appealing sights, sounds and smells; and of great variety and multiplicity of choice.

One can wonder at the insensitive plan arrangement of most U.S. grid cities—with commercial districts sliced apart by wide trafficways, forced asunder by parking structures or compounds, and interrupted by monolithic banks, apartments, or office towers that blank out whole blocks of the shopping street at the pedestrian level. In most U.S. cities one could find almost anything needed if one had the patience and cab fares. But if one should wish to furnish a home or even a room—or to purchase a Swedish lamp once seen and admired—the search can be one of utter frustration. Why? Because shops are so widely scattered within a checkerboard of fuming trafficways and architectonic colossi.

Regional shopping malls are not the answer. Most are anticity aberrations. Increasingly, in the metropolitan context, malls are being recognized as the costly despoilers that they are. Too often have they pulled nearby cities and towns apart—the scattered fragments drawn along to coagulate at the sides of the intervening highways.

The negative impacts of a regional shopping center are seldom foreseen. The perceived benefits are largely an illusion. In the guise of economy-builders they are offered whomping inducements by the local boards and councils which vie to bring them in. They are heavily subsidized. The contingent "improvements"—off-site roadways, ramps, and utility installations—are paid for by the public, including many good citizens whose lives or well-being are jeopardized by the mall's intrusion. Taxes in the surrounding environs are raised, even as life becomes less pleasant. Once-tranquil countryside is subjected to a frenetic rush of uncoordinated development. Meanwhile, back in the affect-

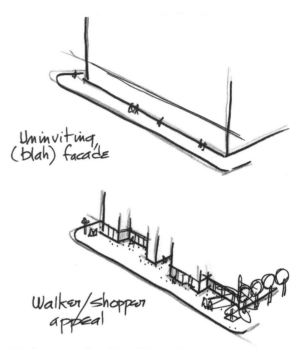

Pedestrian level building frontage

It can be stated as an axiom of urban planning that high-speed, high-volume on-grade through traffic and unified activity areas are incompatible.

ed towns and cities merchants struggle to survive and municipal coffers are drained in the wake of the exodus tide.

A new shopping mall generates an influx of camp-following enterprises and ever-increasing traffic. Things might seem to be booming. But as congestion increases, the shopping experience draws fewer purchasing customers and more of the gawking spectator crowd to paw through trays of trinkets. As sales decline and tariffs are raised, the anchor tenants look elsewhere—to where promoters are planning a new and larger competing mall—farther out and with greater pull and attractions.

When the major department stores move out, the better ancillary shops, and customers, follow—leaving the vacating mall to decline and never fully recover. Much of the exurban United States is now wallowing in such a nondescript backwash.

A new breed of shopping and business office malls is coming into being. More compact and upgraded, they are being planned as integral and integrated elements of balanced town and city centers. Here they have a stable and permanent base. Here, at the center of things, they draw upon the intensity to which they contribute.

One thing to be said for the shopping malls—they have taught some valuable planning lessons. That people will get into their cars and drive for miles to *concentrations* of goods and services. That people are willing to park in compounds and walk considerable distances to traffic-free spaces lined with shops, with things to see and enjoyable things to do. That even the smallest shops can thrive when crowded around and between department stores, office towers, and apartments. That those malls do best which provide for the wide spectrum of community life, activities, and events—within attractive surroundings.

Social intercourse

Humans are gregarious. They like at times to be together, to bustle, to jostle—or just to sit and watch as others go streaming by. For many city dwellers and visitors, shopping is the chief form of group interaction. Most also enjoy meeting together for worship, lectures, concerts, theater, dining, sporting events, and other such group activities. Accordingly, the proper city will provide its cathedral, performing arts center, museum, and stadium as well as its great department stores and restaurants. As the cultural and business center of the metropolitan region, the city is expected to provide crowd attractors.

The measure of the livable city lies not only in the eminence of its structures, but also in the quality of the spaces that surround them or are planned in between. Malls,

---

Shopping without city is as dull as city without shopping.

Some cities are trying to compete with the shopping malls by copying their physical form. What they should be copying is their centralized management.

William H. Whyte, Jr.

squares, and plazas have universal appeal, especially if they are designed expressively to fulfill their particular purpose. Beyond these, how fortunate such cities as Chattanooga or San Francisco, that overlook a dramatic view. Or are oriented to a waterfront, as are San Antonio, Seattle, Chicago, or Toledo.

Perhaps even more fortunate is the city planned around a refreshing open space system of parks—with interconnecting paths, bikeways, and parkways. There are in truth but few examples.

All in all it can be said that the quality of life in a city is no better than the quality of its congregating spaces.

Governance

No peoples have yet failed to find the need for governance to hold them to some code of conduct or some common cause.

What makes for good city government? Historically, there has proved to be no certain way. But Plato in his *Republic*, Henry Adams, Lincoln Steffens in the chronicles of his muck-raking days, and Walter Lippman in his writings have given valuable clues. The common elements are, essentially:

- Clear authority, derived of might, right of lineage, designation by a superior power, or more fortuitously by the will of the people governed
- A compelling goal and objectives
- A dynamic and flexible plan of action
- Clear and equitable regulations
- Authority of enforcement, uniformly exercised
- The respect of the people
- A sense by all citizens that they have a vote that counts

No doubt the latter is one of the most important. The vitality of a city wanes when its people no longer believe that what they do or say matters. Conversely, the strength of a city depends upon the degree to which the governed retain the spirit of individual contribution so directly evident in the old town meeting. This requires leadership integrity, a democratic approach to government, and the delegation of rights and decisions to the city by the state and nation.

More than at first might be realized, there is a direct relationship between the way a city is governed and the way that it looks and works.

Subdivided, as most of our cities are, into a patchwork of wards, boroughs, and/or other political districts, each with its own local officials and special interests, it is little won-

The public uses of plazas have been seen primarily as circulation, as an entrance to a building, and then more recently in terms of gathering or the passive—or even active—enjoyment of places.

MARK FRANCIS

In the contemporary United States, there is little need, reason, or budget for the upkeep of grand plazas or vacuous public spaces created solely to impress.

The *metropolitan region* is a community of persons living within an urban environment and tied together by social and economic bonds but traditionally served by a multiplicity of uncoordinated local governments.

———————————

Most older American cities—and parts of all of them—have the common problem of chronic disorganization. They are in truth a mishmash of fractured and overlapping districts—without discernible boundaries, without focal centers, and without means of convenient access or interconnection.

———————————

der that in their physical form they are so fragmented. Nor is it surprising that so many of their strained resources are wasted in duplicate governance, staff time, fire, and police protection, and other localized services.

Only with a strong central government can a more cohesive, unified, and efficient city be expected. This has led to the concept of a *city manager*. Engaged by the city council and working together with the mayor, the city manager brings to the government the skills of a trained business administrator. This has resulted in many obvious improvements.

A further complication in most metropolitan areas is the fact that crowded around and sometimes impinging upon the city boundaries are a host of more or less independent political entities. These are the boroughs, counties and incorporated towns which draw upon the city services. Many of their citizens gain their livelihood within the city proper, yet almost without exception such districts are protective of their self-interests and reluctant to contribute financial or other support to the host city or to regional endeavors. In looking to a more cooperative and efficient

City and suburbs

Most cities are embedded in a jumble of lesser jurisdictions—each with its own government, schools, street maintenance , fire and police departments, courts and other public services. Each within its legal boundaries strives for its own well-being and special interests at the expense of the central city where many of its residents make their living and whose benefits they enjoy.

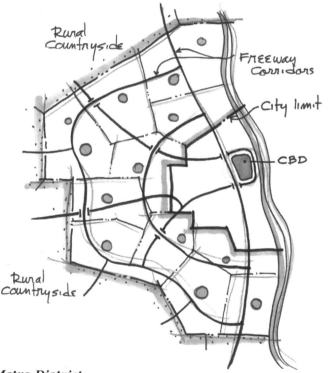

Metro District

Here the scattered municipalities have been consolidated within a Metropolitian District under a Metro Charter that delegates to the Metro Council and staff responsibility for those functions—land and highway network planning, utility systems, education, etc.—which are clearly of regional scope. For Metro to be successful it is essential that local governments are allowed to retain control of those matters of particular local concern.

modus operandi the *Metro* form of government is proving highly successful in some localities. It eliminates duplicative functions and provides a coordinated approach to many aspects of area-wide planning and operation.

A metro government differs from traditional froms in that when granted authority by state charter it takes over from the disparate local governments certain of those functions which are clearly of regional or metropolitan scope and import. Since the sovereignty and power of the local political cadres is thereby diminished, they can be expected to resist—and they do. Where and when voted into being, however, the Metro government has proven the benefits of the broader view, superior planning capabilities, increased influence, and streamlined administrative efficiency. With logic and proven performance so clearly in its favor, it seems destined to become the way of the future. It has faltered only when it has been implemented too abruptly—assuming more duties than could be well handled.

Metro government has succeeded where having been granted broad underlying powers—it has at first exercised only those which are clearly needed to implement programs of metropolitan scope, such as unified systems of transportation, transit, energy transmission, waste treatment, water resource management and comprehensive long range planning. In time, as experience and proficiency are increased, the metro government can assume responsibility for other additional assignments—*while leaving to each local jurisdiction control over its own affairs*.

Chaos or coordination

The development programs and projects within most metropolitan areas are fraught with contradictions and delays. The frustrating state of confusion, conflicts, overlapping regulations, and jurisdictional disputes is wasteful in the extreme; wasteful both of time and of funds.

In searching for an effective mechanism by which to coordinate development, each metropolitan region must put together the one that fits. Those that have worked best have a number of features in common:

- An overview regional council or commission comprised of business, civic, and cultural leaders.

- A central office and clearinghouse with an appointed administrator and staff.

- The dissemination of development guidelines and basic planning information.

- The plotting and description of all significant land-use proposals within or relating to the metro area.

- The conduct of interagency and agency-entrepreneur conferences.

The cities will flourish when suburbanites pay their fair share.

The only reasonable basis of planning for urbanization is the metropolitan area or region. Only by planned control of development in the entire area can unnecessary decentralization be reduced, costly duplication of services precluded, and operational systems assured.

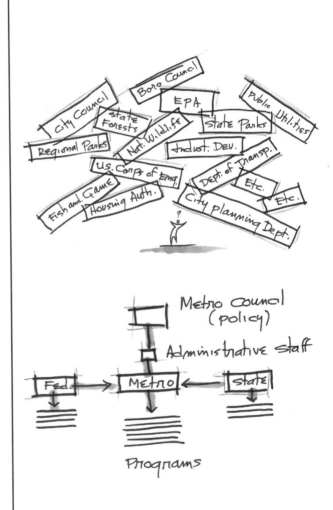

- The resolution of land-use conflicts.
- The right of review and recommendation on all matters affecting the region.

. . .

Within each metropolitan area the focal city has much at stake in regional well-being—for as the region fares, so fares the city. It is therefore incumbent upon the city leadership—political and/or civic—to promote and in all possible ways support a strong and effective regional council and metropolitan action program.

. . .

Within the context of the regional constellation, each city must function and thrive as a working entity. To provide for the needs of its people the city's revenues must equal or exceed funds expended. In this regard its essential productive capacity relates not only to goods, materials and machinery, but to trade, tourism, and ambience as well.

The functioning city will perform efficiently only if designed and constantly adjusted as a functioning mechanism.

The convenient city

Convenience equates with having things needed close at hand and ease in getting around.

Centers

In the convenient city, therefore, it makes sense to provide centers for each of the major types of urban activity—as for example, *financial, entertainment,* or *trade.* Arranged within and around such groupings are those things needed to complement and support them. These will include not only other related types of activity but also the suppliers of necessary goods and services, together with dining and shopping and perhaps lodging for transient clients, patrons, and visitors.

As for getting to and around such centers, the *to* is by car and by rapid transit. Access by bus and automobile is at best to a portal or portals at the perimeter, with ramps to subsurface parking or exterior tiers. The open space ways and places between buildings will be devoted to pedestrians and the things they like to see and do, with concern for the disadvantaged. Where feasible, a transit stop at the edge, or within the core adds a further measure of convenience.

Subcenters

Throughout the metropolitan region the clustering or grouping of like uses and complementary amenities is a

---

Neighborhoods need centers. Communities need centers. Urba-centers need centers. Cities need centers.

Urban transportation alternatives are not all as dramatic as the aerial glideway, hillside funicular, or subsurface "tube." They include such welcome contributors as car and van pools, reserved bus lanes, courtesy buses and trams, the encouragement of bicycle use, and provision for safe and enjoyable walking.

If urban designers were to spend a week in a wheelchair, cities would take new form.

---

mark of superior planning. As is the location around them of planned neighborhoods and communities.

Design for the disabled

Convenience is of heightened concern for those with disabilities.

We are all in our lifetime destined to be disabled in one way or another. From infancy to maturity and beyond there will be times when our ability to see, hear, move, or even to reason clearly will be limited or impaired.

For too long the term "disabled" has been a label applied in the abstract to a group of unfortunates, rather than the recognition of a common, very real, human condition. Until but recently cities confronted the disabled with one dilemma after another. With six to ten street crossings per mile, steep curbs at each trafficway crossing, steps at most building entrances, and inaccessible public conveyances—the whole urban terrain seemed hostile. Much has been done in recent years to make those with handicaps welcome.

With the recent passage by Congress of the Americans with Disabilities Act (ADA) there is now a national mandate to plan all aspects of our physical environment with the handicapped in mind. Not just to provide and designate special facilities and devices (thus emphasizing the fact of disadvantage) but rather to build these aids into our ways and places in such a way as to make them inconspicuous and available to all. Designed into the more caring and comfortable cities will be such features as expanded traffic-free business and shopping centers, low-slung transit vehicles, ample lifts, and gently sloping ramps. There will be "universal" signage, symbols, and easily recognizable signals. Paving and paths will be designed in alignment, profile, width, and texture for ease for movement and repose in cleaner, brighter, safer, and more refreshing surroundings. All people will benefit from such sensitive planning.

The rational city

The rational city makes sense.

It was Descartes, father of the Age of Reason, who in the days of chamber-pot-from-the-balcony-dumping proposed that there must be a better means of sewage disposal. He was further convinced that there must be, all in all, a more reasonable way of urban living than that which he was experiencing. He deplored the prevailing unquestioning willingness to accept the existing condition and set about to reexamine all aspects of life in his city and those of the city itself. Descartes reaffirmed the belief of Hippodamus that a city that followed a well-conceived plan should be better

In the shaping of a more reasonable urban structure it is proposed that the various components be aggregated into well-organized entities—each surrounded by those things most needed to make it work.

"Universal design" which approaches site and facility planning from the perspective of all, not just average, users—considers all degrees of sensory awareness, all types of locomotion and all levels of physical and intellectual function.

SUSAN GOLTSMAN AND DAVID DRISKELL

The size, character, and form of a city are largely influenced by its transportation diagram.

MICHAEL RAPUANO

Cities…their vastness is their most striking feature. Areas that give evidence of planning occupy but a small surface. Disorder predominates. The few green spaces…seem hidden in a maze of grey and shapeless masses.

JOSE LLUIS SERT

Few buildings in the modern metropolis have been designed with any thought of their relationship to others.

The evolutionary planning of the urban metropolis is an interdisciplinary process of *problem-solving* and *possibility realization*. With the base as broad as all of nature and the clientele as inclusive as all of humankind—the challenge is never-ending.

---

than a city that resulted from haphazard growth.

What would Descartes have to say of contemporary U.S. cities? One might believe that he would approve of the fact that the need for comprehensive planning has finally been recognized, but he would no doubt find many accepted urban phenomena open to serious question. Among these are the grid plan block layout, the fronting of dwellings upon trafficways, the omnipresent intrusion of vehicles, unlimited and uncontrolled expansion, single-use zoning, impaction, pollution, and the lack of coherent city form.

Urban form

The U.S. city is amorphous, too often a shapeless aggregation of rigid trafficways and rectangular blocks. The city lacks recognizable and rational structure. It has no coherent plan organization. Could this be because at present there seems to exist no clear concept of what a more reasonable city should be? In these rapidly changing times there is need for a redefinition of "city." Each city for its time, its place, its people, must find its own direction—but find a direction it must. For only with clear and motivating goals can the ideal be visualized and given expressive form.

Problems

In the rational city those responsible will address the whole gamut of problems—existing and potential. Some might seem as incidental as pests, rodents, strays, and impolite pets; others as remote as subsidence, landslides, earthquakes, or floods—any one of which can assume catastrophic proportions should it occur. Geologic instability is often related to sustained fresh water drawdown and the depletion of the underlying aquifers. This can result in soil shrinkage and, in coastal areas, salt water intrusion. Equally as drastic can be the collapse of abandoned shoring or columns in subsurface mine workings. Those who guide a city's growth and construction must proceed in full awareness of all such hazardous conditions. In this age of dawning computer technology, pertinent data, obtained over the years from many sources, can be readily stored and graphically arrayed until the essential base maps are up-dated and complete.

Pollution, in its many aspects, is insidious. Trash, filth, obsolescence, and visual blight are easily detected and eliminated by aggressive clean-up, fix-up campaigns. Not so easily remedied is the progressive contamination of soils by airborne and waterborne chemicals, which in time reach levels of saturation that destroy vegetation and endanger human health. Stagnant air and inversions have become common plagues in most metropolitan regions. Recently the added threat of acid rain has come to have even more alarming implications. Mile upon mile of "Penn's Woods" along the Pennsylvania turnpike, as an example, is lined with trees dead or dying from this aerial pollution. Elsewhere, nationwide, soils and earth-fills contaminated with toxic wastes leach their poisons into the underground freshwater reserves.

It has been well said that our worst problems often present our best opportunities. As a case in point, consider solid waste. In the not too long ago past mountains of garbage were hauled each day from our urban areas to the nearest open "dump site" or barged from port cities as their gift to the sea. As the stench and contamination worsened, the sanitary landfills came into being. They were better but had a way of filling attractive valleys and polluting the sub-surface aquifers from which our water supply is drawn. What was to be done?

The immensity of the problem has led to our current experimentation in *conversion* and *recycling*. By conversion, garbage and human waste are now being processed to produce an amazing array of soil conditioners and nutrients. These give promise of replacing the loss of heretofore irreplaceable topsoil. By recycling, the reclamation and reuse of mineral and forest product derivatives has made it possible to slow, and even in some cases halt, the exhaustion of natural resources.

Thus, recent liabilities have now become valuable assets.

In the teeming cities a far more obvious problem is the breakdown of transportation and utility systems. Peak hour traffic loadings and delays can be as vexing as peak hour water shortages and soaring energy costs.

In the irrational city can be found the whole range of physical woes and abuses. But what, some may ask, does this have to do with planning and design? The answer, of course, should be obvious. Responsible planning and perceptive design are the *only* means by which chaos can be averted and a more agreeable way of city life created and maintained.

Undesirables

What can be done about human unfortunates?? The beggars, bag ladies, trash sorters, and winos; the dope peddlers and addicts; the perverts and prostitutes; the street gangs, vandals and thieves? They are not to be shooed away. Nor beaten. Nor hidden and ignored. All are a fact of city life and must be reckoned with.

Thieves, street gangs, and the violent are to be caught, incarcerated, and retrained where possible—as in constructive work forces, centers, or camps. For beggars, drunks, perverts, prostitutes, and unlicensed purveyors—the plague of every city—the least, and perhaps the best, to be done is

Most people live in a world of split personalities in which business and political actions are dominated by short-run objectives while at the same time personal goals remain long-term. Individuals intensely hope for the future happiness of their children and grandchildren even while responding unknowingly to short-run pressures in ways that jeopardize the future.

More and more newspaper headlines are revealing the accentuation of those pressures— polluted wells, acid rain damage to forests, falling water tables, atomic waste disposal uncertainties, hunger in many parts of the world, and social pressure from crowding, ...terrorism and illegal immigration.

JAY W. FORRESTER
"MODELS AND THE REAL WORLD"
SYSTEMS DYNAMICS REVIEW,
VOL.3, NO. 2, SUMMER 1987

The first garbage crisis came when humans became sedentary. From that point on, the basics of garbage disposal have stayed pretty much the same. You can dump it. You can burn it. You can convert it into something that can be used again. Or you can minimize material goods— tomorrow's garbage—in the first place.

Americans produce 160 million tons of solid waste a year—three and a half pounds a day for every man, woman, and child in the nation. A convoy of 10-ton garbage trucks carrying the nation's annual waste would reach halfway to the moon.

TOMMY EHRBAR

Each week, 40,000 pounds of plastic containers are collected by the Chicago Park District. They are transformed into brightly colored timbers for sandboxes, flower planters, fences and playground liners. The plastic timbers are less expensive, safer (no splinters) and more vandal resistant than wood. But the best part is the community's new appreciation for recycling.

KATHLEEN MCCORMICK

The best way to handle the problem of undesirables is to make a place attractive to everyone else. With few exceptions, center city plazas and small parks are safe places.

WILLIAM H. WHYTE JR.

One of the most virulent types of visual pollution is the spray-painted graffiti that plagues so many cities. With beginnings in the rail yards of New York it was hailed by a few misguided writers as a new indigenous art form. In an atmosphere of permissiveness it was soon to spread as a sickening scourge. It has defaced much of the urban American landscape and lowered property values. It is to be addressed by public officials with vigor—and stamped out for the infection it is.

Inexplicably, even fastidious Scandinavia is smeared from one end to the other with spray-painted crud.

Diminished, contaminated water resources will force us to rethink how we use water. The design and management of the urban landscape to reduce water use, to treat wastewater, and to recharge groundwater will be part of the solution.

ANNE WHISTON SPIRN

There's a movement away from our society's linear blast into the future in favor of a slower, more engaged approach....I think the true centering will be between...humankind and nature.

RICHARD HANSEN

to subject them to regulation and firm control. The halt and diseased among them are to be given treatment, the hungry fed, the ragged clothed, and the homeless provided with housing or shelter. This is a matter of human conscience—an obligation of society and of government at the highest levels.

These "undesirables"—from the vicious to the unfortunate—are too often the product and not the cause of decrepit cities. Most would welcome the chance to help in the cleanup and rebuilding. In the removal of vacant and obsolete structures. In the clearing away of trash and debris. In graffiti eradication. In the regrading and replanting of eroded slopes and drainage ways. In the construction of new trafficways, parking compounds, and plazas. In helping make greenways, bikeways, parks, and allotment gardens. In the creation of a fairer, more wholesome, urban metropolis.

Opportunities

With comprehensive planning the rational city will come to realize possibilities beyond our present fondest dreaming. Plans should start with the preservation and protection of the existing natural features. Water resource management will at last become fundamental to all land planning and development.

Streams, wetlands, water bodies, dominant topographic conformations, and areas of superior vegetative cover will be left intact as elements of an interrelated open space preserve. The built environment will be planned to and around them, bringing people and nature into the best possible relationships. Unstable bearing strata and geologic faults will be avoided. Excavation and grading will be controlled by ordinance and the topsoil conserved. Pedestrians, passenger vehicles, and trucks will be given their own separate routes of movement. Trafficways, structures, and spaces will be sun-, wind-, and climate-responsive. They will avoid the flood, brace to the storms, and utilize the cooling effects of vegetation, water, and the prevailing breeze.

Community plans will evince knowledge of natural systems and their tolerance. Land uses, densities, and floor area ratios will impose no significant stresses by overloading. Residential, production, cultural and recreation centers will be planned together as closely interrelated synergistic entities, conserving travel time, energy, and land.

Urban centers are to be conceived as intensive business, trade, and cultural focal points. They will be created about multilevel transit nodes and interlaced with refreshing garden plazas and courts. Each such complex will be surrounded by lower intensity support facilities such as those providing convenience shopping, restaurants, supplies, and services.

With fixed boundaries (to preclude creep or sprawl) city

centers, in time, will run out of buildable land area. This may have its advantages, as in keeping systems in balance. It may also serve to keep occupancy high and renewal spontaneous. But when the pinch is on, it is to be expected that aerial and subsurface building rights will be explored. Where capacities and tolerances are not a limiting factor many facilities—such as garaging, storage, and goods distribution can well go underground. Out of sight, out of mind. And too, out of weather extremes and traffic.

Another possibility is the utilization of air space—the superimposing of one above-ground use or structure over another. A recreation park or playfield, for example, might be built atop a parking compound or a highway/transitway over railway trackage. Again, a high-rise complex might be built over a truck terminal or freight-yard. There may be several layers of development such as shops at a lower level topped by offices and residential apartments. Thus one property may serve the city in several contributory ways.

Let there be towers and tiered megastructures. They have their place and are needed to house the many primary functions of the centers. But why need they stand so proud and aloof, designed to impress rather than to please? Why need they stand shoulder to shoulder along sterile avenues? Why need they, in fortresslike isolation, seal themselves off from the pulsing life of revitalized cities? Let them rise instead amidst a surrounding of people-friendly places and spaces, with the best of the old and familiar preserved. Let them be opened out onto spaces alive with people and the splendid hubbub and excitement that only a city can give. Let them make room at their edges, atop, and within for people-gathering places. Let them reconnect to the city. Let them rejoin the crowd.

Around the urban centers and subcenters will be clustered the residential neighborhoods, within and around open parklands. The center city and each of its satellite urba-centers will thus be separate, interconnected entities—true urban communities.

The suburban, rural, and outlying wilderness regions will be planned or replanned as a galaxy of towns, villages, communities—each unique to its place and embraced by fields, conservancy lands, lakes, waterways, and forest. The positive values of such a rational approach to land use and urban planning are obvious, and compelling.

The complete city

A proper city is complete—a functioning organic entity. It can be compared to the human body in that it too is a living body—with skeleton, veins, and arteries. The city breathes, drinks, feeds, and gives off wastes. It grows, regenerates, and reproduces. It thinks and acts responsively, having

Towers and megastructures work for the city when, and only when, they intensify, rather than diminish, activity on the pedestrian base from which they rise.

The best-liked urban buildings (and places) are open to the life of the street—either directly as by welcoming entrances and by inside-outside spaces or by people looking out and looking in.

Let us rebuild our cities with reason, and in accordance with natural law.

What a New Yorker especially responds to in Pittsburgh is a sense of city as an organism whose many parts have been made to function as they were designed to.

<small>BRENDAN GILL</small>

Economics

Consider the most basic measure of a nation's economic performance, gross national product. (GNP) In calculating GNP, natural resources are not depreciated as they are used up. Buildings and factories are depreciated; so are machinery and equipment, cars, and trucks. So why, for instance, isn't the topsoil in Iowa depreciated when it washes down the Mississippi River after careless agricultural methods have lessened its ability to resist wind and rain? Because we failed to see the value of growing grain in an ecologically sound manner, we have lost more than half of all the topsoil in Iowa.

Because we have failed to measure the economic value of clean, fresh groundwater, we have contaminated more than half of all the underground reservoirs in the United States with pesticide runoff and other poisonous residues that are virtually impossible to remove.

<small>VICE PRESIDENT ALBERT GORE
EARTH IN THE BALANCE,
HOUGHTON-MIFFLIN, BOSTON, 1990, PP.183–184</small>

To date we have been using advanced computer technology to build cities more suited to life some 600 years ago than to the twenty-first century.

As with any machine that fails to function, one is faced with but several choices. Take a farm wagon, for instance. If it begins to groan and creak you can ignore the problem and ride along until it collapses, and then walk off. You can find the problem and make repairs. Or better yet, use the repaired wagon while building another with improvements to make it work better.

The problems of failing cities are a lot more complicated than those of the old farm wagon— but the choices are the same.

---

mind and spirit. The good city, like a good person, is wholesome, animated, cultivated, and self-assured. The good city is of exemplary character and admirable mien. Like the human, the city has its *élan vital*—its driving force. The city has a need to fulfill many vital functions. For a city to thrive it must be healthy not only physically but economically, politically, and socially as well.

Economic considerations

The economic viability of an urban metropolis depends on its ability to produce a surplus of long-term revenues over expenditures. That this is more difficult than it might seem is evinced by the fact that most cities are presently in dire financial straits. Why?

Some have outgrown their initial reason for being and have failed to find another. Some have exhausted their natural resources or are affected by external forces beyond their control. Others are slowed to a near standstill by constricted trafficways. Others have simply rotted away at the core in the wake of successive outward growth rings.

Obsolescence and vacancies breed all forms of urban ills. When a city is no longer healthful or safe, when it fails to provide more advantage than disadvantage—people leave. At least those who can, and they are usually the more productive ones. When contributing citizens move away, the tax yields are diminished, the needs become greater, and the problems are multiplied.

If there is a law of real estate economics it is this: The resident or entrepreneur will pay all possible to attain that location—be it a city, a neighborhood, or a particular property— which provides the most advantages at the least total cost. Advantages include such things as favorable environment, amenities, trade area, visibility, accessibility, and compatibility. Costs may include acquisition, development, rent, utilities, taxes, travel time, frictions, or energy expended.

Most cities fail simply because their present structure is no longer, or not yet, suited to contemporary city life. The old machine has broken down, and overhauling is not enough. A new model is needed. Usually such a needed change is achieved only with new leadership and better management. There are new techniques and tools to help, such as urban renewal or redevelopment. These have proved highly effective when coupled with knowledgeable planning.

Political aspects

No plan or proposal, however meaningful, can be effected except by political decision. The political machine, for it is a machine, is the mechanism by which communal opinion and public will can be transmuted into action. Political science is the understanding of the means by which this is achieved.

Is the system good or bad? It can be bad if the politicians are bad, for unsavory politicians exploit to their advantage the worst elements of a sinking city. But politicians seem to be as good or as bad as the electorate would have them. Enlightened voters seek enlightened political leadership. Enlightened leaders are the key to a city's improving status and advancement.

How does one work, effectively, as citizen or as planner/designer within the political framework? In practice it has been found helpful to make several assumptions:

- Elected officials seek reelection, which is usually based on their performance.
- Given the opportunity, they seek to support proposals that are in the public good.
- When constituents question their leaders on any issue, the leaders need to be well informed.

It is therefore incumbent upon any group or individual seeking favorable political action to make sure from the start that the facts and merits of the proposal are clear to those who are to make intelligent comments and decisions. Astute political leaders are keenly aware of the needs and opinions of those whom they represent. It is wise to seek the insight, guidance, and support of all possible contributors and build their ideas into the plans.

· · ·

The public agency is the working arm of government. In every department the agency director and staff can bring to bear invaluable experience. They too have the need to be kept informed and are usually glad to contribute background information and advice throughout the planning process.

In sum, politically, the successful plan is one of which the decision makers and their advisors have been kept informed and to which they have made some positive contribution.

Social implications

The city can be likened to a hive of bees. Each type of bee—the worker, soldier, drone, and queen—has its role, as does each individual. Without the bees and their activities, the hive has no intrinsic meaning. The city, too, is meaningless except as a manifestation of the life of the people within it.

As an expression of bee society the hive is an intricate marvel of efficient function. Nothing has been overlooked. Nothing is superfluous. Nothing is wasted. All is in balance.

Observation of many such hives in nature reveals that without exception they are located near the base of resource—the flowers of orchard, field, or forest—and attuned to the sweep of the sun and play of the wind. The specific site of the hive in nature is equally well-considered. The fix in the crevice of rock or hollow trunk is so selected as to minimize the natural constraints and to make optimum use of all possibilities.

When the colony outgrows the limits of a good working bee society, the hive is not enlarged to unmanageable size, converted to less efficient form, or abandoned. It is kept in repair, with meticulous care, and a new bee community and hive is formed at another propitious location. Is it expecting too much that in the planning and design of cities as much care be given to site selection, articulate structural form, and to the living needs and communal life of its inhabitants?

Human habitat

The literature of cities is as rich and varied as it is voluminous. Sometimes glorious, sometimes tragic, sometimes poetic, it is the timeless saga of the interaction of humans in their hived habitations.

From the earliest cuneiform records pressed into tablets of wet clay to the hieroglyphic inscriptions of scribes on papyrus; from the hand-lettered writings of medieval monks on illuminated parchment to the critical observations of our current authors, laser-printed in softback paper editions and distributed by the thousands—the story of the city continues to unfold. Its wonders are extolled, its failings damned in writings, art, and music. From the time of the first human settlements, the city has been under scrutiny by a host of sagacious observers. What do these poets and pundits have to tell us as we lurch into the planning and rebuilding of our twenty-first-century cities?

There are points of agreement. Few would dispute, for instance, the premise that a city should *not* be unsafe, unsanitary, unhealthful, uninviting, insolvent, inefficient, ugly, or a blight on the landscape. A city should not be, in short, what most of our cities presently are in part—and some in very large measure. Conversely, a city *should* be safe, clean, healthful, agreeable, attractive, financially solvent, efficient, productive, well-structured, handsome of form, and fitted harmoniously into its natural setting. Clearly, these are qualities for which to strive.

If there is general agreement on what a more livable city might be, there is far less consensus on the means by which to make it so. Among urbanologists—critics and aficionados—there is sharp and sometimes acrimonious dissension as to the best planning/replanning approach.

In the earliest handwriting we can read, hieroglyphic, the ideogram meaning "city" consists of a cross enclosed in a circle...The cross represents the convergence of roads, communication and trade; the circle, a moat or wall for togetherness and protection.

ROBERT S. LOPEZ

The garden city proposals of Sir Ebenezer Howard have been misconstrued by many to be an abandonment of the city, and flight to the country. Howard's proposals have recently come under attack by those who misunderstand his recommendations. Those who read into his writings a plea for compatible urban-regional integration are staunch and ardent believers.

Daniel "Make no little plans" Burnham was an advocate of the *city beautiful* concept of the great white and shining classical city. His was an art-and-architecture ideal. Le Corbusier, too, with his inventive mind and lifelong quest for expressive form, conceived the *radiant city,* a vast architectonic expanse of boulevards and spaced out colossi, the whole of which was dashed with unending streams of cars and dotted with inconsequential antlike people. His was an altogether too prophetic vision of where our society then seemed to be heading.

Scholarly Lewis Mumford was more moderate. He drew upon years of research and writing to conclude that the best system was one of disciplined order—an order to be established by trained professionals. It was a concept of promise. Unfortunately, the discipline came to be imposed by a band of erudite theoreticians seemingly committed to providing for the uninhibited movement of traffic at the expense of everything else. The emphasis of Mumford and his followers tended more toward cold geometric form and order than warm, people-togetherness—or people-nature considerations.

There have followed proponents of architectural cities, engineered cities, materialistic and political cities, park cities, and unrestrained, free-for-all, anything-goes cities that have exploded far out-of-bounds. The chaotic results have led to "can't-do" cities—of artificially contrived zones of single use, each zone color-coded and overlaid with outmoded regulations and deadening restrictions. *Zoning,* conceived as an answer to the rampant uncontrolled misuse of property, was designed to help ensure the "highest and best use of the land." Its result, however, was to change at one stroke the national attitude toward the value of land—from that based on *current productive yield* to that of *potential speculative profit*. The higher the zoning category, the higher the land owner's anticipated sales price and gain. As could be predicted, zoning designations were soon to be based less on reason than on raw political pressure.

Zoning as a concept is fairly new. In its continuing evolution it is taking promising new directions—as in planned unit and planned community development, land-banking, phased "build-out" or "contour" zoning, multiple-use designations, and performance incentives. But in its initial form (still extant in many municipalities) it was, and can be, stifling and counterproductive.

The real tragedy of urban design around the world, and urban design education, was that it did not ever deal with the issues of the Earth and its natural processes.

ROBERT HANNA

Is it not expecting too much of urban planners to fit a city to its environs when few in their schooling have taken as much as a single course in the natural sciences?

---

*There is a wistful myth that if only we had
enough money to spend— the figure is usually
put at a hundred billion dollars—we could wipe
out all our slums in ten years, reverse decay in
the great, dull, gray belts that were yesterday's
and day-before-yesterday's suburbs, anchor the
wandering middle class and its wandering tax
money, and perhaps even solve the traffic problem.*

*But look what we have built with the first sever-
al billions: Low-income projects that become
worse centers of delinquency, vandalism and
general social hopelessness than the slums they
were supposed to replace. Middle-income housing
projects which are truly marvels of dullness and
regimentation, sealed against any buoyancy or
vitality of city life. Luxury housing projects that
mitigate their inanity, or try to, with a vapid vul-
garity. Cultural centers that are unable to support a good bookstore. Civic centers that are
avoided by everyone but bums, who have fewer
choices of loitering place than others.*

*Commercial centers that are lackluster imita-
tions of standardized suburban chain-store shopping. Promenades that go from no place to
nowhere and have no promenaders. Expressways
that eviscerate great cities. This is not the rebuilding of cities. This is the sacking of cities."*

Jane Jacobs
The Death and Life of Great American Cities,
Randon House, Inc., New York, 1961, p.5.

The idea of *urban redevelopment* was soon to follow that of zoning. It was devised as a therapeutic aid to ailing cities. As first put into practice, however, the process was irrational and brutal. Instead of serving as a healing and restorative agent it was applied in areawide cauterization and sterilization. It was a city destroyer of blitzkrieg propor-tions. Whole neighborhoods and communities designated as "substandard" were condemned, the properties expropri-ated, the structures razed and bulldozed out of existence. In the name of "slum clearance" the landowners and ten-ants were driven out, with minimal compensation, to fend for themselves. Those with small businesses were left with no means of livelihood. In time, often years in duration, the vacated lands would be improved with public funds and sold or leased to developers. The rich became richer, the poor became desolate, and dreaded *redevelopment* became a dirty word. It was a terrible start for a well-meant proce-dure of such promise.

Urban redevelopment as an element of comprehensive regional planning has since become more civilized. When coupled with renewal and self-help programs, when selec-tively applied and phased in turn-over increments—and when administered by a socially sensitive and nonpolitical governing body—it is often the welcome key to the regen-eration of an entire declining district.

Planning, too, as a discipline, is slowly but surely gain-ing respect and public acceptance as a necessary and posi-tive force. It has taken a while. It would have taken much longer were it not for a vocal spokeswoman, Jane Jacobs, who in the early 1960s sounded a clarion call of protest against city planning as it was then being mispracticed. Her powerful and perceptive *Life and Death of Great American Cities* turned a spotlight on the havoc being wrought. Further, she made a convincing case for the posi-tive values of the turbulent in-city street life of low- to moderate-income families left to their own creative devices and given but minimal help and support. She had little use for urban green or even too much urban clean—and cer-tainly none for the gleaming towers raised at the cost of widespread people-displacement. Although short on solu-tions to the city dilemma, she was dead set against whole-sale clearance and planned monotony. She and others to follow—Von Eckhard, Whyte, Clay, Spirn, Hiss, Kay, and Gore among them—have introduced the human element into the planning equation, an infusion that is bound to persist.

With the ensuing era of environmental concern it was only to be expected that ecological factors were soon to be introduced. Their consideration is now a mandatory prereq-uisite of comprehensive planning.

And so the wheel turns—from the bucolic city to the classic, the monumental, the orderly, the mechanistic, the materialistic, the political, the social, the humane, and the ecologically sound. What next? Where do we go from here? Where do we find the examples? Abroad, we have much to learn from such transition cities as Seoul, Chambery, Stuttgart, Vienna, Paris, Lucerne, and Stockholm. All, and many like them, have managed to maintain their traditional vitality and appeal while moving enthusiastically into the age of advanced technology and environmental responsibility. Here at home are cities, too, in which there are striking examples of both misguided and excellent urban readjustment. We have only to look about us with a clear and critical eye to discern the failures and the successes. Failures, so that we can analyze their cause and avoid their recurrence. Successes, that we may understand the conditions that brought them about and learn to emulate and extend them. Such trial-and-error experimentation is a hallmark of our U.S. pioneering culture. Our bent for experimentation is both a weakness and a strength—a weakness if we blunder along haphazardly, a strength if we continue to build upon the gains we have made, and the lessons to be learned.

Prescribed procedures

How is it done—this planning or replanning at such a large scale and with so many things to consider? Each city or region must find its own way and formulate its own program. But whatever the approach, the following summary guidelines might well be brought to bear:

- *Know what is there.*

  Too much so-called city planning is done over existing zoning maps, without the foggiest notion of what they represent—without a first-hand knowledge of how the neighborhoods work or how they feel. There can be no substitute for on-site reconnaissance to the point of empathic understanding.

- *Know the working parts*

  To improve each city component—the center city, inner city, outer city, and suburbs—it is necessary to understand each component's nature and function. Only then can each be better formed and all brought together in more synergistic relationships.

- *Strengthen the neighborhoods.*

  Each neighborhood under consideration is to be studied to discover its positive and negative features. What would it take to improve it—to make it more workable and complete? One effective approach to any improve-

As we look to a strategy for urban revitalization the planning process would teach us that to find solutions we must first define the problems. Then, with needed data at hand, the alternative possibilities can be explored and refined into action recommendations.

———————————

ment program is to eliminate or ameliorate the negative features and accentuate the positive.

▪ *Build the people into the plan.*

Strive to devise for all existing and future city dwellers and workers the best possible living experiences. Gratifying conditions are seldom imposed. They evolve out of discussions and meetings with those involved, with planners responding to the residents' needs and aspirations and incorporating the thinking of the community leadership.

▪ *Preserve the best of existing features.*

These might include a historic building, an old stone bridge, a narrow alley or passageway, a stream, pond, or venerable oak. Such features might include a row of main street gas lamps, a tavern, a civil war monument, or memorial horse trough in the park. It may be only the name of a lane or street. If a feature speaks of time and place in a favorable way, try to build it into the plans.

▪ *Accommodate the automobile.*

In some form or other the personally operated motor vehicle will long be with us, presumably no longer a despoiler of the city and countryside, but as a welcome attribute. We are learning that innovative trafficway systems can be planned for the freer and safer movement of vehicles while at the same time creating traffic-free urban activity centers of many various types. New land use and trafficway diagrams will establish the outlines of more agreeable future cities.

▪ *Use transit to link metro centers.*

Multimode rapid transit will assume a key role in the intracity movement of passengers when, at last, it is preplanned together with compact communities, for center-to-center linkage.

▪ *Combine transport, transmission, and energy corridors.*

Such broad, multipurpose swaths can be planned to avoid sensitive land/water areas and communities and to serve new and receptive manufacturing, fabrication, and warehousing districts. By the phased consolidation of scattered plants and routes a less disruptive and far more efficient regional production complex can be brought into being.

▪ *Preclude all forms of pollution.*

Pollution—of the air, soil, or water or by roadside clutter

Our communities, cities, and countryside must be made more, not less, accessible to the automobile. This involves improved trafficway alignment, new land-use patterns, and the elimination of pedestrian–motor car conflicts.

or building scatteration—is to be prevented and eliminated. This ties closely with an enlightened metropolitan policy of land, water, resource, and growth management.

- ### *Plan integrated systems.*

A city without systematic organization resembles the floor of a disarrayed machine shop with parts scattered everywhere. Only when the disparate parts are fitted together into working entities can each component operate. Only when all are competently assembled and in balance can the total machine function. A city is a highly complex mechanism in need of constant fitting, refitting, and adjustment.

- ### *Create an open space framework.*

It is around such a system of interconnecting roadways, institutional grounds, parks, forest preserves, agricultural lands, and waterways that the better cities take form. Each contributing space is to be planned to best fulfill its purpose. All together are combined to provide paths of movement, areas for recreation, means of storm water drainage, climate moderation, and a salubrious landscape setting.

- ### *Apply the P-C-D approach.*

This lets people use and enjoy the best features of their land/water surroundings without doing lasting harm. Simply stated, it means that in considering the use of any property the best features are outlined on the ground and *preserved* intact. A protective *conservation* band of limited use is then described around them. Finally, on the least sensitive upland reaches, potential *development* areas are defined within the preservation-conservation lobes.

- ### *Plan the city and region together.*

A city in isolation is like a gem without a setting—or an engine without its mounting and related automotive parts. It is the *interaction* between city and metropolitan region that generates trade and prosperity for both. Only by sustained metro planning can a coactive operational fit be achieved and sustained.

- ### *Provide for flexibility.*

A rigidly detailed and officially adopted master plan for a community, city, or region can stultify progressive enterprise and design creativity. Better that the conceptual long-range plan delineate the general land-use areas, fix population and floor area caps, diagram the circulation network, and establish environmentally sound perfor-

Reservoirs and retention ponds within and outside the city are too often fenced and "off-limits" to the public. Opened up as attractive features of the open space system, they can provide welcome passive recreation and refreshment for the surrounding community.

A distinguished psychiatrist, Dr. Herbert E. Thomas, has noted that, "A person's sense of well-being is proportionate to the flow of energy focalized and directed to constructive ends, rather than being dissipated."

So, too, is it with a city.

In *A Distant Mirror,* author Barbara Tuchman makes a cogent comparison between the 14th and 20th centuries, as follows:

"...the 14th century, like the 20th, commanded a technology more sophisticated than the mental or moral capacity that guided its use."

Experience has shown that downtown renewal can best be initiated by a nonpolitical civic action council and best implemented by an inter-agency office under the mayor's wing.

---

mance standards. Better to set only the conceptual diagram and controls, while encouraging creative individual expression.

. . .

The guidelines listed are far from complete. No matter, for it might seem that they are but wishful thinking. Certain it is that few modern U.S. cities have been planned with even these basics in mind. Most contemporary urban planning appears to follow no guidelines at all—save for the compulsion to clear and rebuild, with ever wider streets, ever more in-city parking, and ever more monumentality.

The sad fact of the matter is that city planning as commonly practiced today falls far short of its potential. There are glowing exceptions. But, although planning technology is advancing by leaps and bounds, the work of many planning departments today is uninspired and uninspiring. Why? Because too often city planning, renewal, and redevelopment have become the tools of entrenched politicians who use them to their political advantage and to the gain of supporters and friends. Again, the department is often directed and staffed by technicians trained in abstract planning "methodology"—with no sense whatsoever of mission, of how the city functions, or of what the people need. Moreover, the planning by one agency is frequently conducted without regard for, and often in conflict with, that of related agencies or jurisdictions. Contention and chaos ensue.

The new regionalism

It has become evident that many of the more pressing urban problems can be tackled and solved only on a *regional* basis—for streams and rivers flow, traffic rambles, and utility systems span many town and city borders. Yet local governmental officials are understandably reluctant to relinquish control over all that happens within their bailiwicks. By what means, then, can regional issues be studied and resolved?

In the U.S. a promising phenomenon has been the initiation of civic action groups working at a regional level. Usually nonpolitical, they are comprised of concerned citizen leaders from all walks of life. They are privately funded and nonprofit, with a director and staff to define priorities, engage consultants, and prepare recommendations. They exert their prestigious influence where it counts. Such civic action groups have within the past several decades had remarkable success in effectuating the continuing renewal or renaissance of many metropolitan areas.

Again, the regional problems of other areas have been approached by a coalition of local governments working through appointed representatives. With or without a professional staff they are publicly funded and report their findings and recommendations to their local councils. Such regional study groups have the advantage of more direct relationship with the political decision makers—but also the disadvantage of divisive political points of view.

Perhaps the most promising of regional planning mechanisms is an evolving form of metropolitan or Metro government. There are many successful examples. In the best, elected officials are granted broad powers by charter, but initially assume limited assignments. These specifically delegated responsibilities cover only those areas of study and administration which are clearly of *regional* scope. Such may be comprehensive land planning, transportation, utility systems, waste disposal, and resource management. Other issues of more local concern—such as community police and fire protection, schools, and recreation—are left to the local councils. The savings effected by the elimination of overlapping staff work and positions is clearly evident, as are the benefits of a broader, more professional approach to regional problems and possibilities.

Prospectus

Looking ahead, what features will be the common denominators of tomorrow's more livable cities? It is proposed that most will be distinguished by a long range *preservation, conservation,* and *development* plan—with provisions for topographic restoration and reforestation. Their plan diagram and three-dimensional structure will express a more logical disposition of use areas. The cities' plans will intensify the activity centers, ring them with the required supply and service facilities, and provide for the creation of new or redeveloped residential neighborhoods, which will be formed around an interconnected open space system of in-city recreation lands, forest, and wildlife preserves. These cities will be blessed with direct rapid transit and parkway interconnection of the urba-centers and linkage with their suburban-rural environs and the wilderness beyond.

The cities will respond to the urging of the land; preserve the integrity of the surrounding natural and constructed landscape; and conserve the ecological, agricultural, scenic, and historic superlatives. They will impose no significant disruption to such natural systems as rivers, streams, and drainageways, fresh water aquifers, plant and animal communities, or to the vital food chain.

City plans will so address each topographical area and

Ecology: A subdivision of the science of biology that deals with the dependency and interaction between the Earth's living and nonliving systems.

———————————

The art of living is neither taught nor encouraged in this country.

All great ages of art spring from a coherent view of the world, a shared language.

GRAY BRECHIN

———————————

In the field of earth science, the present decade will long be remembered as the time in which environmental protection became more than the interest of a few and emerged as a popular movement.

———————————

No perfect city has yet been built. It is extremely doubtful that any will ever attain perfection. The best that can be expected at a given time is an orderly evolution toward the then-current ideal. This being so, it is the planning process that counts.

———————————

Even though a measure of environmental consciousness has today become almost universal, political decisions are still being made at the expense of the environment.

MICHAEL HOUGH

feature as to discover and reveal its highest qualities.

Given such hopeful possibilities, how do we get from here to there? How do we make the transition?

Action guidelines

Some of our leaders—governmental, civic, and professional—are working hard and well at the task. Others are moving to join the crusade toward improving our living environment. Why now, at last? Perhaps because we Americans are spurred by crisis, and a crisis is clearly at hand; conditions have in fact reached the point where there's no other rational way to turn. Perhaps because public dissatisfaction with the status quo has become so widespread and vocal. Or perhaps because proven means of remedy are in place and available. And because we are seeing across the land more and more successful examples of what can be and is being done.

Wise political leaders have learned to read and respond to the public will. They are sensing that for the first time in history the U.S. people are coming to put the quality of living for their families and progeny on a par with, and often ahead of, economic gain. This past decade in America, as elsewhere in the world, has come to be recognized as the era of awakened environmental concern.

How is concern to be transposed into positive action? How, in short, are our cities to be rebuilt and reshaped in more workable and agreeable form? How is our fragmented regional and rural landscape to be protected and reestablished as a more productive and wholesome base? Not in one great cataclysmic sweep—but, rather, in many ways, by many participants, and in many progressive phases.

Governmental

In the federal government it will take a change in priorities. There are presently a plethora of uncoordinated activities but no clear statement of policy and no clear direction. The EPA (Environmental Protection Agency) helps and has made a telling contribution. As an agency it has served somewhat like the Inspector General of the armed forces, empowered to cut across departmental lines and act at the highest levels.

Needed at the presidential and Congressional level is a new and resounding declaration of commitment—a statement of purpose and policy to transcend existing directives and serve as a mandatory all-governmental guideline. Such a manifesto could well be formulated by a nonpartisan task force comprised of our nation's top thinkers and experts. As an ongoing source of input each succeeding president would do well to follow the lead of others in appointing a panel of distinguished citizen advisors for counsel on such issues as urban revitalization, growth management, and land and resource planning. Congress will and must have its own councils, commissions, and committees—and its United Nations cadre—all working within the scope of the national policy goal. With a newly appointed cabinet member chief, such efforts could lead to focused action—and to more effective participation in environmental programs on a global scale.

State action

State action plans and approaches vary. Among the most effective have been those of Virginia, California, Oregon, Connecticut, and Florida. Early on, Connecticut produced a pathfinder plan for the development and conservation of the state's human and other resources. California, too, places emphasis on the environment and its cities. The Virginia General Assembly, concerned with the state's tilt toward urban sprawl and disruption, formed a blue chip study commission to confer with regional leaders and citizens and to build on their ideas. It came up with "The Virginia Plan" which condensed into one concise document a summary of recommendations, 2- and 5-year budgets, and an outline draft of enabling legislation. It is still considered the chart by which the course of state action is guided.

Florida, with unprecedented problems of rapid urbanization, developed its own mechanism for dealing with them. With the help of an environmental aide and staff, the governor and cabinet secretaries met periodically as a group to discuss and act upon the more pressing state planning issues.

Each state must find its own way of producing an action plan best suited to its needs. What matters is that there *be* a plan and that it be implemented.

It no longer seems germane to point out that every state, and every jurisdiction within it, has need of a planning commission and staff. It seems obvious, too, that responsible officials should know and work to support those planning recommendations designed for the public good. At the conclusion of their term in office and when bidding for reelection let our officials be judged on the basis of *performance* rather than campaign promises.

> *By their* deeds
> *shall ye know them.*

Civic action

It can be stated categorically that the most effective thrust provided to date in the crusade for urban and environmental improvement has been that of the various foundations,

Perhaps we are ready at last for a national land use plan and policy. A broadly defined P.C.D. plan, if you will, by which those areas of public and private ownership which are of exceptional ecologic, scenic, or historic value are preserved and put off-limits to disruptive development. By which they are protected by buffering lands and waters of limited uses that conserve their essential landscape character. The remaining lands would then be designated for phased development consistent with their highest and best use potential, and in accordance with the long range goals and controls of the governing jurisdictions.

councils, clubs, committees, and other civic action groups. They have pointed and led the way. Amongst them, as examples, are such stellar performers as Cry California, Florida Defenders of the Environment, the Allegheny Conference on Community Development, the Sierra Club, and the American Conservation Foundation.

Smaller citizen groups have been formed for such worthy causes as block by block clean-up programs, housing rehabilitation, roadside care, saving a stream, and city street tree planting.

Individuals

Individuals, on their own or banded together, have been a telling force in bringing about a change for the better in their communities and urban surroundings. Some seemingly minor acts—such as the sorting of cans and bottles for recycling, the picking up of roadside trash, or the planting of a memorial tree in a schoolyard—make a difference. Their effects are accumulative. They set an example. They generate momentum.

Again, it helps just to share one's thoughts with family members and friends—to write letters to the Editor, to Council members, or the Mayor. To attend and express one's views in public meetings. To petition. To stand up and be counted...

With the possible exception
of the vote, there is no
force on Earth as powerful
as a good idea.

Breakthrough

The field of urban and regional planning has witnessed in the past few years the introduction of many innovative approaches, tools, and techniques that have transformed the profession. No longer essentially an art form such as that which promoted the "city beautiful" concept of the Columbian Exposition days, planning has now become a broadly based science. Not that it has turned its back on design—for the comprehensive planning of cities and the countryside is *design* in its fullest, truest sense. Planning is the bringing together of diverse and multitudinous elements into harmonious relationships. Planning is an art and science that embraces and applies the principles of architecture, engineering, and landscape architecture. Planning brings into play the contributions of such disciplines as law, sociology, economics, and political science. Planning deals with health, safety, sustenance, employment, finance, education, and recreation. There is hardly a single aspect of contemporary life and living (or life in generations to follow) that is not a consideration in the design of a modern metropolis.

Techniques

In the field of land-use planning alone we have now accepted and apply such relatively new techniques as those of comprehensive planning and resource management. We are learning the benefits of land leasing, monitoring, mitigation and the transfer of development rights. Defined "urban improvement districts" and contour zoning are helping to preclude the havoc of urban sprawl. There is movement, too, toward coordinated transportation and long-range regional planning. At a larger scale there is at last the recognition of the logic and need for intensive river basin and coastal zone planning. A number of such study reports and action plans are exemplary.

The requirement of an environmental impact statement for all federally aided projects helps to ensure that negative impacts will be ameliorated or eliminated; that positive values will be optimized; and that the proposed project, on balance, will impose no significant long-term damage to the affected community. This idea has been expanded by some municipalities to provide a set of performance standards which preapply to *all* development proposals.

A further test of project suitability is that by which each development proposal is weighed against a current and flexible conceptual plan for the region. Passing muster, it is then presented for discussion in open public meetings before approval or rejection by the elected decision makers.

Computer application

Most new approaches to urban design rely heavily on the use of computers to reduce vast quantities of information to manageable form. They are invaluable in producing coordinated base mapping upon which a wide range of variables can be readily displayed and analyzed.

Aside from its functions of mapping, data storage and comparative analysis, computer technology is making many new contributions to creative urban design. The three-dimensional modeling, visual simulation, and the related image editing and projection enable the designer to present ideas in a more facile and realistic way. Digital sketching—or freehand sketching over a computer-justified base—gives the creator the advantage of artistic expression within the context of the actual project environs. Thus the proposed improvements are made more understandable and community-specific.

Although computer technology has wide application in city and regional planning, it is to be recognized as an aid

The *city beautiful* movement was an attempt to subjugate the functions of city to a preconceived aesthetic ideal.

The *beautiful city* concept is that of a metropolitan region in which all the elements are in balance and working together in harmony.

Cities have failed because we have had no way to see or study them as a functional entity. We are now on the verge of a breakthrough.

With the failure of traditional zoning to prevent undesirable development, preclude sprawl, or protect the nation's farmlands and scenic/historic resources, a new means of land-use control was bound to emerge. It has come in the form of performance standards.

Under the provisions of a typical performance code, a development plan is reviewed and approved on the basis of its meeting positive criteria developed by each local government to meet its long range goals. It is based more on incentives than restrictions, more on protection than consumption, more on innovation than conformity, and more on community values than on vested rights.

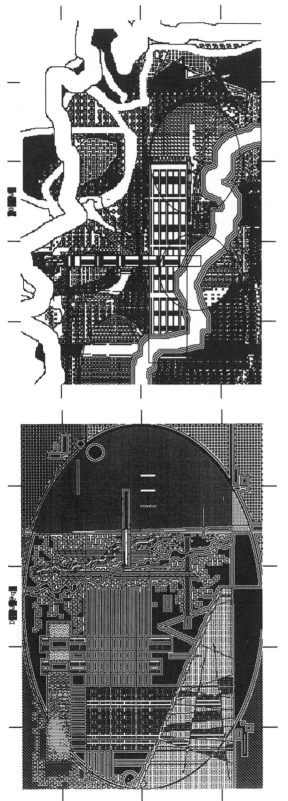

Computer Generated Images by Architect Kevin V. O'Brien

Hypothetical urban patterns suggesting the integration of structural forms in response to natural "givens."

to, *but not a substitute for,* the experienced planner and intuitive designer. The computer has no way of knowing, for instance, that a line being drawn represents a road or that roads have variable dimensions, sections, materials, costs, and scenic qualities. The computer can array sheet after sheet of mapping—each showing by area or parcel differing characteristics—without the ability to assess the information displayed. It can plot the extent of a 20-year flood, with no thought of preventive measures or consequences.

The computer can help to display concepts graphically, but it cannot conceptualize. It sometimes comes close, as when applied in the McHargian method of route selection by means of a series of graphic overlays to suggest alignments and areas affording the least physical, social, or economic restriction. In all such instances, however, there is need for supplementary expert opinion and discussion of such unquantifiable factors as those of aesthetics, historical significance, regional preferences, and such value judgments as the long-range public good.

Of interest in the search for more articulate form is experimental work exploring the symbiotic relationships between the built and the natural in the urban landscape. Prototype studies have produced a series of computer-generated overlay images of a city on a hypothetical site. The evolving patterns simulate structured development and open space land in well-ordered systems.

In the graphic models opposite are forms suggesting streams, rivers, and open water. Other unbuilt-upon areas might well represent wetlands, hills, mountain uprisings, forest preserves, or parkland. Within this natural framework are portrayed geometric structural patterns that suggest the lines and outlines of advanced types of trafficways, neighborhoods, superblocks, or urban activity centers.

In these early portrayals the "plans" are two-dimensional and fictitious. In progressive studies—with comparable criteria programmed to introduce topographical and climatological factors, and expanded to include solid planning data—the possibilities are intriguing.

Systems dynamics

The planning or replanning of a city is as complex a problem as could possibly be imagined. It involves not only the wise use of the land and resource base, it directly affects in many ways the well-being of all people within its sphere of influence. City planning deals with such diverse personal issues as health, housing, employment, and recreation, with schools, shopping, and safety on the streets. City planning involves a broad spectrum of social, political, and economic concerns, including the provision of cultural facilities and the production of sufficient revenue to run the city and fund improvement programs. Plans must be time, place, and climate-responsive. They must be ecologically and environmentally sound. They must be sensitive to the topography.

How can one get one's arms around such complexities, which keep changing day by day? Many enthusiastic urbanists have come to believe that a new breakthrough has come with the advent of *systems dynamics.* In layperson's terms, systems dynamics is a process for conceptualizing, representing, and testing assumptions about the structure and interrelationships in a complex system. It is a research or decision-making process by which alternative approaches to overall design or to a problem are considered in order to arrive at a system that provides optimum performance with respect to established criteria.

Regardless of the subject area, all system dynamics studies share the need for a holistic understanding of how the discrete parts of the system interact. Only when the assumptions about these interrelationships—usually represented in the form of a computer model—have been validated and the model intuitively refined can it be used as an effective aid in policy-making decisions. But first there is need for the conceptual model—the ideal toward which the planner/designer is striving. As the study progresses, the "ideal" may be modified or refined, but it is always the best-case performance against which the evolving resultant is tested and toward which the study moves.

In the systems dynamics process the computer is but an analytical tool. Its function is to test, quantify, and represent the consequences of proposed alterations to the systems components or their relationships. The changes proposed, or alterations, are in the form of new input by intuitive planner/designers seeking to improve performance in the total system. As the study progresses, the conceptual models may be modified or refined to reflect the "feed-back" findings. But first there is need for the *concept*—of what the subject entity is and what it might better be.

How, for example, could one improve, say, a dynamo, without first knowing how a dynamo works? How could one plan a better community without understanding the parts of a working community and their interrelationship, how each part might be better fashioned, and the whole might be better conceived? How could one get a true sense of the urban metropolis—of its working parts and their interaction—without such a tool as systems dynamics? If with its help our scientist-technologist-designers can put an astronaut on the moon and launch interspatial satellites, there is yet hope—a bright future—for our cities.

To understand that an urban metropolis functions as a *system* is to recognize that the relationship of the various

The last century has been devoted to exploring the frontier of physical science. The next century will be the time for exploring the dynamic nature of social systems and using the resulting knowledge for improving institutions and economies.

Jay W. Forrester
"Models and the Real World"
Systems Dynamics Review,
vol.3, no. 2, Summer 1987

Systems analysis is the determination of causative relationships.

Systems dynamics in the urban planning context is the determination of the effects of bringing those relationships together, in toto, at any given point in time.

A static picture of a city at any given moment is merely the by-product of a complex, dynamic system in a state of perpetual evolution. The success of an urban area is a function of understanding and leveraging the dynamics that underlie its structure.

GREG J. SCHOLL

components has a bearing the upon performance of not only each component but upon also the city as a whole. This is a premise hard to refute. If, for example, the city's commercial core were to be relocated to or beyond the perimeter, all other elements of the city and its surrounding region would be affected and would tend to adjust.

It can be seen then that a city not only is systematic (by definition), it is dynamic. Further, the degree of operational efficiency is a function of improving the parts and optimizing relationships. The better the relationship of its various parts, the better a city works.

As noted, in order to commence the systems dynamics process in any study—as for the restructuring of a city and its surrounding region—there is need for an initial concept, or first rough draft, of a preconceived "ideal." It may be in the form of a descriptive text, a mathematical formula, or a visual representation such as a sketch or diagram. It is a *conceptual plan,* or conceptual model.

Appraisal

Today as we head into the twenty-first century we share with Sir Ebenezer Howard of England his assessment of the urban scene a hundred years ago:

> *...the overgrown and over-congested metropolis, penalized in its health by its slums and in its efficiency by ill-sorted and misplaced industries; given to extravagant wastes in time, energy, and money merely to transport its goods and people over distances that had been expanded to no good human purpose; desolate in its lack of social facilities, though possessing, in its central institutions, the chief organized forms of social life.*
>
> *Ebenezer Howard, London, 1898**

Today we have the same problems, and more. Then, settlements were relatively stable within their traditional bounds. Urban sprawl, the U.S. plague, had not yet become infectious. Pollution was largely confined to industrial cities. The locust swarms of automobiles had yet to invade the cities or the rural countryside.

Gains

Are we losing ground? In appraising our metropolitan areas today it might seem that the past hundred years have seen little progress. That, however, is not the case, for there have been remarkable gains. To prove the point we need only

---

*As paraphrased by Lewis Mumford, in *An American Introduction to Sir Ebenezer Howard's "Garden Cities of Tomorrow." Pencil Points Magazine,* 1945.

mention such urban highwater marks as Radburn, Reston, Columbia, the Chicago lakefront and forest preserves, the park city of Milwaukee, the San Antonio Riverwalk, the Embarcadero of San Francisco, or Washington's L'Enfant Plaza.

Or how about such innovative features as parkways, freeways, national parks, river basin studies, air rights, rapid transit, the monorail, or urban renewal?

Again, a few key words or phrases will suffice to suggest a significant breakthrough in urban land planning proficiency—such terms as *zoning, eminent domain, mitigation, transfer of development rights, environmental impact statement, growth management,* and *comprehensive planning.* Or even new public attitudes toward such issues as pollution control, conservation, and ecology.

In truth we have come a long way in reshaping and resuscitating our cities. There are such bright spots as in-city parklets, conference centers, new stadia, and waterfront improvements. There are new public squares, plazas, and pedestrian shopping streets. There are sculpture courts, fountains, benches, murals, and planters. The centers of many cities have been transformed and interlaced with inviting walkways. Minitrams, scooting shuttleboats, and other new forms of transit provide pleasant interconnection. In many neighborhoods, repaved and relighted streets—freed of overhead wires and their blizzard of signs—now sparkle under a canopy of foliage. Historic districts are being restored and brought to life as community centers and tourist attractions. Canals and streams are being rediscovered as frontage for shops, dining courts, and new apartments.

The present status

These are welcome developments. As multiplied and expanded they presage what the future can hold. They are, however, too few and too far between. Even in those fortunate cities achieving a "renaissance" they are still but refreshing oases in an encompassing desert of obsolescence. Without exception, U.S. cities are in deep and deepening trouble—the troubles of abandoned homes, boarded storefronts, or pollution, poverty, the homeless, raging crime, and staggering debt. Why? How could such things happen?

They happen largely because in the war to save our foundering cities we are engaged mainly in half-hearted skirmishes and rear-guard actions. Our leaders seem more intent on retrenchment than launching an all-out attack. It is not enough. There is need in each city for a concerted long-term battle plan—for bugles, a flag, and a rallying call. There is need to regenerate a sense of civic pride and the will to create a model urban metropolis.

America is a beautiful country of ugly cities.

The battle for downtown has been waged against the symptoms not the sources of its troubles...

James ROUSE

Howard's ideas (those of Sir Ebenezer Howard as proposed in "Garden Cities Of Tomorrow") have laid the foundation for a new cycle in urban civilization: one in which the means of life will be subservient to the purpose of living, and in which the pattern needed for biological survival and economic efficiency will likewise lead to social and personal fulfillment.

LEWIS MUMFORD

———————————

Diagrams are made to be modified.

———————————

When reason has finally come to prevail, city centers and the suburban-rural hinterlands will be planned, and largely governed, as a metropolitan unit.

———————————

Model

A more workable, more livable, urban metropolis....Where does one find the model? It would be hard to surpass one already at hand. This is the prophetic garden city concept of Sir Ebenezer Howard, a visionary whose time may well have come. His was an idea so intriguing and promising that when introduced to a public thoroughly disillusioned with cities and city living it was greeted with unbridled enthusiasm. Although too advanced for full implementation in its time, it has proved to be an idea of such appeal that it can be said to have had a positive influence on all subsequent urban planning.

Graphically, the Howard concept is expressed in several disarmingly simple diagrams. Being diagrams they are subject to change and varying interpretations. Are the garden city diagrams still valid? Not in detail. Not without modification. But many distinguished urbanists agree that their central idea may hold the key to vastly superior city building.

The figures which follow are reproductions of the original Garden City diagrams, a segment of a hypothetical satellite community of some 5,000 acres with a projected population of some 32,000 persons. As can be seen, it is essentially a residential complex, but one in which schools, shopping, cultural amenities, and workplaces are provided and in balance.

"Garden cities of tomorrow"
These four conceptual diagrams are from a treatise by Sir Ebenezer Howard, first published in London in 1898.
1. *The Three Magnets.* This diagram from *Garden Cities of Tomorrow* expresses the dynamic tensions of the urban metropolis, which have changed little in 100 years. It would be hard to convey the idea more clearly.

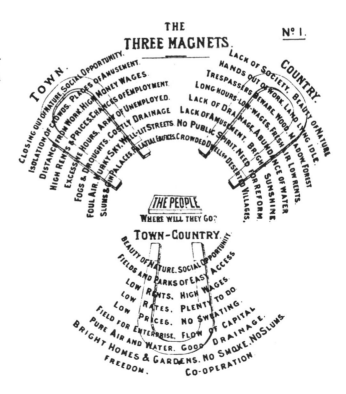

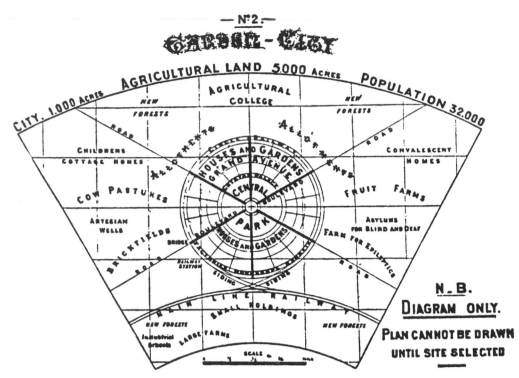

The garden city

2. Here an intensive urban activity center has been organized as a near-complete and nearly self-sustaining community complex. Essentially it groups the normally dispersed components into a more workable plan arrangement. It provides both hub to hub and peripheral access to other city centers and the central business district. It features a central community park and open space frame. It includes an extensive agricultural preserve within which only compatible uses may be located. It recognizes the need for fixed boundaries and a stable population, to keep all systems in balance.

Garden city center

3. The third diagram is an enlargement of the developed center. It features a focal park and garden plaza around which major buildings are grouped. The main circumferential avenue with its widened open space corridor serves to separate and buffer the inner band from the outer band—which extends to the settlement limits. The widely spaced trafficways define extensive superblocks as locations for unified residential, cultural, commercial, and manufacturing neighborhoods.

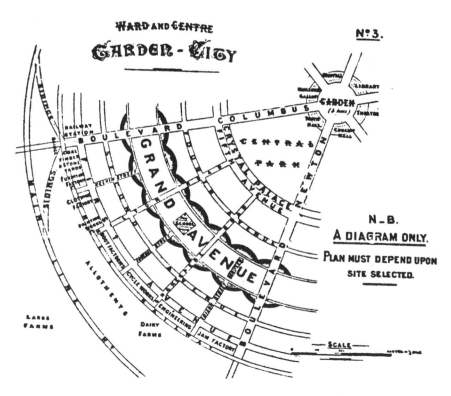

Satellite centers

4. A fourth diagram (No. 5 in Howard's work) shows the disposition of various types of activity centers as satellites of the center city core. The sun and satellite planets of such a metropolitan constellation are interconnected by rapid transit and free flowing trafficways. Each is positioned within a protected preserve of agricultural, park, and conservation lands interspersed with planned residential neighborhoods. This simple land-use concept has influenced most urban planning from the time of its inception. It is still an idea to be realized.

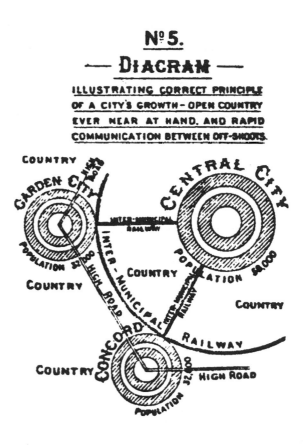

The original drawings and text presented a convincing case for garden cities of a new high order. Not a new type of suburban retreat, as some have supposed. Not only cleaner, greener, more efficient communities themselves. Essentially what Howard proposed was *the planned integration of the cities with their supporting regions.*

Would not this result in a further dispersion of urban elements—further sprawl—a further invasion of the rural landscape? Quite the contrary. For Howard's premise—and the premise of this centennial book—is the urgent need for consolidating the scattered elements into more self-contained and workable activity centers. These are to be regrouped and interconnected, all within a restored farmland and nature surrounding. Further, fundamental to a harmonious integration, the whole of the metropolitan region is to be planned, and to a large extent administered, as a unified entity.

Garden city 21

Building upon the garden city model of Sir Ebenezer Howard—and upon the plans of countless communities and cities in which they have since been applied—an updated version is offered. (See color section.) It bears the title *Garden City 21,* for it could presage a new order of cities in the twenty-first century.

As a concept the Garden City 21 model is consistent with both the thinking of Sir Ebenezer and the most advanced urban planning technology of our times. Various aspects of the garden city proposals have been tried with consistent success. The central idea, however—that of a coordinated regional planning approach—has yet to be implemented. It has been widely accepted and acclaimed in theory, but until recently we have had neither the necessary legal powers, technical capacity, nor the dedicated resolve to pull it off in a meaningful way. We now have the capability and the urgent need. At long last it may well be the time to put it all together.

What good is a diagram? It could never be built—nor is it so intended. It does, however, show the idealized relationships of the major plan components—the center city, the jurisdictional city, urban activity centers (urba-centers) and the embracing suburbs, together with the principal routes of highway and transit interconnection.

A comparative analysis

This comparative diagram shows a quadrant of the original Ebenezer Howard *Garden City* plan (circa 1900) superimposed on an updated garden city model proposed for the twenty-first century. There are notable similarities.

Garden city 21
(a comparative analysis)
Here a section of the original Sir Ebenezer Howard conceptual diagram has been superimposed on its contemporary counterpart.

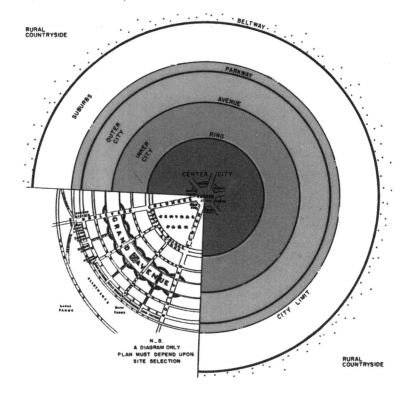

1. In both, the *center city* is the principal business, government, and cultural center for the metropolitan region. It includes government offices, a "galleria," library, hospital, concert hall, theaters, and museum—all surrounding a pedestrian garden plaza.
2. The *inner city* provides worker and management housing and services in support of the center city, from which it is separated by a (depressed or elevated) traffic distributor ring. Its outer limit is bounded and contained by a broad, parklike band embracing "The Avenue," schools, and recreation.
3. In both diagrams the *outer city* provides ample space for compact urban activity centers of various types together with related and integrated residential neighborhoods, shopping, and services.
4. The *suburban areas,* beyond the city limits, are allotted to larger homes, estates, market gardens, and orchards.
5. The *rural countryside* is in turn designated for protected farmland, forest, and conservation areas. New education, recreation, or other activity centers are welcome where needed and compatible.

Further common denominators are the well-defined limits to scatterization and the provision of broad zones within which a wide variety of mixed uses are permitted. The use of superblocks eliminates much of the friction and waste of the conventional gridblock street system. In total, both diagrams provide a planned environment within which a far more agreeable and rewarding mode of city living might be experienced. The differences between the two proposals, which span 100 years, are mainly those resulting from advances in means of travel and transportation and from the population explosion.

Transition

The evolving conceptual plan is brought on phase by phase through renewal, redevelopment, restoration, and new construction. During the unending years of transition and advancement, new needs and conditions are bound to arise and require adjustment and updating of the conceptual plan.

Howard's plan for the "Garden City of Tomorrow" had the power of simplicity. It was easy to understand, and when understood had great energizing thrust. It made eminent sense when first proposed. With minor modifications it makes even more sense today.

What makes the idea so timely? First, the urgent need for a positive guide to give promise and clear direction. Second, it is a holistic approach that recognizes and addresses the full range of urban problems and possibilities. It has the flexibility to move with the times. It provides for a phased and orderly evolution. It is entirely feasible. The garden city idea is supported by the most creative thinking of our scientists and practitioners. It embodies an awakened social consciousness, political know-how, and sound economic policy. The garden city is the answer to the conservationists' dream and the ecologists' prayer.

Various aspects of the garden city concept have been tested and applied with modifications in the more successful new communities throughout the modern world. Only within the past several decades, however, have we had the legal and technical capability to implement the central idea—that of *planned and phased metropolitan integration.* To "gather up" the similar and synergistic uses now dispersed throughout megalopolis; to regroup them into well-planned satellite communities of various types around the center cities. To restore, in time, the lands between as enveloping farmland, field, and forest. This is the hope of our ailing cities if they are to be restructured as the crowning achievement of the twenty-first century. In such bold measures are to be found our one best chance. None better, or as promising, has yet been put forward.

. . .

In sum it is proposed that the notable cities of tomorrow will continue to be those which to their users seem expressive, functional, convenient, rational, and complete. They will be more livable.

In our ignorance and hunger and rapacity, in our dream of a better material life, we laid waste the continent and diminished ourselves before any substantial number of us began to feel, little and late, an affinity with it, a dependence on it, an obligation toward it as the indispensable source of everything we hope for.

WALLACE STEGNER
AMERICAN PLACES,
WALLACE AND PAGE STEGNER
UNIVERSITY OF IDAHO PRESS,
MOSCOW, IDAHO, 1983.

" 'Virtue,' said Marcus Aurelius, 'What is it, only a living and enthusiastic sympathy with Nature?' Perhaps indeed the efforts of the true poets, founders, religions, literatures, all ages have been, and ever will be, our time and times to come, essentially the same —- to bring people back from their persistent strayings . . ."

WALT WHITMAN
THE PORTABLE WALT WHITMAN,
EDITED BY MARK VAN DORN
PENGUIN BOOKS, NEW YORK, 1977, P. 640

Beauty

But what of that evasive quality, beauty? Is it not also basic to urban design? Yes, and the well-designed city must, above all, be beautiful. But, contrary to common understanding, beauty is seldom consciously contrived. Nor is it to be construed as mere decoration or effusive ornamentation. *Beauty, the perceived harmonious relationship of all the elements, can only be inherent. In the urban context, it is that magical quality experienced when the total city and each of its components are perceived to be appropriate, in harmony, in balance, and working well together.*

. . .

The ultimate test

The ultimate test of urban design, as of all design, is its effect upon the lives and experiences of its users. The ultimate city will be, for its time and place, the ultimate human habitation.

There is no beauty unless there's a need fulfilled.

Thomas Hart Benton

True simplicity comes at the end of an exploration of complexity, from a concise summing up of all that really needs to be said.

Benjamin Thompson

The diagrammatic models and conceptual plan in the color section are offered as a point of reference, and departure, for the planners of tomorrow's more livable cities and metropolitan regions.

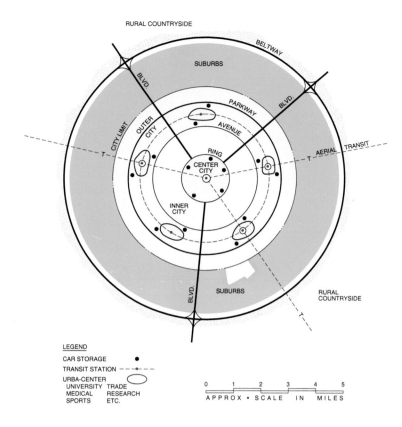

LEGEND
CAR STORAGE
TRANSIT STATION
URBA-CENTER
UNIVERSITY TRADE
MEDICAL   RESEARCH
SPORTS   ETC.

0   1   2   3   4   5
APPROX • SCALE IN MILES

Garden City 21
(A Conceptual Model)

This conceptual model of a city for the 21st century shows a more workable plan arrangement of the urban components. Adjusted to fit the topography and implemented by phased evolution, it holds much of promise.

Variations in urban form

With a diagrammatic model in hand—modified as deemed desirable—it is to be adjusted to the underlying topography and human-built features of the site and its environs.

The possible variations in the plan diagram of an urban metropolis are limitless. There are, however, tested relationships of the key elements that have proven their validity at this point in time. The goal is to best relate each to the other and to the dominant features of the natural and built environs.

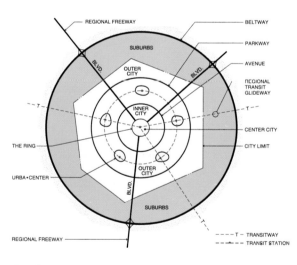

Garden City 21
(A Diagrammatic Model)

This diagrammatic layout is intended to indicate theoretical plan relationships only. To have application, it must be adjusted in response to topography and other siting factors.

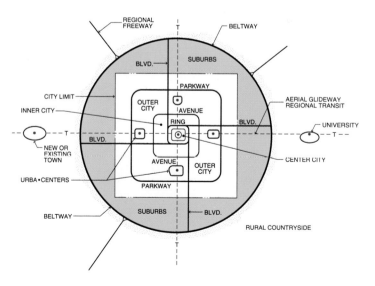

Garden City 21
(Squared Diagram)

A rectilinear version is well adapted to the transformation of an established urban metropolis with an existing grid street layout.

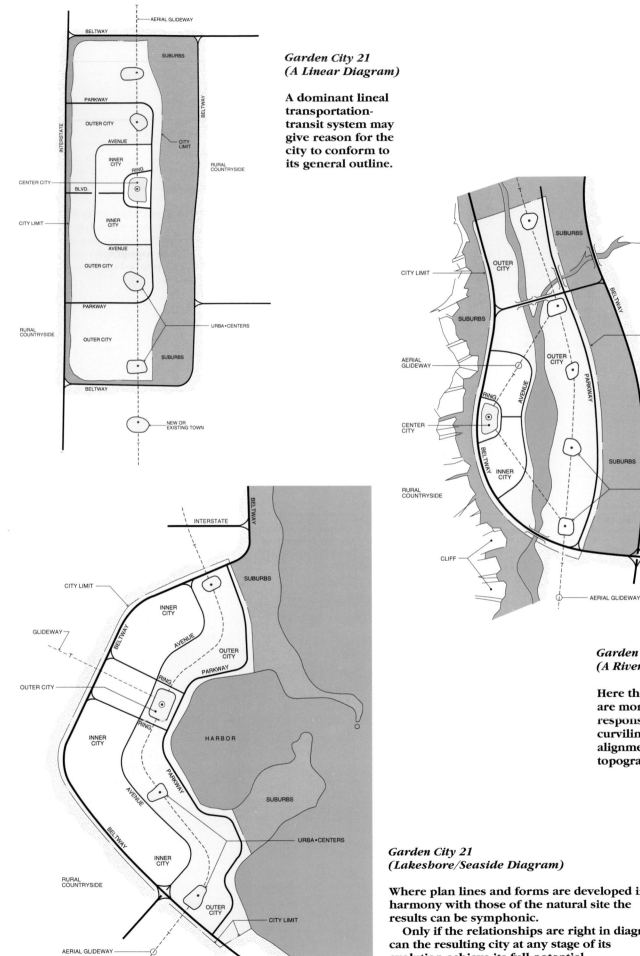

**Garden City 21
(A Linear Diagram)**

A dominant lineal transportation-transit system may give reason for the city to conform to its general outline.

**Garden City 21
(A Riverine Version)**

Here the plan forms are more fluid in response to the curvilinear river alignment and topography.

**Garden City 21
(Lakeshore/Seaside Diagram)**

Where plan lines and forms are developed in harmony with those of the natural site the results can be symphonic.

Only if the relationships are right in diagram can the resulting city at any stage of its evolution achieve its full potential.

Topographic Framework

The fitting of a selected diagram to an actual urban site, new or existing, is an ongoing task and can be accomplished effectively only by application of the comprehensive planning process. This begins with gaining a keen understanding of, and feeling for, the topography and landscape environs. It involves the PCD approach by which those features to be preserved and conserved are outlined for protection with compatible development allocated to appropriate intervening lands.

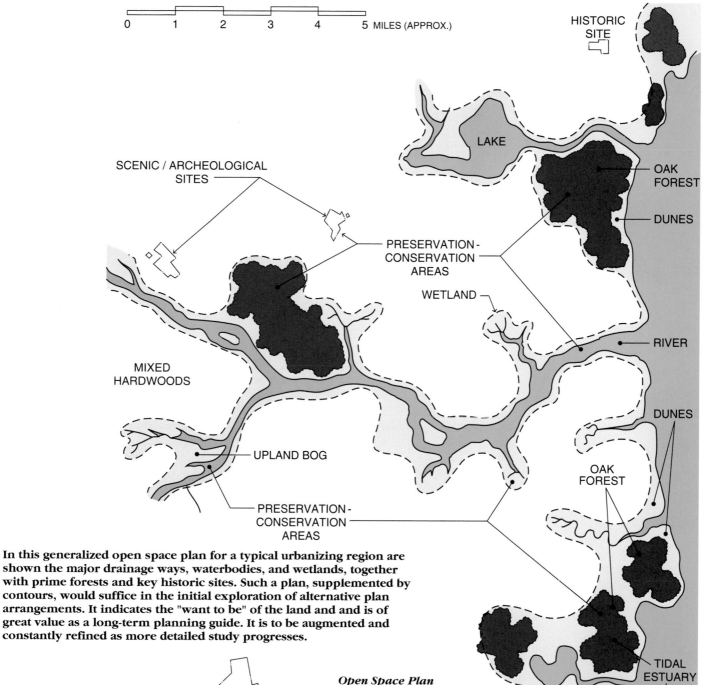

0   1   2   3   4   5 MILES (APPROX.)

HISTORIC SITE

SCENIC / ARCHEOLOGICAL SITES

LAKE

OAK FOREST

DUNES

PRESERVATION-CONSERVATION AREAS

WETLAND

RIVER

MIXED HARDWOODS

DUNES

UPLAND BOG

OAK FOREST

PRESERVATION-CONSERVATION AREAS

TIDAL ESTUARY

In this generalized open space plan for a typical urbanizing region are shown the major drainage ways, waterbodies, and wetlands, together with prime forests and key historic sites. Such a plan, supplemented by contours, would suffice in the initial exploration of alternative plan arrangements. It indicates the "want to be" of the land and and is of great value as a long-term planning guide. It is to be augmented and constantly refined as more detailed study progresses.

EXISTING SETTLEMENT (TO BE PROTECTED)

Open Space Plan
(The "Want-to-be" of the Land)

Here, by site analysis, the open space frame has been established for a new or existing city. The dominant landscape features have been outlined for preservation or restoration as a sound ecological base.

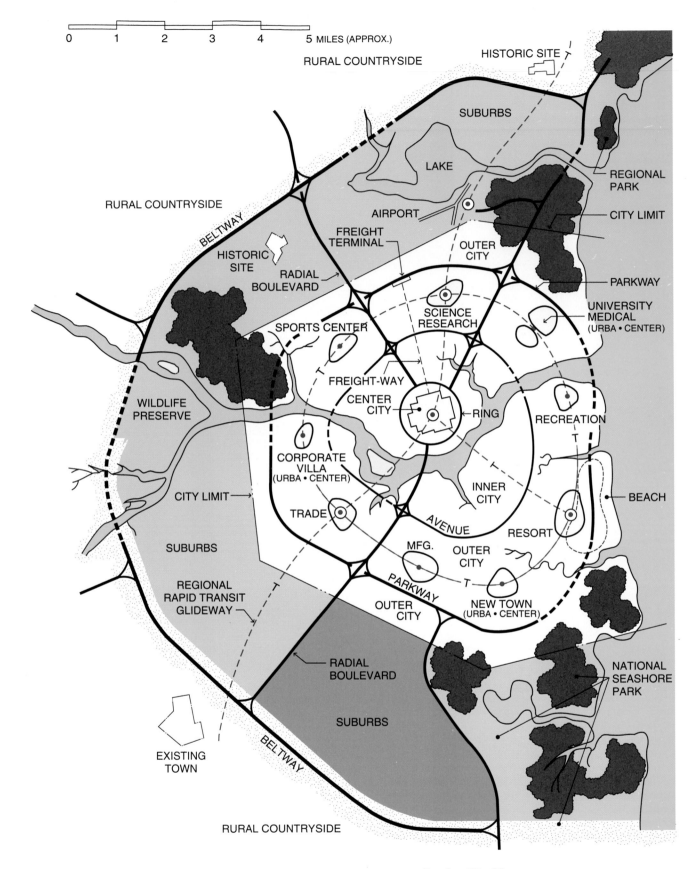

SCALE: 0 1 2 3 4 5 MILES (APPROX.)

RURAL COUNTRYSIDE

HISTORIC SITE

SUBURBS

LAKE

REGIONAL PARK

CITY LIMIT

RURAL COUNTRYSIDE

AIRPORT

BELTWAY

HISTORIC SITE

FREIGHT TERMINAL

OUTER CITY

PARKWAY

RADIAL BOULEVARD

SCIENCE RESEARCH

UNIVERSITY MEDICAL (URBA · CENTER)

SPORTS CENTER

FREIGHT-WAY

CENTER CITY

RING

RECREATION

WILDLIFE PRESERVE

CORPORATE VILLA (URBA · CENTER)

INNER CITY

BEACH

CITY LIMIT

TRADE

AVENUE

RESORT

SUBURBS

MFG.

OUTER CITY

REGIONAL RAPID TRANSIT GLIDEWAY

PARKWAY

NEW TOWN (URBA · CENTER)

OUTER CITY

NATIONAL SEASHORE PARK

RADIAL BOULEVARD

SUBURBS

EXISTING TOWN

BELTWAY

RURAL COUNTRYSIDE

Shown is a long-range conceptual plan, or model, for a typical urbanizing region. As can be seen it preserves and conserves (protects) the best of the dominant topographic features. Development areas and routes of interconnection are to be fitted compatibly with the natural landscape enframement.

Garden City 21
(A Prototype Conceptual Plan for Phased Long-Range Development)

This example shows the integration of a diagrammatic model adjusted to the topographical setting.

Further Reading (A sampling)

Appleyard, Donald: *Livable Streets,* University of California Press, Berkeley, 1981.

Barnett, Jonathan: *Ambition and Miscalculation,* Harper & Row, New York, 1986.

Berry, Thomas: *The Dream of the Earth,* Sierra Club Books, San Francisco, 1988.

Branch, Melville C.: *Comprehensive City Planning,* Planners' Press, APA, Chicago, 1985.

Breen, Ann, and Dick Rigby: *Waterfronts: Cities Reclaim Their Edge,* McGraw-Hill, New York, 1993.

Capra, Fritjof: *The Turning Point,* Bantam, New York, 1982

Carson, Rachel: *Silent Spring,* Houghton Mifflin, Boston, 1962.

Chan, Yupo: *Facility Location and Land Use,* McGraw-Hill, New York, 1992.

Clark, Kenneth: *Civilisation,* Harper & Row, New York, 1969.

Clay, Grady: *Right Before Your Eyes: Penetrating the Urban Environment,* Planners' Press, APA, Washington, D.C., 1987.

Collins, Richard C., Elizabeth B. Waters, and A. Bruce Dotson: *America's Downtowns: Growth, Politics, and Preservation,* Preservation Press, The National Trust for Historic Preservation, Washington, D.C., 1990.

Council of Planning Librarians: *Urban Planning: A Guide to the Reference Sources,* Chicago, 1989.

Fein, Albert (ed.): *Landscape Into Cityscape: Frederick Law Olmsted's Plans for a Greater New York City,* Cornell University Press, Ithaca, N.Y., 1968.

Garreau, Joel: *Edge City: Life on the New Frontier,* Doubleday, New York, 1991.

Gore, Vice President Al: *Earth in the Balance: Ecology and the Human Spirit,* Houghton Mifflin, New York, 1993.

Gratz, Roberta Brandes: *The Living City,* Simon and Schuster, New York, 1989.

Harris, Charles W., and Nicholas T. Dines: *Time-Saver Standards for Landscape Architecture,* McGraw-Hill, New York, 1988.

Hiss, Tony: *The Experience of Place,* Vintage/Random House, New York, 1990.

Hough, Michael: *City Form and Natural Process,* Van Nostrand Reinhold, New York, 1984.

Howard, Ebenezer: *Garden Cities of Tomorrow,* F. J. Osborne (ed.), MIT Press, Cambridge, Mass., 1965. (Originally published in London, 1898.)

Jackson, J. B.: *Discovering the Vernacular Landscape,* Yale University Press, New Haven, Conn., 1983.

Jacobs, Jane: *The Death and Life of Great American Cities,* Modern Library, New York, 1993. (Originally published by Random House in 1961.)

Katz, Peter: *The New Urbanism: Toward an Architecture of Community,* McGraw-Hill, New York, 1993.

Lebovich, William L.: *Design for Dignity: Accessible Environments for People with Disabilities,* Wiley, New York, 1993.

Levitt, Rachelle (ed.): *Cities Reborn,* Urban Land Institute, Washington, D.C., 1987.

Little, Charles: *Greenways for America,* Johns Hopkins University Press, Baltimore, Md., 1990.

Little, Charles: *Hope for the Land,* Rutgers University Press, New Brunswick, N.J., 1992.

Lyle, John Tillman: *Design for Human Ecosystems,* Van Nostrand Reinhold, New York, 1985.

McKibben, Bill: *End of Nature,* Random House, New York, 1989.

Marsh, George Perkins: *Man and Nature,* David Lowenthal (ed.) Harvard University Press/Belknap Press, Cambridge, Mass., 1967. (Originally published in 1864.)

Mills, Edwin S., and John F. McDonald (eds.): *Sources of Metropolitan Growth,* Center for Urban Policy Research, Piscataway, N.J., 1992.

Moudon, Anne Vernez (ed.): *Master-Planned Communities: Shaping Exurbs in the 1990's,* Urban Design Program, University of Washington, Seattle, 1990.

Mumford, Lewis: *The City in History,* Harcourt, Brace, Jovanovich, New York, 1961.

Mumford, Lewis: *The Culture of Cities,* Greenwood Publishers, Westport, Conn., 1981. (Originally published by Harcourt, Brace and Co., New York, 1938.)

Naar, John: *Design for a Livable Planet: How You Can Clean Up the Environment,* Harper & Row, New York, 1990.

Oehme, Wolfgang, and James van Sweden: *Bold Romantic Gardens,* Acropolis Books, Herndon, Va., 1991.

Simonds, John Ormsbee: *Earthscape: A Manual of Environmental Planning and Design,* second edition, Van Nostrand Reinhold, New York, 1986. (Originally published by McGraw-Hill, New York, 1978.)

Simonds, John Ormsbee: *Landscape Architecture: A Manual of Site Planning and Design,* second edition, McGraw-Hill, New York, 1983.

Smith, Herbert H.: *The Citizens Guide to Planning,* second edition, Planners' Press, APA, Chicago, 1979.

Spirn, Anne Whiston: *The Granite Garden, Urban Nature and Human Design,* Basic Books, New York, 1984.

Spreiregen, Paul D.: *Urban Design, the Architecture of Towns and Cities,* McGraw-Hill (For the American Institute of Architects), New York, 1965.

Trancik, Roger: *Finding Lost Space: Theories of Urban Design,* Van Nostrand Reinhold, New York, 1986.

Whyte, William H., Jr.: *Rediscovering the Center City,* Doubleday (Anchor), New York, 1990.

Wilkes, Joseph A. (editor-in-ehief), and Robert T. Packard (associate editor): *Encyclopedia of Architecture: Design, Engineering and Construction,* Wiley, New York, 1988.

Other publications:
(Bookstore Catalogs Available)

American Institute of Architects
1735 New York Avenue, N.W.
Washington, DC 20006

American Planning Association
1313 E. 60th Street
Chicago, IL 60637-2891

American Society of Landscape Architects
4401 Connecticut Avenue, N.W.
Washington, DC 20008

Community Builders Handbook Series
Urban Land Institute
625 Indiana Avenue, N.W.
Washington, DC 20004-2930

Process Architecture Publications
Process Architecture Publishing Co., Ltd.,
1-47-2-418 Sasazuka, Shibuya-Ku
Tokyo, Japan

Sierra Club Books
2034 Fillmore St.
San Francisco, CA 94115

INDEX*

*See also Acknowledgments.